4 PB

NOV 29 2002

i2
12/03
5
4/06
9/07 ✓ 6/07
15 x 8/09 ✓ 9/09
17 x 2/10 ✓ 10/10
22 x 7/11 ✓ 12/11
22 x 2/11 ✓ 3/14

110633111

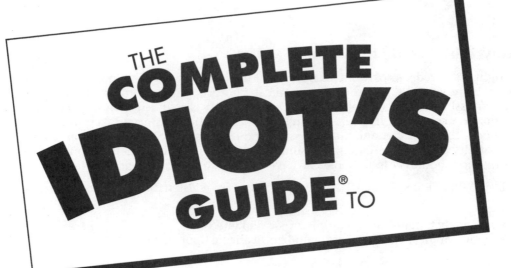

THE COMPLETE IDIOT'S GUIDE® TO

Playing Drums

by Michael Miller

WITHDRAWN

alpha books

A Pearson Education Company

SAN DIEGO PUBLIC LIBRARY
PACIFIC BEACH

Copyright © 2000 by Michael Miller

All rights reserved. No part of this book shall be reproduced, stored in a retrieval system, or transmitted by any means, electronic, mechanical, photocopying, recording, or otherwise, without written permission from the publisher. No patent liability is assumed with respect to the use of the information contained herein. Although every precaution has been taken in the preparation of this book, the publisher and author assume no responsibility for errors or omissions. Neither is any liability assumed for damages resulting from the use of information contained herein. For information, address Alpha Books, 201 West 103rd Street, Indianapolis, IN 46290.

THE COMPLETE IDIOT'S GUIDE TO and Design are registered trademarks of Pearson Education, Inc.

International Standard Book Number: 0-02-863940-5
Library of Congress Catalog Card Number: Available upon request.

03   02   8   7   6   5   4

Interpretation of the printing code: The rightmost number of the first series of numbers is the year of the book's printing; the rightmost number of the second series of numbers is the number of the book's printing. For example, a printing code of 00-1 shows that the first printing occurred in 2000.

Printed in the United States of America

Note: This publication contains the opinions and ideas of its author. It is intended to provide helpful and informative material on the subject matter covered. It is sold with the understanding that the author and publisher are not engaged in rendering professional services in the book. If the reader requires personal assistance or advice, a competent professional should be consulted.

The author and publisher specifically disclaim any responsibility for any liability, loss, or risk, personal or otherwise, which is incurred as a consequence, directly or indirectly, of the use and application of any of the contents of this book.

NOV 29 2002

Publisher
Marie Butler-Knight

Product Manager
Phil Kitchel

Managing Editor
Cari Luna

Acquisitions Editors
Mike Sanders
Susan Zingraf

Development Editor
Tom Stevens

Senior Production Editor
Christy Wagner

Copy Editor
Krista Hansing

Illustrator
Jody Schaeffer

Cover Designers
Mike Freeland
Kevin Spear

Book Designers
Scott Cook and Amy Adams of DesignLab

Indexer
Amy Lawrence

Layout/Proofreading
Angela Calvert
John Etchison
Ayanna Lacey
Heather Hiatt Miller
Stacey Richwine-DeRome
Nancy Wagner

Contents at a Glance

Part 1: Let There Be Drums!   **1**

  1 So You Want to Play Drums ...   3
*What does it mean to be a drummer? Read this chapter to find out
what you're getting yourself into ... and it isn't all fun and games!*

  2 Before You Play, You Have to Pay: Buying Your First Drums   13
*Everything you need to know about buying a snare drum, a drumset,
cymbals, sticks, and heads—it's the only drumset reference you'll ever
need!*

  3 Plugging In: Using Electronic Drums and Drum
Machines   45
*Not all drums are made from wood—you can expand your percus-
sion possibilities with an electronic drumset.*

  4 Bongos and Claves and Vibes, Oh My!: The Rest of
the Percussion Family   51
*A drummer is often called upon to play other percussion instru-
ments; learn about them here!*

  5 Heads, Shells, and Lugs: Tuning and Caring for
Your Drums   57
*How to get the perfect sound from your drums—and keep them in
tip-top shape.*

  6 A Brief History of Time: Drummers to Listen To   71
These are some of the most influential drummers of all time.

  7 King of the Studio: An Interview with Drumming
Legend Hal Blaine   81
*Hal Blaine is the most recorded drummer in history and has played
on thousands of hit records. Find out how he got started and what
advice he has for today's beginning drummers.*

Part 2: Bang the Drum Slowly: Snare Drum Basics   **95**

  8 Wholes, Halves, and Quarters: Notes and Notation   97
*Before you can play, you have to read—and this chapter teaches you
everything you need to know about reading music.*

  9 Get a Grip: Holding Your Sticks   109
*Learn the right way to hold your sticks and hit the drum—with
either matched or traditional grip.*

  10 A One and a Two and a Three: Playing Your First Notes   115
*This is the chapter you've been waiting for—you finally get to play
some music on the snare drum!*

  11 Playing Offbeat: Syncopated Rhythms and Triplets   125
Learn how to play notes when people are least expecting them ....

  12 The Big Bounce: Open and Closed Rolls   133
Fill in those long spaces—with a snare drum roll!

13 Twenty-Six Things You Need to Know: The Rudiments   141
Teach yourself the basic building blocks of all drum music—from flams to paradiddles to ratamacues.

14 Marching Along: Basic Rudimental Beats   153
Apply the rudiments with some fun exercises—and a snappy solo.

Part 3: You Got the Beat: Drumset Basics   159

15 In the Driver's Seat: Moving Around the Drumset   161
Find out how to set up your drums—just make sure everything is within reach.

16 For Your Hands Only: Playing Drums and Cymbals Together   167
Before things get too complicated, learn to play on top of your set with your right and left hands.

17 Stepping Out: Adding Your Feet   173
Take two hands, add two feet, and all of a sudden you're playing the entire drumset!

18 In the Pocket: Basic Rock, Country, and R&B Beats   179
Bookmark this chapter—with 64 different rock grooves, you'll never run out of beats to play.

19 Swing Time: Basic Jazz Beats   193
Swing your way through 16 different jazz grooves—plus one terrific jazz solo!

20 Take Five: Playing in Odd Times   199
Learn how to count to five (and seven and nine) with this primer on odd time signatures.

Part 4: Wipe Out: Advanced Drumset Techniques   205

21 Setting It Up: Fancy Fills   207
Learn how to fill at the end of a phrase—and kick an accented figure in a big band!

22 Take the Spotlight: Drum Solos   213
A good drum solo is more than just playing really fast and loud; learn the right way to solo, and then practice with three fun full-page solos.

23 Less Is More: When Not to Play   221
You don't always have to play on two and four; the best drummers know when to lay out and when to play a different beat.

24 Different Strokes: Beyond Sticks   227
Learn how to play with brushes and Wood Whacks—and find out the difference between a rimshot and a rimclick.

25 Parting Advice from One of Today's Hottest Drummers: An Interview with Kenny Aronoff   233
Kenny Aronoff might be the hardest-working drummer today; we catch him between tours and get some practical advice on how to become a solid and successful drummer.

Appendixes

A Drum Words: A Drummer's Glossary   241

B Drum Records: Recommended Listening   245

C Drum Books: Supplemental Instruction Books   249

D Drum Links: Other Percussion Resources   253

   Index   257

Contents

Part 1: Let There Be Drums!   **1**

1 So You Want to Play Drums ...   **3**

Why Do You Want to Be a Drummer? 3
What Do Drummers Do? 5
Different Drummers 6
   Get Funky: Rock, Country, and R&B Drumming 6
   Get Swingin': Jazz Drumming..7
   Get Serious: Symphonic Drumming..8
   Get in Step: Drum Corps Drumming 8
   Get Supportive: Percussion and Ethnic Drumming 8
   Get Versatile: Studio and Show Drumming 9
How to Become a Drummer—in Three Easy Steps 9
   Step One: Find a Teacher 9
   Step Two: Practice, Practice, Practice..10
   Step Three: Learn to Read 11
It's Not Just a Job—Well, Okay, Sometimes It's Just a Job................11

2 Before You Play, You Have to Pay: Buying Your First Drums   **13**

Before You Buy: Evaluating Different Options 13
   Snare Drum vs. Drumset: Should You Buy It All Now? 13
   Spend a Lot or Spend a Little: What Do You Get for Your Money?....14
   New vs. Used: Can You Save Some Bucks with a Previously Owned Set? 16
   Name Brand vs. No Name: Which Is the Best Deal? 16
The Big Purchase: Buying a Drumset..21
   How to Evaluate a Drum 23
   Choosing a Snare Drum 25
   Choosing a Bass Drum 27
   Choosing Your Tom-Toms 28
   Choosing Stands and Pedals 30
   Choosing Cymbals 32
Hit It: Choosing the Right Sticks 34
Meet Mr. Drum Dealer: Choosing Where to Buy 36
Advice from a Pro: A Drum Dealer Talks About Buying Drums 37
The Bottom Line: How Much Should You Spend? 39
   Putting Together an Entry-Level Set 40
   Building a Semi-Pro Kit 41
   Spending the Bucks for a High-End Professional Set......................42

3 Plugging In: Using Electronic Drums and Drum Machines   **45**

I Play the Body Electric: Electronic Drum Kits 45
   How Electronic Drums Work..46
   Drop Out, Plug In: Different Types of Electronic Drums................46
   The Pros and Cons of Electronic Drums 47
Pull the Trigger: Making Your Acoustic Drums Electric 48

4 Bongos and Claves and Vibes, Oh My!: The Rest of the Percussion Family   **51**

Laying Down a Latin Groove...51
Groove to a World Beat 53
Where Do They Get Such Wonderful Toys? 54
Orchestrate Your Way to the Top..55
Some Percussion Is Melodic 56

5 Heads, Shells, and Lugs: Tuning and Caring for Your Drums   **57**

Time for a Cleaning: Keeping Your Set in Tip-Top Condition 57
    Cleaning Your Drums...58
    Cleaning Your Cymbals 58
    Cleaning Your Stands and Pedals 59
    Make Like a Boy Scout—and Be Prepared! 60
Perfect Pitch Not Required: Tuning Your Drums.............................60
    Choosing the Right Heads...61
    Changing Heads..62
    How to Tune a Wild Drum 63
    How to Muffle a Ringy Drum 65
    Tuning Your Snare 67
    Tuning a Tom 68
    Tuning Your Bass Drum 68

6 A Brief History of Time: Drummers to Listen To   **71**

Straight-Ahead Stylists: Great Jazz Drummers...................................71
Drum Starrs: Great Rock Drummers 74
Groove Masters: Great Studio Drummers 77
Musical Chameleons: TV Drummers 78

7 King of the Studio: An Interview with Drumming Legend Hal Blaine   **81**

What Makes a Drummer Great 81
The Hal Blaine Interview 83

Part 2: Bang the Drum Slowly: Snare Drum Basics   **95**

8 Wholes, Halves, and Quarters: Notes and Notation   **97**

Taking the Measure of Things 97
Taking Note—of Notes 98
    Whole Notes 98
    Half Notes 98
    Quarter Notes..99
    Eighth Notes 99
    Sixteenth Notes 100
Taking Count 100
Taking a Rest..101

Taking a Note—and Dotting It 102
Taking Two Notes—and Tying Them Together 102
Taking the Beat and Dividing by Three..102
Taking Time—Signatures 103
Taking the Pulse 103
Taking It Up—and Taking It Down 105
Taking a Do-Over 106

9 Get a Grip: Holding Your Sticks   109

Shake Hands with Your Sticks 109
Make a Match: Learning Matched Grip..*109*
Not Quite the Same: Learning Traditional Grip *110*
Bang a Drum: Learning the Stroke 112

10 A One and a Two and a Three: Playing Your First Notes   115

Playing Quarters..115
Playing Eighths..116
Playing Sixteenths 116
Playing Accents 116
Drum Solo: *Taking Back the Beat* 117

11 Playing Offbeat: Syncopated Rhythms and Triplets   125

Skipping a Beat: Syncopation 125
Three for Two: Playing Triplets 126
A Syncopated Solo: *Freddie's Feet* 126

12 The Big Bounce: Open and Closed Rolls   133

Keep It Clean: Open Rolls 133
The Five-Stroke Roll *134*
The Seven-Stroke Roll *134*
The Nine-Stroke Roll..*134*
The Eleven-Stroke Roll *135*
The Thirteen-Stroke Roll *135*
The Fifteen-Stroke Roll *135*
The Seventeen-Stroke Roll *136*
Make a Buzz: Closed Rolls 136
Exercising Your Rolls 137
A Rolling Solo: *Rollin' the Hay* 137

13 Twenty-Six Things You Need to Know: The Rudiments   141

Getting Started: The First Thirteen Rudiments 141
1: The Long Roll *142*
2: The Five-Stroke Roll *142*
3: The Seven-Stroke Roll *142*
4: The Flam *143*
5: The Flam Accent *143*
6: The Flam Paradiddle *144*

7: The Flamacue 144

8: The Ruff 145

9: The Single Drag 145

10: The Double Drag 145

11: The Double Paradiddle 145

12: The Single Ratamacue 146

13: The Triple Ratamacue 146

Finishing Up: The Second Thirteen Rudiments 147

14: The Single-Stroke Roll 147

15: The Nine-Stroke Roll 148

16: The Ten-Stroke Roll 148

17: The Eleven-Stroke Roll 148

18: The Thirteen-Stroke Roll 149

19: The Fifteen-Stroke Roll 149

20: The Flam Tap 149

21: The Single Paradiddle 150

22: The Drag Paradiddle No. 1 150

23: The Drag Paradiddle No. 2 151

24: The Flam Paradiddle-Diddle 151

25: The Lesson 25 151

26: The Double Ratamacue 151

14 Marching Along: Basic Rudimental Beats   **153**

Rudimental Exercises 153

A Rudimental Solo: *Rudimentary, My Dear Watson* 154

Part 3: You Got the Beat: Drumset Basics   **159**

15 In the Driver's Seat: Moving Around the Drumset   **161**

Take a Seat 161

Spread Your Feet..162

Spread Your Toms...163

Stack Your Cymbals 164

Get Ready to Play! 165

16 For Your Hands Only: Playing Drums and Cymbals Together **167**

Keeping Time 167

Lines and Spaces: Reading Drumset Notation..................................168

Put Your Hands Together: Practicing Independence 168

A Two-Handed Solo: Tom-Tom Time..168

17 Stepping Out: Adding Your Feet   **173**

Pedal Pushing: How to Play Your Bass Drum and Hi-Hat Pedals 173

Drum Dancing: Exercising Your Feet..174

Your First Drumset Solo: *Top to Bottom* 175

18 In the Pocket: Basic Rock, Country, and R&B Beats   **179**

Groovy, Baby! 179
   Basic Eighth-Note Grooves 179
   Four-to-the-Floor Grooves 180
   Sixties Grooves 180
   Quarter-Note Grooves 180
   Funky Grooves 180
   The Three-Legged Dog Groove...180
   Dance Grooves 181
   Sixteenth-Note Grooves 181
   Ethnic Grooves 181
   Shuffle Grooves 182
A Groovy Solo: *The Groove Machine* 183

19 Swing Time: Basic Jazz Beats   **193**

Swinging the Beat: Jazz Exercises...193
A Solo in Swing Time: *Jazz Jump* 194

20 Take Five: Playing in Odd Times   **199**

Counting to Something Other Than Four: Odd-Time Exercises................199
   Playing in 3/4 200
   Playing in 5/4 200
   Playing in 7/4 200
   Playing in 9/8 and 12/8 200
An Odd-Time Solo: *Basic Math*...201

Part 4: Wipe Out: Advanced Drumset Techniques   **205**

21 Setting It Up: Fancy Fills   **207**

Sounds Great! More Filling! 207
Kick the Licks: Setting Up a Big Band 208

22 Take the Spotlight: Drum Solos   **213**

It's Your Turn: How to Play a Drum Solo 213
   The Good, the Bad, and the Really Loud: Why Some Solos
    Are Better Than Others..213
   The Best-Laid Plans of Mice and Drummers: How to Structure Your Solo......214
   When in Doubt, Roll: What to Do When You Get Stuck 215
   Flash with the Pans: How to Add Sizzle to Your Solo......................216
Solo Practice: Three Drumset Solos 216
   Ringo's Right Foot: The Beginning 216
   Gene's Toms: Sing³ 216
   Danny Around the Drums: Made Ya Smile 217

23 Less Is More: When *Not* to Play   221

Play a Different Beat..221
Lay Out—Until the Chorus 223
Drop the Ride 224
Ignore the Snare...224
Leave Your Kit at Home...225

24 Different Strokes: Beyond Sticks   227

Shots and Clicks: Using Your Sticks in Different Ways.............227
  A Softer Backbeat with Rimclicks 227
  A Louder Backbeat with Rimshots...228
Sweeping the Head: Playing with Brushes................................228
Rolling Along: Playing with Mallets 230
Different Sounds: Other Types of Beaters 231

25 Parting Advice from One of Today's Hottest
Drummers: An Interview with Kenny Aronoff   233

My Kenny Aronoff Story 233
The Kenny Aronoff Interview 235
Learning from the Pros 239

Appendixes

A Drum Words: A Drummer's Glossary   241

B Drum Records: Recommended Listening   245

C Drum Books: Supplemental Instruction Books   249

D Drum Links: Other Percussion Resources   253

Index   257

Foreword

People don't dance to the guitar, the bass, or the vocals. People dance to the drums! In the spirit of Rodney Dangerfield, let me say this (as I loosen my collar): Drummers need more respect! After all, according to many ethno-musicologists, drums are supposed to be the second-oldest instrument known (the first being *vox humana,* the human voice).

Mike Miller's *The Complete Idiot's Guide to Playing Drums* is a fantastic and extremely comprehensive book on the drums (my favorite instrument and Mike's, too, I think!). Mike is obviously a very good and well-schooled drummer with lots of professional playing experience. He definitely knows firsthand what he is talking about. His book is a must-have for any drummer on any level. It not only has a wealth of information about virtually every aspect of the drums, but it also contains two great interviews with two of my favorite world-class drummers, Hal Blaine and Kenny Aronoff. I especially love the fact that he has given so much attention and credit to Ringo Starr, one of the greatest drummers in the world.

In this great and well-thought-out book, Mike Miller shows you how to play in a band. This book is also of great value to the parents and friends of the drummer-to-be. It has an entire section on how and where to pick out the ideal drumset, how to set it up, and how to maintain it properly. Mike covers how to select sticks, cymbals, drumheads, and pedals, and who to listen to for inspiration. He even talks about hearing protection, and I always wear earplugs to protect the ears that God gave me.

The Complete Idiot's Guide to Playing Drums also gives an in-depth look at electronic drums, ethnic percussion, classical percussion, tuning the drums, playing different styles of music, playing drum solos, drummers' musical responsibilities, and tons of other crucial drumming topics. There is also a tremendous interview with Harry Cangany, who is a very knowledgeable vintage-drum expert. Mike includes a list of recommended CDs, drum videos, drum books, and drum-related Web sites.

Hal Blaine (one of my biggest drumming influences) and Mike really stress the importance of reading music. I couldn't agree more, as 90 percent of the work I do involves some type of reading. Mike's rudiment section is great, too.

The phenomenal drummer Terry Bozzio once said as he looked at his drums, "There's a lot of dignity to this instrument!" I think that after reading this book, anyone who considered him- or herself a complete drumming idiot will have a new respect for this great instrument—the drums!

Gregg Bissonette

Gregg Bissonette has played drums for such people and groups as Maynard Ferguson, David Lee Roth, Santana, Don Henley, Joe Satriani, Gino Vannelli, Toto, Andy Summers, Christopher Cross, The Mustard Seeds, Brian Wilson, Linda Ronstadt, Ray Charles, and Duran Duran, among others. He also has recorded motion-picture scores for Hans Zimmer, Michel Colombier, and many others, as well as the TV shows *Mad About You, King of the Hill,* and *Friends.*

He has produced two instructional videotapes (also available on book and play-along CD), *Private Lesson* and *Playing, Reading, and Soloing with a Band.* Gregg's latest solo CD, available on Favored Nations Records, is titled "Submarine."

Introduction

Drumming is in my blood. No matter what my various business cards have said through the years, at heart, I am and have always been a drummer.

I don't remember why I started playing drums. Maybe it had something to do with watching Cubby play drums on the original *Mickey Mouse Club;* you can't ignore the influence of television on impressionable children. (I certainly couldn't ignore how Cubby's playing seemed to impress Karen, who I personally liked more than Annette.) All I know is that my parents have a picture of me at age five playing a little toy drumset. The die was cast.

The author at age five—my father didn't seem too enthusiastic about my drumming!

I started taking drum lessons when I was in fifth grade in the back of the Wurlitzer store in our local mall. My teacher was a guy named Jack Wagley, and his method for taking the ring out of the store-supplied practice snare was simply to toss his billfold onto the drum head. Crude, but effective.

When I started taking lessons, my parents bought me a Ludwig Acrolite snare drum on a flat-tripod stand; I used Ludwig 2B laminated sticks with plastic tips. Jack took me through all the old standby method books, Harr and Podemsky and Wilcoxin. I learned to play my rolls, not bounce them, and I memorized all 26 rudiments, diligently counting my way from measure to measure: "One-and two-and three-and four-and."

I got my first drumset in sixth grade; before then, I would set up my snare together with some chairs and lamps and pound on a metal lampshade like it was a ride cymbal. My first set, purchased one weekday evening for just $150, was a red sparkle Polaris from Japan (Japanese sets were the cheapies back then—that was before Yamaha and Pearl got big), with a 20-inch bass, a 13-inch small tom, and a 16-inch large tom. The hi-hat cymbals were so cheap that if I pressed too hard with my left foot, the top cymbal inverted; I was constantly snapping that trashcan cymbal back into shape until I bought my first set of Zildjian New Beats later that year.

By seventh grade I was playing in a garage band ("Walk Don't Run" and "Brown Sugar" were our two big covers) and was the drummer in the junior high choral club. I was also the top drummer in our school's A-list concert band, one of just two seventh graders in what was typically an all-ninth-grade group. The other seventh grader was another drummer, a short blonde kid named Mike Richards, whom I met when we were both auditioning for the band. We two Mikes became fast friends and remain so today. I can remember many lazy summer afternoons in the basement of Mike's parents' condo, listening to Blood, Sweat & Tears and Chicago and Chase, while trading licks on his silver sparkle Ludwigs and wondering if we could get lucky with any of his sister's friends.

When I was in eighth grade, Jack Wagley, still my drum teacher, was trying to teach me how to play jazz using the Chapin and Morello books. I could play all the notes, technically, but I couldn't get the feel down. Jack became increasingly frustrated at my lack of swing and finally asked me if I had ever actually listened to any jazz. I answered no, of course, and he prescribed The Dave Brubeck Quartet's *Time Out* as the antidote to my swing problem. That evening I called up my father and asked him to pick up a copy of *Time Out* from the local Lyric Records store on his way home from work. I spent the entire evening huddled over my GE portable stereo with my headphones on, listening to Joe Morello swing his way through "Take Five," "Blue Rondo a la Turk," and all those other odd-time marvels. It was an awakening.

The very next day—*the very next day!*—Phyllis Earnshaw, my school's choral teacher, came up to me after choral club rehearsal. (Truth be told, I had a major crush on Mrs. Earnshaw and was always lingering after class.) She asked me if I'd be interested in getting together with her (on piano), Gene Smith (the band director and an alto sax player), and Brian Siemers (a ninth-grade bass player) and playing some Brubeck tunes after school. Today I'm still amazed at the cosmic coincidence or divine intervention that triggered the Brubeck invitation; then, at that moment, the only thing I could say was: "Yes!"

Our little Brubeck get-togethers ultimately led to us performing "Take Five" for a school concert. I played the Morello solo note for note, or as note for note as I could do in eighth grade. I just remember kicking the bejeezus out of my bass drum during the opening bars of the solo and hearing that sound reverberate through the entire gym. Of all the gigs I've ever played, that is the only one that I can still recall in complete detail.

I entered high school with a brand new drumset, a custom-ordered set of Ludwig blue-tint Vistalites. Unfortunately, I was playing in the high school's jazz band, and I never could get those damned Vistalites to sound right. Their boomy sound may have been perfect for John Bonham and Led Zeppelin, but they couldn't have been more wrong for Stan Kenton and Woody Herman. I *hated* those drums!

My first really good kit, a set of blue-tint Ludwig Vistalites—they'd be worth a fortune to a collector today!

The Vistalites lasted my sophomore year, after which I replaced them with an off-the-shelf Fibes five-piece set. These fiberglass drums had a beautiful antique copper finish, sounded terrific live, and were powerful enough to cut through just about any band I was playing with. I still have those Fibes today, and they still sound great.

I played for a lot of different bands in high school and on into college, where I was accepted into the Indiana University School of Music's Jazz Studies program. At one time I was playing in no fewer than six different groups—a four-person wedding reception band, a large Weather Report–like fusion band, an avant-garde jazz quartet, a Dixieland band, the Singing Hoosiers (IU's world-renowned swing choir), and one of the school's many orchestras. Frankly, I don't know where I got the energy!

Time went on, and my musical endeavors eventually gave way to a business career. Even though the number of gigs I played dwindled away to nothing, I still had my drums set up in the spare bedroom, and I still practiced my chops regularly. From time to time I'd replace an old piece of hardware, try out a new type of head, or add a new cymbal to my kit. I may have been a business-man by profession, but I was still a drummer at heart.

My current business card says I'm a writer, and now I'm writing a book about playing drums. Things have come full circle, through no grand plan of my own. I just replaced my now-vintage Fibes drums with a state-of-the-art custom Drum Workshop six-piece set, and my friend Mike Richards and I have started trading patterns back and forth again—this time via mail, as I'm still in Indianapolis and he's several moves removed in Kansas City. Drumming is still in my blood.

The author today—the best kit I've ever played, natural-finish Drum Workshop drums with brass hardware all around.

Some of the best times in my life have come behind the drumset or while hanging out with fellow drummers. Unlike other professional communities I've dealt with throughout my life, the drumming community is one of the most friendly and helpful bunch of folks you'll ever come across. Whether it's the owner of my local drum shop, a product manager at a big drum company, or a drumming legend like Hal Blaine or Kenny Aronoff, everyone has time to talk and lend a helping hand. Drummers are friendly folks.

Why This Book Is for You

You're reading this book because you want to be a drummer. That's great—the world needs more drummers. I wish I could be there to see every one of you pick up the sticks for the first time, struggle through learning how to count, beam with the purchase of that first drumset, and feel that special feeling that comes when everything clicks in and the band starts to groove. There's nothing better.

Of course, to get from here to there takes a lot of hard work. You have to learn how to hold the sticks, how to hit the drum, how to count, and how to *play*. You'll have to spend many long hours practicing the same patterns over and over and over until your hands hurt. You'll have to learn how to play along with others, and you'll have to learn to *listen*.

In short, you have to learn how to be a drummer, and this book is the place to start. Know, however, that you can't do it alone. You'll need a good teacher, someone who can take you through this book—and many others—and show you the proper technique for playing different types of music. With the help of this book and a good teacher—along with lots and lots of practice—you can become as good a drummer as you want to be.

What You'll Find in This Book

The Complete Idiot's Guide to Playing Drums is composed of 25 chapters, each of which concentrates on a different aspect of playing drums. The chapters are organized into four general parts, as follows:

Part 1, "Let There Be Drums!" describes what it means to be a drummer, how to buy your first drums, and how to tune and take care of your drums. You'll also discover some of the more influential drummers in history and learn what advice drumming legend Hal Blaine has for beginning drummers.

Part 2, "Bang the Drum Slowly: Snare Drum Basics," shows you how to read music, how to hold your sticks, and how to play basic patterns on snare drum. You'll progress from quarter notes to rolls to the rudiments, using a series of exercises and drum solos to hone your skills.

Part 3, "You Got the Beat: Drumset Basics," puts you behind the kit and teaches you how to play all those drums and cymbals at the same time. You'll learn all sorts of different beats that you can use on your own gigs, including rock, country, soul, jazz, and odd-time grooves.

Part 4, "Wipe Out: Advanced Drumset Techniques," goes beyond basic beats into fills and solos. You'll even learn how to play with brushes and mallets, and when *not* to play on a song. This section includes an interview with hot studio and touring drummer Kenny Aronoff.

At the very end of the book are four useful appendixes: a glossary of musical terms, a recommended listening list, a list of supplementary learning materials, and a list of other drum-related resources, including Web sites.

How to Get the Most out of This Book

To get the most out of this book, you should know how it is designed. I've tried to put things together in such a way as to make reading the book and learning how to play both rewarding and fun.

This book mixes information and instruction. The information you can handle on your own—just read the text and look at the pictures. The instruction, however, is best accomplished with the help of a qualified drum teacher. You can practice all you want on your own, but you'll get more out of your studies—and progress faster—with someone helping you along.

There's a lot of instruction in this book, so you'll see a lot of music on these pages, beginning in Part 2. Most of the instructional chapters include a series of practice exercises, followed by a solo that applies everything you've learned in that chapter. You should play each exercise one at a time, starting slowly and deliberately, and repeating the exercise over and over and over until you can play it properly. The goal is to learn the pattern (along with the proper sticking, on snare drum)—*not* to see how fast you can play it! After you've mastered the exercise at a slow speed, *then* you can start playing it faster.

Once you get to Parts 3 and 4, the exercises reproduce actual drumset beats played by real drummers on real songs. You can use the beats in these exercises in your own playing—or combine bits and pieces of different exercises to create your own unique grooves.

The solos in this book are meant to reinforce the concepts you've learned in each chapter and to take you the next step beyond. That means that you'll find a few patterns and techniques in the solos that were not presented in that chapter's exercises. When you encounter something new, look it over and work it out *before* you try to play it. You should be able to figure out anything you run into by applying the basic skills you learned previously—and then have some fun wailing through the solos!

Throughout the entire book you'll see a number of little boxes (what we in publishing call *sidebars*) that present additional advice and information. These elements enhance your knowledge or point out important pitfalls to avoid. Here are the types of boxes you'll see scattered throughout the book:

Drum Note

These boxes contain additional information about the topic at hand.

Drum Tip

These boxes contain tips and advice to help you add more power to your playing.

Drum Word

These boxes contain definitions of words or terms you may encounter in a particular playing situation.

Drum Don't

These boxes contain warnings and cautions about things *not* to do when you're playing.

There's More on the Web

If you're not sure what a particular exercise or solo in this book is supposed to sound like, you can go to the *Complete Idiot's Guide* Web site (www.idiotsguides.com) or to my personal Web site (www.molehillgroup.com/drums.htm) and listen to the exercises in digital format. Each exercise and solo is in its own unique file; just click on the link to play the exercise on your own computer!

Let Me Know What You Think

I always love to hear from my readers—especially when the readers are fellow drummers! If you want to contact me, feel free to e-mail me at books@molehillgroup.com. I can't promise that I'll answer every e-mail, but I will promise that I'll read each one!

If you want to learn more about me and any new books I have cooking, check out my Molehill Group Web site at www.molehillgroup.com. Who knows—you might find some other books there you'd like to read.

One, Two, Ready, Go!

Still here? It's time you learned how to be a drummer, so pick up your sticks and get ready to play!

Dedication

This book is dedicated to Phyllis Fulford, a.k.a. Mrs. Earnshaw, my junior high school choir director and music teacher. Phyllis, you inspired me as much as Hal, Buddy, Joe, Bobby, and all the terrific drummers I've ever listened to, but on a much more personal level. I can honestly say that I wouldn't be writing this book today if you hadn't seen something special in that brash eighth grader and then offered a world of encouragement and opportunity. You have my heartfelt thanks, appreciation, and admiration—you did good.

Acknowledgments

I had assistance from dozens of individuals in the creation of this book and would like to thank the following for their help:

Thanks to the usual suspects at Alpha Books, including but not limited to Marie Butler-Knight, Mike Sanders, Tom Stevens, Christy Wagner, Krista Hansing, Renee Wilmeth, and Susan Zingraf, for helping to turn my manuscript into a printed book.

Thanks to numerous individuals representing the major drum and cymbal manufacturers, including Wayne Blanchard (Sabian), James Catalano (Ludwig), Sara Griggs (Roland), David Levine (Drum Workshop), James Rockwell (LP Music Group), Paul Speck (Tama), Josh Touchton (Mapex), and Lisa Surace (ddrums/Armadillo Enterprises), for their assistance in providing information and photographs used throughout the book.

Thanks also to my old friend Mike Richards, who over the years put many ideas into my head that ultimately took form in this book. Mike was also the technical editor for this book, which means that he ensured that what I wrote was true, more or less, and that what I composed was playable. He also offered much useful advice on how to present basic information and exercises in the best way possible for beginning drummers. His input now and in the past has been invaluable.

Special thanks to Harry Cangany, well-known drum historian and president of Drum Center of Indianapolis, for taking the time to offer his opinions and advice, for providing photographs of Gene Krupa and Buddy Rich, for getting me hooked up with Kenny Aronoff and Gregg Bissonette, and for selling me my new Drum Workshop set!

Special thanks also to Kenny Aronoff, drummer extraordinaire and all-around great guy, for taking time from his busy schedule of touring and studio dates to sit down for an interview and share his experience and advice.

More special thanks to Gregg Bissonette, of exceptional technique and even more exceptional attitude, for writing the foreword to this book and for sharing his wisdom and enthusiasm.

Finally, my heartfelt thanks to my idol, the legendary Hal Blaine, for taking the time to talk with me for this book, for being so entertaining and such a gentleman, for sharing some wonderful stories and advice, and for allowing this long-time admirer to share in some of the magic.

Special Thanks to the Technical Reviewer

The Complete Idiot's Guide to Playing Drums was reviewed by an expert who double-checked the accuracy of what you'll learn here, to help us ensure that this book gives you everything you need to know about playing drums. Special thanks are extended to Mike Richards for his assistance and contribution.

Trademarks

All terms mentioned in this book that are known to be or are suspected of being trademarks or service marks have been appropriately capitalized. Alpha Books and Pearson Education, Inc., cannot attest to the accuracy of this information. Use of a term in this book should not be regarded as affecting the validity of any trademark or service mark.

Part 1

Let There Be Drums!

Learn what it means to be a drummer—from buying your first drumset to tuning and caring for your drums. Find out what kind of drums and cymbals you can get for your budget, as well as what kind of set is best for you. Then, learn how to take care of your new drums and how to change heads and tune them so they sound just right. Special bonus in Part 1: An interview with drumming legend Hal Blaine!

Chapter 1

So You Want to Play Drums ...

In This Chapter

➤ Some good reasons—and bad ones—to be a drummer

➤ Things drummers are responsible for

➤ Different kinds of drummers

➤ The way to become a drummer

You've thought it over long and hard, and for whatever reason, you've decided that you want to play drums. If you're serious about it, you'll find that being a drummer is one of the most artistically fulfilling things you can do in your life—and even if you're not serious, you can still have a lot of fun!

Before you spend a lot of money on drums and cymbals, however, let's take a closer look at what it really means to be a drummer. (And it isn't all fun!)

Why Do You Want to Be a Drummer?

There are all sorts of reasons why you might want to be a drummer. Some of the reasons are pretty good, and others are pretty bad. See if you can recognize yourself in the following list:

➤ **You have a good sense of rhythm.** Okay, this is a good start. Drummers have to have a good sense of rhythm and be able to keep a steady beat. The drummer is the time-keeper of the band and has to be able to feel—and express—a solid pulse *and* play intricate rhythms around that pulse.

➤ **You can't carry a tune.** This isn't the best reason in the world to be a drummer. Just because you can't play any other instrument doesn't mean that you should play the drums; drummers aren't the rejects of the musical world, you know! In fact, some of the best drummers are also accomplished composers or arrangers or know how to play

Drum Note

You'll hear a lot of different words and phrases used to describe a set of drums. My favorites are *skins, traps, kit, rig, gear,* and *tubs.*

other, more melodic instruments. That doesn't mean that you need to be a piano virtuoso before you pick up your sticks, but it does help to have an understanding and appreciation of the other instruments and musicians around you.

➤ **You always liked listening to drummers.** Here's another good reason to pick a seat behind the skins. If you're really interested in something, you'll stick with it longer. When you find yourself listening to your favorite CD and picking out the interesting drum parts, you're well on your way to imitating those parts for real.

➤ **You like to play "air-drum" solos.** Some folks like to play air guitar; others like to play air drums. (Very few like to play air oboe for some reason.) However, just because you like to wave your arms around and pretend that you're playing a crowd-pleasing drum solo doesn't automatically make you drummer material. Sorry.

➤ **You'd rather be in the background than in the spotlight.** If you're somewhat on the shy side and think you're too bashful to front a band (like a lead guitarist does), sitting behind the relative security of a big drum set might sound appealing. The problem is, even though drummers tend to sit in the back, they're really the most important member of the band—everyone depends on them to keep the beat and drive the band forward. It's hard to do this if you're timid and lack self-confidence. Just think of some of the most famous drummers in history and count up how many shy guys are on the list—no one ever accused Buddy Rich of lacking self-confidence!

➤ **You'd rather be in the spotlight than in the background.** On the other hand, the drum throne probably isn't the right place for you if you're a glory hog. Being a drummer is about being part of the team and working with your fellow musicians to create a great-sounding whole. If you're in it only for the spotlight, the rest of the band will suffer. Playing drums isn't about soloing all the time, you know—most of my favorite "drum records" don't have any solos at all, just a great beat!

➤ **You like to pound out your aggression.** Okay, I'll admit that a good session behind the toms is a decent way to release some stress (and it's good aerobic exercise, to boot!), but you shouldn't use the drums as a replacement for a trained therapist. If you're all aggression, your playing will be aggressive, too, and drumming needs to be a mix of loud and soft, of power and of sensitivity. When you play to let off steam, you're shortchanging your fellow musicians (and your audience!).

➤ **Your brother/father/mother/sister/friend played drums, and you want to follow in that person's footsteps.** This isn't a bad reason to play the drums, but make sure you're doing it because you want to—not because others expect you to. I'm not sure that drumming talent is inherited (although **Ringo Starr** and **John Bonham** both sired decent drummers), but if you grew up around drums, chances are good that you picked up something useful along the way. (Besides, you can play someone else's drumset for free—and you might even inherit some hand-me-down skins!)

➤ **You like the way you look (or the way it feels) sitting behind a shiny new drumset.** Hey, who doesn't? Still, just because you can sit inside a sports car doesn't make you Mario Andretti—and sitting behind a set of drums won't make you **Buddy Rich,** either. Drumming isn't about appearances (all the glossy drum company ads aside); it's about talent and feel and groove. So, if you look good and feel powerful sitting behind the drums, make sure you can walk the walk before you decide to make it a full-time thing.

➤ **You want to pick up lots of chicks (or guys).** Let me disillusion you. Drummers don't get groupies. Guitarists and singers get groupies. Think about it. How many fans standing by the stage door at a Rolling Stones concert are waiting for Mick Jagger, and how many are waiting for **Charlie Watts?** I rest my case.

➤ **You appreciate the artistic expression capable with mastery of the instrument.** Now you're talkin'! Not that you can't have fun, but playing drums is serious stuff, and you'll find a lot of *really* serious cats out there. Just listen to a **Kenny Aronoff** or a **Neil Peart** talk about roots and technique and musicianship, and you realize that there is a lot of ground to explore if you're sincere about taking up the instrument. Drums are real musical instruments, and drummers are real musicians. If you're serious about music, being a drummer (or the more formal *percussionist*) is as valid a choice as being a concert pianist!

➤ **You think playing drums would be "fun."** Read the previous paragraph. *Of course* playing drums is fun, but it's also serious business. If you don't mind mixing hard work with your fun, then you have the right mind-set to be a successful drummer.

Perhaps the best reason to play drums, though, is that you love drums. You love the way they sound, you love listening to other drummers, and you love picking up the sticks and playing. If you have a love for drums, then you're well on your way to being a successful drummer!

What Do Drummers Do?

Can you be sure that you want to be a drummer if you're not really sure of what drummers do? Sure, drummers drum, but what does that really mean?

Here are some of things that the best drummers do—and that you'll be doing if you're serious about playing drums:

➤ **Keep the beat.** The drummer is the pulse of the band. You set the tempo, and you make sure that the band *keeps* the tempo. You have to be rock solid all the time and not speed up when you get excited or slow down when you get bored (or when the music gets complicated!).

➤ **Drive the band.** Beyond keeping the beat, you have to make that beat *exciting*. You have to drive the band forward, creating a groove that makes the audience want to get up and dance. (This is tougher than it sounds, since you have to drive forward without speeding up!)

➤ **Set things up.** The drummer is the timekeeper and, in many cases, the conductor. When there's something big coming up—the chorus of the song, the climax of a big solo, or a change in dynamics or instrumentation—it's the drummer's job to set things up and lead into the next section. These setups and fills help propel the band from one part to another and give a little punch to the parts that need it.

➤ **Complement and interact with other players.** A good drummer makes everyone else sound better. It's not enough to sound good yourself and keep a solid beat; you have to play little licks and flourishes that pull the best out of your fellow musicians—

without drawing undue attention to yourself! When the guitarist is soloing, you have to listen to what's going down and anticipate what's coming next—and then add the right fills and accents and crashes to push the soloist to greater heights. When you're laying down a groove, you have to work with the bass player to create the most solid beat. I've always thought of drummers kind of like point guards in basketball: both drive their teams, feed other players, and make everyone else look good—which sometimes means you make more assists than points!

➤ **Add color and variety to the music.** If all you wanted was a solid beat, you could program a drum machine and skip the gig yourself. The best drummers, however, go beyond simple timekeeping to make the song sound that much better. Listen to any hit record from the 1960s that featured **Hal Blaine** on drums, or listen to any of **Dino Danelli's** old Rascals tunes, or listen to any big-band charts from **Buddy Rich** or **Gene Krupa**. These cats laid down a solid beat *and a little bit more,* making the music come alive in a way that less competent drummers couldn't even dream of. (For kicks, listen to The Rascals' "Girl Like You," and try to imagine it with *just* the beat, no other licks or fills. All of a sudden that hit song sounds a little less special, doesn't it?)

➤ **Play an occasional solo.** Oh, yeah, and every now and then you get to step to the forefront (figuratively) and play a little on your own. A little flash, a little crash, and you're a star!

Drum Word

A **gig** is a paying job for you and your band—anything from playing at a wedding reception to performing a standing-room-only concert at a big outdoor stadium.

Of course, these are just the musical things that a drummer does. A drummer also drives a lot (to and from *gigs*), carries a lot of heavy equipment, sets up and tears down that heavy equipment, sits around waiting for the next set to start, and worries about making enough money to buy that next new piece of gear.

There's one more thing that drummers do: practice. We can't forget practice. Good drummers practice a *lot*. Even when you're famous, you still practice—an hour or more a day, every day. (That's because there's always something new to learn!)

So, if you don't like practicing, don't like carrying around heavy equipment, and don't like playing with and interacting with other musicians, don't be a drummer. (Maybe you should play harmonica—not much to carry there!)

Different Drummers

If you're serious about playing drums, sooner or later you'll need to decide what kind of drummer you want to be. "What's that?" you're saying. "I thought all drummers were pretty much the same!" Not that I want to overly complicate your life (and delay your immediate drumming gratification), but no two drummers are alike; there are lots of different types of drumming that you can pursue.

Get Funky: Rock, Country, and R&B Drumming

The drumming you're probably most familiar with is the kind you hear on the radio every day. Rock drummers (and country drummers and *R&B* drummers—the styles are amazingly similar) play a big beat behind popular songs, typically in 4/4 time with straight eighth notes on either the hi-hat or the ride cymbal, and a heavy two and four backbeat on the snare drum. Rock drumming is all about groove, setting the beat for the rest of the band, and playing a little fill at the end of each eight bars. (You'll also have to learn a shuffle beat for a few tunes, but straight eighths is the rule of the day.)

This type of drumming is typically loud and hard and more about feel than finesse. A rock drummer typically plays a five-piece set with a bass drum, a snare drum, two small toms, and one floor tom (although some rock drummers have monster sets with multiple toms and double bass drums); you'll also find a big ride cymbal, a hi-hat, and two or more crash cymbals. The drums in a rocker's drumset are typically bigger than those in a jazz set, which often means deeper shells—and, in many cases, larger head diameters.

If you're a rock drummer, you probably play *matched grip* because that makes it easy to play around the toms. You'll also play with heavier sticks, for both increased volume and a fuller sound on the toms. (You can learn more about rock, country, and R&B drumming in Chapter 18, "In the Pocket: Basic Rock, Country, and R&B Beats.")

Get Swingin': Jazz Drumming

Some rock drummers might take issue with this, but I find that jazz drumming takes a little more technique than other types of playing. You run into a greater variety of musical styles when you play jazz, and you have to play with a greater dynamic range (from really soft to really loud).

There are several different types of jazz drumming, however. Acoustic jazz with a small group means playing in small clubs without a lot of amplification—and playing really soft, in a lot of cases. Drummers playing in small groups typically play small sets—a four-piece set (a bass drum, a snare drum, one small tom, and one floor tom) is common, as are smaller drum sizes (both in depth and diameter). Smaller, dryer cymbals (especially for the ride cymbal) are normal, as are lighter sticks.

Drummers playing in fusion groups or big bands will typically play a bigger, more rocklike set than do small-group drummers. This type of jazz—while still requiring a broad dynamic range—also gets very loud and very powerful, and bigger drums and louder cymbals help cut through the mix.

In all cases, if you're playing jazz, you must master all sorts of beats. In the course of a single gig, you may have to play a little rock, some funk, some straight-ahead swing, a slow blues, a light bossa nova, and a soft ballad. That's a broad repertoire, most of which requires a level of finesse not always necessary in other types of playing.

You can learn more about jazz drumming in Chapter 19, "Swing Time: Basic Jazz Beats."

Drum Word

R&B stands for **rhythm and blues,** otherwise known as soul or urban music.

Drum Note

Whoa! What's all this 4/4 and eighth notes jive? We're talking standard music notation here, and if you're not familiar with it, flip over to Chapter 8, "Wholes, Halves, and Quarters: Notes and Notation," to get up to speed.

Drum Word

Matched grip is a way of holding your sticks so that both your left and right hands are identical. This is in contrast to **traditional grip,** where the left hand is turned up and turned sideways. Learn more about matched and traditional grips in Chapter 9, "Get a Grip: Holding Your Sticks."

Drum Note

You'll find most older jazz drummers playing traditional grip and most younger jazz drummers playing matched grip. It used to be common knowledge that you could coax finer notes out of the snare drum with traditional grip, but this isn't really true—a drummer born and raised with matched grip is just as sensitive on the snare as a traditional-grip guy. Whichever grip you use, just make sure you have lots of left-hand control!

Get Serious: Symphonic Drumming

A drummer doesn't always play a drumset. Symphonic or concert drumming requires you to master a full complement of percussion instruments—from snare drum to tambourine to triangle to timpani to marimba. You'll be playing a classical repertoire—which means symphonies and chamber works from Bach, Beethoven, and other respected composers.

Symphonic drumming is very disciplined and is all about reading, playing, and interpreting—but *not* about improvising. You play what's written, not what you make up. Symphonic drumming can also be very formal; if you're playing a symphony gig, make sure that you have a tux and that your shoes are shined!

You can learn more about timpani and xylophones and other symphonic percussion in Chapter 4, "Bongos and Claves and Vibes, Oh My!: The Rest of the Percussion Family."

Get in Step: Drum Corps Drumming

I sometimes think of drum corps drumming as kind of like symphonic drumming, but with more exercise. That's a little misleading, of course, since drum corps are all about drums. (Symphonic playing, on the other hand, sometimes requires you to rest for 10 or 15 minutes at a time.)

When you play in a drum corps, you need really good chops. You have to be able to play intricate rudimental patterns fast and loud—while marching around in a precise formation! Of course, just because you're in a drum corps doesn't mean you're playing snare drum; drum corps feature a full range of drum parts, from tenor drums to timp-toms to cymbals to several different sizes of bass drum. The corps plays together as a unit, with each part dependent on the other. You'll find playing in a drum corps a lot of work, but it's *terrific* training for your instrument—and a great way to make a lot of lasting friends!

To learn more about drum corps and rudimental drumming, turn to Chapter 14, "Marching Along: Basic Rudimental Beats."

Get Supportive: Percussion and Ethnic Drumming

Many bands of all types—even jazz and country—feature a percussionist in addition to the drummer. In fact, some forms of music—Latin, in particular—feature multiple percussionists and relegate the drummer to the background!

Playing percussion is fun because you get to play a lot of different instruments. You may find yourself switching from congas to maracas to timbales to a bell tree—all in the same song! Your job as a percussionist is to add color to the music and to reinforce what the drummer is doing. You won't play every note in every song, but the notes you play will be very important ones.

You can learn more about ethnic percussion instruments in Chapter 4.

Get Versatile: Studio and Show Drumming

It's one thing to play live in front of an audience and to play off the energy of the band and the crowd. It's another thing to go into a recording studio, put on a set of headphones, *sight-read* your way through a complex score, and play perfectly precise through take after take after take until the song is in the can.

Studio recording is possibly the most challenging type of drumming you can do. A studio musician may be called upon to do virtually *anything*—from laying down a heavy rock beat to swinging through some uptempo jazz to navigating through a complicated symphonic snare drum part to shaking a tambourine. In the studio—or when playing for a TV show or a Broadway musical—you have to be able to do it all.

Drum Word

Sight-reading is the ability to read through and play a piece of written music without ever having seen it before. It's an essential skill for studio and symphonic drummers.

You also have to be able to do it quickly, which means that being a good sight-reader is essential. Plus, you have to do it cleanly because the microphones in the studio will pick up every little buzz or rattle coming from a poorly maintained or tuned kit—as well as any mistakes you might make. In other words, you have to be versatile, quick on the draw, and perfect.

If it sounds like I have a lot of respect for studio drummers, I do. Some of my favorite drummers are studio gods who have helped to define the drum sound of several generations. I'm talking about cats like **Hal Blaine**, **Earl Palmer**, **Benny Benjamin**, and **Roger Hawkins**—guys who could play just about anything you put in front of them, and provide the extra punch to turn an average song into a top 10 hit. (Learn more about these kings of the studio in Chapter 6, "A Brief History of Time: Drummers to Listen To"; find out more about history's most prolific studio drummer in Chapter 7, "King of the Studio: An Interview with Drumming Legend Hal Blaine"; and read about studio drumming today in Chapter 25, "Parting Advice from One of Today's Hottest Drummers: An Interview with Kenny Aronoff.")

How to Become a Drummer—in Three Easy Steps

You still want to be a drummer? Then read on for the one-two-three on how to get to where you want to go.

Step One: Find a Teacher

Although you *can* teach yourself how to play drums (and this book is a good first start for that approach), a better way to learn is with a qualified drum teacher. As painful as it might be to get criticized from time to time, a drum teacher can show you the right (and wrong) ways to stand (or sit), hold your sticks, breathe, and hit the drums. While an instruction book can show you what to do, a teacher can demonstrate how to do it.

If you're serious about playing drums, go to your local music store (or to your music teacher or band director at school) and find a compatible teacher. Spend an hour a week at a drum lesson, and pay attention to what your teacher tells and shows you.

Drum Note

Even full-time drummers take lessons on occasion. It's not uncommon for working drummers to take lessons from a pro when they're in town—because you're never too old to learn!

As your playing matures—or if you want to learn different things—you'll probably find yourself switching teachers. While there's nothing wrong with keeping the same teacher for several years, different teachers have different strengths and weaknesses. You might find one teacher who's terrific at snare drum and drum corps stuff, but you might need to switch to a different teacher when it's time to move to the full set. Most drummers I know have had several teachers throughout their careers—and have learned something important from each and every one of them.

Step Two: Practice, Practice, Practice

In the life of a drummer, actually playing live is only a small part of the playing you do. The vast majority of notes you play will be during practice—either practicing with your band or practicing your own instrument, by yourself. To learn your instrument, you need to practice. To get better on your instrument, you need to practice. To discover new licks and styles, you need to practice. To stay in shape, you need to practice. In short, get ready to spend a lot of time practicing.

If you're just starting out, practicing probably sounds boring. I won't lie to you—it is. But it's also necessary. You have to train your hands (and your feet) to play specific things, and you have to train your mind to react and interact in specific situations. Practicing helps you prepare for anything that comes up in a live playing situation, and it ensures that you have the chops necessary to get the job done.

There are many different ways to practice. When you first start out (in Chapter 10, "A One and a Two and a Three: Playing Your First Notes"), you'll want to set up a snare drum or a practice pad, a music stand, and a metronome. At first, you'll not only be practicing specific music exercises, but you'll also be practicing how to hold your sticks, how to hit the drum, and how to keep a steady beat.

Once you get a little more experienced, you'll be practicing behind a full drumset. You'll still be practicing patterns and exercises, but you'll also pop in a CD from time to time and practice by playing along with various songs. Not that you want to mindlessly copy the beats recorded by the pros; rather, you need to learn how to play with other instruments, and you want to learn from what the pros played. (Too many drummers just play along in their own style, without ever listening to the terrific grooves laid down by legendary drummers—what a waste of practice time!)

You'll eventually get to the point where you're practicing with other musicians, either in your school band or orchestra or with a group of your friends. While this feels very different from practicing alone in your room, until you're playing in front of a paying audience, you're still practicing—and learning.

After all, that's what practice is all about: learning how to play your instrument and learning how to play in a band. Just as you'd never try to fly a commercial aircraft without a lot of hours in a flight simulator, you can't sit down and expect to play the drums without practicing first. As the old adage says, practice makes perfect—there's something to that.

Step Three: Learn to Read

Yeah, I know that you know how to read *words*—now you have to learn how to read *music*.

I can already hear some of you saying, "I don't have to read music to play" or "So-and-so was a great drummer and *he* didn't know how to read music." Both of those statements may be true, but I still contend that you'll get farther in your musical life—and have more opportunities open to you—if you know how to read music.

Imagine this scenario: A big-time producer calls you up and asks you to play drums for an important recording session (or TV show or Broadway musical). You get there, set up your kit, and introduce yourself to the producer. The producer hands you a sheet of music and tells you that the session starts in five minutes. You have no time to listen to the music before you play, you've probably never even heard this stuff before, and you're expected to start playing—for real!—without a lick of practice. All you have is a piece of paper with lots of little black dots on it.

This may sound intimidating, but it's precisely how real musicians work. Unless you play in one band for your entire life, you'll be "the new guy" on a gig sometime in your career. The way "new guys" learn the music is by *reading it*. In fact, most big-time gigs have no rehearsal—you just sit down and start reading.

Of course, if you can't read, you're out of luck. This is why I say it's *essential* to learn how to read—and why I devote an entire chapter (Chapter 8) to reading music.

It's Not Just a Job—Well, Okay, Sometimes It's Just a Job

Okay, now you know what's involved with being a drummer and how to get started. That's just Step One in what could become a lifetime of drumming.

What's life like for a career drummer? Well, the first thing to know is that drumming *is* a career—and, like any job, it has its good days and its bad days. The best days—when everything clicks, the music is great, and you're "one" with your band mates—are like heaven. The worst days—when the music sucks, your hands have a mind of their own, and your band mates are so square that they have corners—are just dreadful. (And, to be honest, you'll probably have more bad days—and average days—than you will great days.)

Professional drumming is a job. Drummers go to "work" every day, just like guys in suits do—it's just that the work is a little different. You put in your time; you deal with all sorts of work-related issues; and you pick up your paycheck. Of course, not too many blue-suit guys get to do their jobs in front of a screaming audience, but that's one of the good points about being a drummer.

Even though professional drumming is a job, when it's good, it's very, very good. There's nothing like the feeling you get when you kick a band into overdrive, when everything is cooking and your fills are perfect and the audience is grooving it. Those days are gold and make everything else—even those long hours practicing by yourself—worthwhile.

The Least You Need to Know

➤ Even though drumming is fun, drummers are serious musicians—and drumming is serious business.

➤ There are many different kinds of drumming, including rock/country/R&B, jazz, symphonic, drum corps, studio, and percussion and ethnic drumming.

➤ Drummers are responsible for keeping the beat, driving the band, setting up important parts of a song, complementing and interacting with other players, adding color and variety to the music, and playing an occasional solo.

➤ If you want to be a drummer, find yourself a good teacher, start practicing, and learn how to read music.

Chapter 2

Before You Play, You Have to Pay: Buying Your First Drums

In This Chapter

➤ How much money should you spend?

➤ What should you look for in a new set?

➤ What brand should you buy?

➤ Where should you shop?

There is no greater thrill for a drummer than unpacking a brand-new set of drums—seeing how the light reflects off the finish, marveling at the untouched white or clear heads, figuring out how to position the stands and the toms just so, giving each of the drums its first tentative hit, and listening to that out-of-the-box sound that is so hard to capture afterward.

Yet, I digress. Before you take receipt of your new drumset, you have to do your homework and figure out which set to buy—and where to buy it. That's what this chapter is all about—helping you spend your money wisely when you decide to buy your first drums.

Before You Buy: Evaluating Different Options

As you consider buying your very first drums, there are several things you need to think about, over and above your budget. While the amount of money you can spend is definitely a deciding factor in what you buy, every price range offers several choices that deliver different bangs for your buck, so to speak.

Snare Drum vs. Drumset: Should You Buy It All Now?

The first thing to decide if you're a beginning drummer is whether you should buy a complete set of drums or just a snare drum. Naturally, you *want* to buy the whole drumset, but if you're just starting out, it may be weeks or months before you progress from simple snare drumming to using the complete set. (In other words, you have to learn how to play one drum before you can play all of them!)

If you buy a drumset before you're ready, you'll be tempted to start pounding the entire kit when you should be concentrating on your snare drum studies. Moving to the full set before you're ready could actually stunt your growth, and few beginning drummers have the discipline to ignore that great-looking set of drums sitting within easy reach!

An approach I recommend—and the one I followed when I was first starting out—is to buy a snare drum first. In fact, buy as good a snare drum as you can afford, since it's the drum you'll be hitting most often, even after you buy the rest of the kit. Then, after you've progressed in your snare drum studies—typically several months down the road—you can buy a complete set (minus snare drum, since you already have one). This approach helps you focus on necessary reading skills and stick technique and also helps you get started with less cash expenditure.

You'll find that many drum manufacturers offer "starter kits" for beginning snare drummers. These kits typically offer a snare drum, a snare drum stand, and a pair of sticks for a special combined price. (Some of these kits also include a snare drum case.) Beginning-level snare drum kits can be found for around $200, although you might want to spend a little more to get a snare that will last you through the first stages of your drumming career.

Drum Note

If you're really unsure about this drumming thing, you might not even want to invest in a snare drum. It's perfectly acceptable to start off with a relatively inexpensive practice pad (typically a piece of rubber mounted on a wood or metal base) until you decide whether it's worth your while to spend the bucks for a good snare drum or drumset. You can buy a practice pad, a stand, and a pair of sticks for around $75, which is a cheap way to find out if you're serious about playing drums.

Spend a Lot or Spend a Little: What Do You Get for Your Money?

Whether you decide to buy a complete drumset or just a snare drum, you'll be faced with a very wide range of equipment. In the case of snare drums, models run from $200 to $1,000 or more, and hit virtually every price point in between. For a complete drumset, you can get by for as little as $300 (without cymbals), or you can spend $7,500 or more for a custom set from a quality company.

Given this broad price range, just what do you get for your money?

It goes without saying that the more you spend, the more you'll get. Higher-priced drums are built better, sound better, and will last longer than lower-priced drums. That said, there are several features you need to look at:

Drum Note

Drumsets typically fall into three major price ranges. *Entry-level* sets sell for $300 to $800 (with basic hardware but without cymbals); *semi-pro* sets fall into the $1,000 to $2,500 range; and *professional* sets sell for $2,500 and up. See "The Bottom Line: How Much Should You Spend?" section later in this chapter for more information about specific sets in these price ranges.

➤ **Shells.** While you'll learn more about different types of shells later in this chapter, know that higher-priced drums typically use higher-quality woods—which produce a better, more resonant sound. Low-end sets typically use woods like basswood or Philippine mahogany (luan), while higher-end sets use maple or birch.

➤ **Finish.** Beginning-level sets typically come in a limited range of finishes—depending on the manufacturer, you might have a choice of three or four basic colors. As you progress to higher-end sets, the range of finishes increases geometrically; some of the high-end stains and painted finishes available for custom sets are one-of-a-kind pieces of art!

➤ **Hardware.** Cheap sets typically have cheap stands—cymbal stands, tom-tom stands, and bass drum pedals that just won't stand up to any heavy-duty playing or gigging. When you spend more money, you get stands that are double-braced and that will stand up to any pounding you can dish out. (I find that some of the first things beginning drummers upgrade are their stands—just to improve the overall sturdiness of their kits.) Another feature to look at on your stands is a "memory lock" that uses a collar of some sort to "remember" your stand's height and angle settings, making it easier to set up your kit to the exact same specifications every time you play.

➤ **Tom-tom mounts.** Lower-priced drumsets feature tom holders that extend into your bass drum, and (in many cases), inside your small toms. While this is a historically accepted practice, anything you hang on or poke into a drum can dramatically effect the resonance of that drum. A better solution is to use so-called suspended tom mounts, such as the RIMS system or similar mounts produced by other manufacturers. Suspended tom mounts don't poke into or attach directly to any of your drums; instead, they suspend a tom by its rim or tuning rods, thus letting the drum vibrate and ring freely. These suspended tom mounts cost more than simpler traditional mounts, however, so you won't find this option on many entry-level kits.

Notice that I didn't talk at all about cymbals, since cymbals are typically not included in drumset packages and must be purchased separately (They're also discussed separately later in this chapter.) However, the general comments I made about low-priced/high-priced drums apply to cymbals; when you spend more money, you get a better-sounding, more durable set of cymbals. In fact, if you have a few extra bucks to spare, put it in your cymbal budget and go for a higher-end hi-hat and a better-sounding ride—the two cymbals you'll use the most.

Drum Tip

Here's something real musicians know: The better your equipment, the more you'll play it. Obviously, a great musician can make even a cruddy instrument sound good, but most musicians (beginning or experienced) find that the sound and feel of a high-quality instrument inspire them to spend more time with that instrument. If you have a world-class drumset, I guarantee that you'll spend more time playing and practicing—the best instruments are just so enjoyable that you can't pull yourself away. On the other end of the scale, a poor-quality instrument can be a chore to play—you have to work harder to produce a sound that isn't quite as good.

That's not to say that everyone should invest in the highest-priced drums available. Nothing can be further from the case—after all, a lousy driver in a Ferrari is still a lousy driver. Still, if you're serious about playing drums, save up a little bit more and buy the best-quality set within your budget. A better-quality set *will* make a difference in your playing and dedication!

New vs. Used: Can You Save Some Bucks with a Previously Owned Set?

Here's a very real option that too few drummers take advantage of. Let's say you have $800 to spend on a set. When you visit your friendly neighborhood drum dealer, you see a handful of no-name kits at this price and even a few entry-level kits from Ludwig, Mapex, and other name manufacturers. However, if you ask, you'll also find a selection of *used* kits in the same price range, and these will typically be higher-end kits than what you're looking at new. In other words, you can often get more bang for your buck in a used set.

Used drums aren't like used cars—you don't have to worry about lots of moving parts wearing out or breaking down. In fact, unless the kit was used for a cross-country tour by a big-name heavy metal drummer, you'll probably find that the drums and accompanying hardware are in pretty good shape—and have probably been restored to some degree by the drum dealer. You'll likely also find that the quality of the drums themselves—the wood and the resultant sound—is much better than what you can find in a new kit in the same price range. (You may even get lucky and find a real high-quality vintage set in your price range—which could make you the envy of all the other drummers in your town!)

So when you're looking for a new snare drum or drumset, make sure you look through the previously owned section. You might like what you find!

Name Brand vs. No Name: Which Is the Best Deal?

Once you know what to look for in a kit, how do you compare two similar kits at a similar price point? One important thing to look at is the drums' manufacturer—and that manufacturer's reputation.

Drum Note

Vintage drums are old drums that, for one reason or another, have some inherent value to collectors. Not every old drum is a collectable; some old drums are just old drums. But certain brands and lines and models have taken on collectible status over the years and thus are worth a great deal of money to vintage drum aficionados.

Many of these vintage drums feature unique hardware or finishes, were produced in very low quantities, or have some historical significance—they were played by a famous drummer or were the first to introduce specific features.

Back when these drums were new, few drummers thought about their value as vintage instruments—most drummers just wanted the instruments to hold up and sound good for their next gig! This means that many vintage drums got "repaired" and modified with nonstandard equipment and heads, thus diminishing their value to collectors. (Naturally, collectors want to collect things in their original state whenever possible.)

Logically, this means that if you have a unique set of drums—sorry, but typically not entry-level sets—you should avoid modifying them with nonstandard equipment. If you keep them pristine, they may be worth a little extra to a collector some day.

If you want to learn more about vintage drums—such as the Ludwig Black Beauty or Slingerland Radio King snare drums—check out a book called *The Great American Drums (and the Companies That Made Them),* by Harry Cangany, available at a drum shop near you. (You can also turn to the end of this chapter to read an interview with Mr. Cangany and find out what he recommends to drummers buying their first drums.)

If you're looking at entry-level sets, you'll find a lot of equipment from "no-name" manufacturers. These kits, while appearing to be good bargains, might prove disappointing in the long run. That's not to say that no-name sets aren't necessarily good drums, but rather that no-names are also "no value" sets when it comes to selling them or trading them in for a better set at a later date. You might also find that it's difficult to find spare parts or extra drums for a no-name kit. In other words, you'll probably be stuck with what you bought when you go no-name—which isn't necessarily a bad thing, especially if the price is right.

On the other hand, most brand-name drum manufacturers make some very affordable entry-level kits—often in the same price range as no-names. Even though these entry-level kits may have limited features or may be manufactured to different tolerances than the rest of that manufacturer's line, you'll have the backing of a major drum company in case anything goes bad or you need spare parts—and these low-end brand-name kits typically have a higher resale or trade-in value than similarly priced no-name kits.

So, what are the most popular names in the drum business today? The top five brands in the United States, in order, are Pearl, Ludwig, Tama, Mapex, and Drum Workshop. These big five offer sets at various levels and in various price ranges—as do a half dozen other major manufacturers. Here's a quick list of the top dozen name players in today's drum market, in alphabetical order:

➤ **Drum Workshop (DW).** DW is the Mercedes of drum manufacturers. This company's bass drum pedals, hi-hats, and cymbal stands are standard equipment for a significant number of drum pros (even those who play and endorse other manufacturers' drums), and its drums, if you can afford them, are among the best you can find. Each DW set is pretty much custom-made; you can specify the size, finish, and lug/rim finishes of each drum in your kit and choose among a staggering variety of custom-made snare drums in various exotic woods and metals.

One of Drum Work-shop's typical high-quality custom sets.

(Photo courtesy of Drum Workshop, Inc.)

➤ **Fibes.** Not quite the same company that was around in the late 1960s and 1970s (and that made the vintage fiberglass kit I've played since 1974), the new Fibes is a small manufacturer of high-quality wood and clear acrylic drums. The company uses much of the old Fibes hardware and still makes the fiberglass snare drum that so impressed Buddy Rich and other drummers through the years.

➤ **GMS.** This is a relatively new, higher-end American drum company. Its top-of-the-line Grand Master Series (GMS) features eight-ply maple shells and all-brass hardware.

➤ **Gretsch.** Even though Gretsch makes a full line of sets, the company is still known for its great-sounding small jazz kits—and remains the drum of choice for traditional jazz drummers.

➤ **Ludwig.** Ludwig is a full-line percussion company—and even manufactures timpani and marimbas through Musser, a sister company. Ludwig's kits range from the entry-level Accent line to the semi-pro Rocker and Rocker Pro/Classic Birch series, to the top-of-the-line Classic series. Ludwig's Black Beauty snare drums remain the choice of many pro drummers, just as the company's low-priced snare drum kits appeal to large numbers of beginners.

Quality maple drums from Ludwig's Classic series.

(Photo courtesy of Ludwig Drum Co.)

➤ **Mapex.** Mapex is an up-and-comer, producing a full line of drums at all price points. The company's entry-level V-series and M-series kits represent a terrific value to beginning drummers, and their top-of-the-line Orion sets are among the best available in the industry.

A quality six-plus-one piece set from Mapex's Orion line—complete with a second snare drum!

(Photo printed with permission by Mapex USA, Inc.)

➤ **Pacific.** Pacific is a division of Drum Workshop, with drums and equipment designed by DW and manufactured overseas. Pacific's entry-level sets are unique in offering RIMS-type suspended tom holders—in the same price range as low-quality no-name sets.

A pretty good low-end set from Pacific—note the suspended tom holders.

(Photo courtesy of Pacific Drums and Percussion, a division of Drum Workshop, Inc.)

➤ **Pearl.** This is the largest drum company in the United States, with a wide variety of drum lines—from the entry-level Forum and Export series to the top-of-the-line Masters sets.

➤ **Premier.** This is a British drum company with an 80-year-old tradition, playing in the mid- and high-end of the market.

➤ **Sonor.** The high-quality sets from this German company are known for their thick shells (would you believe 12-ply large toms and bass drums?) and massive hardware—very sturdy equipment overall.

➤ **Tama.** Tama is one of the "big five" drum companies, with a wide variety of quality sets—from the low-end Swingstar line to the high-end Starclassic series.

A great-looking six-plus-one piece Starclassic set from Tama—some of the best drums and hardware in the business.

(Photo courtesy of Tama)

➤ **Yamaha.** This division of the Japanese conglomerate has a variety of sets—from entry-level Debut series to the pro-level Recording Customs.

There are other brands you'll run into, of course. Some, such as CB, Peace, and Sunlite, offer lower-level sets; others, such as Ayotte, Brady, and Noble & Cooley, are smaller manufacturers offering custom and semi-custom drums. If you're unsure about a particular manufacturer, ask your local drum dealer and any drummer friends what they think—you'll quickly find out if a manufacturer has a good or bad reputation.

The Big Purchase: Buying a Drumset

Buying a drumset is a major purchase, with lots of component parts. A full set includes a snare drum, a bass drum (played with a bass drum pedal), one or more small toms (also called riding toms), one or more large toms (also called floor toms, even if they're suspended off the floor!), a variety of cymbals, and all the stands and holders necessary to put everything in its place.

A drumset is typically described as having a certain number of "pieces," where each piece is a separate drum. (You don't count cymbals or stands as pieces.) For example, a set with a snare drum, a bass drum, one small tom, and one large tom is a four-piece set; add a second small tom, and you have a five-piecer.

The following diagrams show several typical setups. Note that there is no such thing as "the" correct setup; every drummer sets up his or her drums differently. Also note that these diagrams show traditional right-handed setups; if you're a lefty, you can reverse the setups, reverse part of the setups (maybe moving the snare to the other side), or play left-handed on a right-handed set.

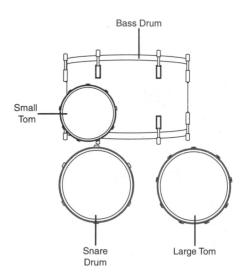

Bass Drum

Small Tom

Snare Drum

Large Tom

A traditional 4-piece setup—typical sizes are a 5-inch × 14-inch snare drum, a 14-inch × 22-inch bass drum, an 8-inch × 12-inch or 9-inch × 13-inch small tom, and a 16-inch × 16-inch large tom.

The very popular 5-piece setup—a 5-inch × 14-inch snare drum, a 14-inch × 22-inch bass drum, an 8-inch × 12-inch and a 9-inch × 13-inch small tom, and a 16-inch × 16-inch large tom.

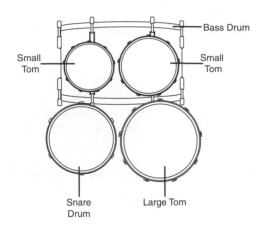

One type of 6-piece set, with an extra small tom (typically in the 10-inch × 14-inch range).

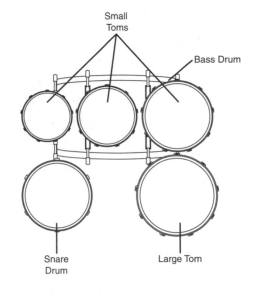

A variation on the 6-piece set, with a 16-inch × 18-inch large tom instead of a third small tom.

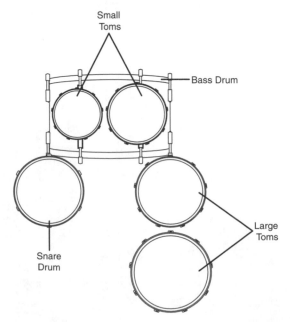

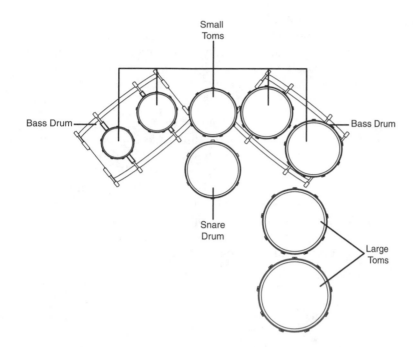

Small
Toms

Bass Drum

Bass Drum

Snare
Drum

Large
Toms

A double-bass set, with a full rack of toms.

How to Evaluate a Drum

Whether you're looking at bass drums, tom-toms, or snare drums, several common elements affect the sound of the drum. These include the size of the shell, the thickness of the shell, the type of wood used for the shell, and how much stuff is hanging from or poking through the drum. Beyond the drum itself, you also need to consider what types of heads are used and how the drums are tuned (discussed in Chapter 5, "Heads, Shells, and Lugs: Tuning and Caring for Your Drums").

Drum sizes are normally expressed with the shell depth first and the head/shell diameter second. A snare drum with a 5-inch depth and a 14-inch diameter is described as a "5 × 14" drum; a tom with an 8-inch depth and a 12-inch diameter is an "8 × 12." The larger the diameter of the drum, the lower the pitch, so you'll see a typical set of toms progressing from 12-inch to 13-inch to 14-inch to 16-inch diameters, with the resulting pitches moving from high to low. When examining the depth of the drum, note that shallower depths offer very good sensitivity (the ability to play quietly and still produce a full tone), while deeper toms have a greater low-end range but require more force to generate a full tone.

"Standard" tom sizes are 8-inch × 12-inch, 9-inch × 13-inch, 10-inch × 14-inch, and so on. So-called "power" sizes go for more depth, with 10-inch × 12-inch, 11-inch × 13-inch, and 12-inch × 14-inch sizes fairly common.

Most drums are made of multiple layers—or plies—of wood. Thin shells (typically with four plies) are quite popular, as they resonate easily and generate a very rich and deep "woody" tone; these drums are preferred for recording and other close-miked situations.

Drum Note

Another, slightly more technical, element to consider is the drum's bearing edge. This is the edge of the shell upon which the drum head is placed. Rounded bearing edges sound a little different than sharper bearing edges; it's all about how much head touches the shell. In addition, lower-priced drums are apt to have rougher or uneven bearing edges, which can dramatically impact the quality of the drum's sound.

Drum Note

Some manufacturers use different plies on different sizes of drums in an attempt to produce a more even sound around the kit. For example, Drum Workshop uses fewer plies on its smaller tom-toms and more plies on its large toms and bass drums.

Medium-thick shells (typically six-ply) are stiffer and have less vibration but with greater projection. Thick shells (eight or more plies) don't have as much ring but have really great projection and a higher pitch; they're ideally suited to loud rock playing in large venues. Go with a thinner shell for a lower pitch; go with a thicker shell if you're playing in a really loud band.

The wood used in the plies also contributes to the sound of the drum. Maple is the favorite wood of many drummers, as it produces a fairly even and rich sound across the entire frequency spectrum. Birch drums have a slightly stronger high-frequency response while maintaining a good low-end punch and are preferred by many studio drummers. (Yamaha's birch Recording series have been studio staples for close to two decades.) Mahogany (actually Philippine mahogany, or luan), which is used in many low-end sets, produces a warm sound with decent bottom and punch but with less high-end.

Drum Note

Wood isn't the only material drums are made of. Back in the 1970s, the old Fibes company made a popular series of fiberglass drums that lacked warmth but had tremendous projection; today's new Fibes company is still making that cutting fiberglass snare drum. (I have a set of Fibes fiberglass drums made in 1974, and I can vouch for their ability to cut through just about any mix!)

Another 1970s trend having a millennial resurgence is the clear acrylic drum, popularized back then by Fibes, Zickos, and Ludwig's Vistalite series. Acrylic drums are known for their unusual looks and a big, boomy sound—popularized by **John Bonham** of Led Zeppelin fame. (I had a set of blue-tinted Ludwig Vistalites before I bought my Fibes; I found it impossible to tune those things for anything *but* a boomy sound!) Today both Fibes and Zickos still make acrylic drums, and the old 1970s acrylics are very popular among vintage collectors.

While the majority of today's drums have shells of either wood plies or solid wood, Remo makes all its shells from a material it calls Acousticon. Acousticon is a resin-impregnated wood fiber material that is lighter than a traditional wood-ply shell, with greater weather-resistance and good projection. It's wood, but it isn't. I find that these Remo drums sound surprisingly good.

Of course, snare drums are available in just about any material you can think of. You can find snare drums with shells of maple, various exotic woods, brass, steel, copper, and bronze. Each material has a distinctive sound, and you have to hear some of these drums to get a good feel for their strengths and weaknesses.

In general, the more a drum vibrates or resonates, the fuller the sound. Anything that keeps a drum from vibrating (such as more plies in the shell) works to deaden the drum's natural sound. The primary cause of deadening vibrations is the hardware attached to or hanging off the drum. Big, heavy lugs (used to attach the head and rim to the drum) dampen a lot of vibrations, as do tom-tom holders—especially those that actually poke through the shell of the tom or bass drum.

To work around this hardware problem, many manufacturers produce low-mass lugs that minimize contact with the drum shell. In addition, so-called suspended tom mounts—such as the popular RIMS system—hang toms by their rims or tuning rods, thus avoiding any direct hardware contact with the shell itself. If you go with a suspended tom mount, you should also think about using separate tom-tom floor stands, as opposed to a bass drum–mounted tom holder; getting rid of the tom holder enables the bass drum to resonate more fully than otherwise.

Choosing a Snare Drum

The snare drum is the most important drum in your kit. In fact, you may want to buy your snare drum before you buy the rest of your drumset; in any case, you should invest as much money as you can afford in this particular drum.

The following diagram shows the parts of a snare drum. You hit the top (batter) head, which is typically coated with a rough finish to facilitate playing with brushes. The bottom (snare) head is much thinner, to better vibrate the wire snares that give the snare drum its distinct buzz.

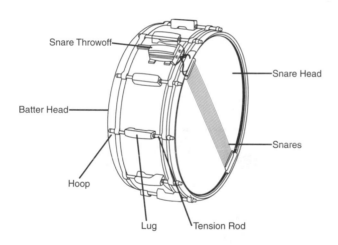

The most important drum in your kit—the snare drum—viewed from underneath.

The snare assembly itself is key to the sound and usability of the drum. The snare throwoff should operate smoothly and completely disengage the snares (making the drum sound more like a tom-tom) when in the off position. The snare assembly should also facilitate quick and easy tuning of the snares; tighter snares produce a crisper sound, while looser snares produce a buzzier, thicker sound.

Most snare drums are 14 inches in diameter, although some drummers use 12-inch and 13-inch "piccolo" snare drums to produce a higher-pitched sound (with a lot of "crack"). Typical depth for a snare used in a drumset is in the 4½-inch to 5½-inch range, although deeper drums can be employed for a "fatter," deeper sound.

Popular steel-shelled snare drums from Ludwig.

(Photo courtesy of Ludwig Drum Co.)

Snare drum shells can be made from a variety of woods and metals, each of which produce a slightly different sound, as detailed in the following table. It's safe to say that most beginning-level snare drums are steel, although wood-shelled snares are quite popular among professional drummers.

Sound Characteristics of Snare Drum Shells

Shell	Sound
Maple (multiple-ply)	Dark and warm
Maple (solid-wood)	Low body, strong midrange focus, solid high-frequency crack
Steel	Powerful yet sensitive, medium pitch and tone
Bronze	Pleasant midrange sound, capable of being loud and aggressive
Brass	Bright, higher-pitched

Drum Note

Since different types of snare drums produce dramatically different sounds, many pro drummers own multiple snare drums and use different drums for different types of music. Some drummers (myself included) will use two snare drums in their "live" setup, with the second snare positioned to the left of the hi-hat. (As an example, my personal setup includes a 6½-inch × 14-inch solid-maple model as my main snare and a 5-inch × 13-inch bronze model as a secondary snare; the larger drum produces a big and fat sound, while the secondary snare is higher-pitched with a really loud and ringy crack.)

A selection of wood-shelled snare drums from Drum Workshop— from 10-inch × 14-inch to 4-inch × 14-inch.

(Photo courtesy of Drum Workshop, Inc.)

When you're looking at wood snare drum shells, consider, also, how the shell is constructed. Most wood shells are made of several different plies of wood; fewer plies create a thinner shell that has more resonance and a lower pitch than thicker shells. Some high-end snares feature solid-wood shells, made from a single sheet of wood. These solid-wood snare drums produce a sound that combines low-end warmth with a strong high-end crack.

Snare drums come in a variety of sizes, types, and prices and are available from every major manufacturer as well as a lot of small, custom manufacturers. Prices range from around $200 to $1,000 or more, depending on the shell material and size, types of lugs, snare assembly, and other equipment.

Choosing a Bass Drum

The bass drum is the punch at the bottom of your kit, the boom-boom-boom that drives the music forward, works with the bass player to establish a groove, and kicks out important accents. You want a bass drum with a good low thud, enough ring to cut through the mix without sounding excessively boomy, and enough presence to make itself felt as well as heard.

What size bass drum you choose depends on the type of playing you're doing. If you're playing in an acoustic jazz group, go with a smaller, punchier drum, such as a 14-inch × 18-inch or a 14-inch × 20-inch. For more popular music, 14-inch × 22-inch or 16-inch × 22-inch are fairly versatile sizes—although some "power" setups are going with an extra-deep 18-inch × 22-inch bass drum. If you're playing heavy metal or other arena rock music, go all the way up to a 16-inch × 24-inch or 18-inch × 24-inch, which will give you a very loud, very boomy sound.

If you're buying an entry-level kit, chances are good that your small tom holder will be mounted on top of your bass drum. This is a traditional practice—and very convenient—but can serve to stifle your bass drum's vibrations and deaden the drum's sound. A better solution is to mount your toms from a floor stand, thus allowing the bass drum to freely resonate—and produce a deeper, fuller sound.

Drum Note

Drum Workshop and some other manufacturers make snare drums that feature a three-part shell. The outside rings—nearest the top and bottom heads—are typically maple ply, while the center ring is brass. These drums purport to combine the best qualities of different types of shells—the warmth and depth of maple with the brighter qualities of brass.

The bottom of your set—
the bass drum.

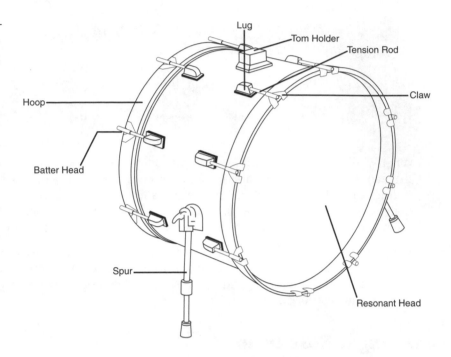

Lug
Tom Holder
Tension Rod
Claw
Hoop
Batter Head
Spur
Resonant Head

The other major pieces of equipment on the bass drum are the spurs. These are two forward-angled rods with either grippy rubber or pointed metal ends that help to keep the bass drum from lurching forward as you play. Look for spurs that fold up or detach for easy packing—and that have enough grip to keep your drum from getting away from you!

Choosing Your Tom-Toms

Tom-toms are the color in your kit. A typical drumset will have two or more toms; the more toms you have, the more options you have when playing fills or solos around the set.

Toms mounted above your bass drum—even if they're hanging from a separate stand—are called small toms or riding toms. If you have only one small tom (like a traditional jazz setup), look for an 8-inch × 12-inch or 9-inch × 13-inch model. If you have a dual small tom setup, you can go with several different combinations, with two-drum combinations of 10-inch and 12-inch, 12-inch and 13-inch, 12-inch and 14-inch, or 13-inch and 14-inch diameters. As previously discussed, you can go with standard shell dimensions or with deeper "power" toms for a fuller sound.

There are various types of holders available for your toms. Most holders today use some sort of ball or ratchet device to enable an almost limitless number of positions; some include memory locks to "remember" the tom position each time you set up. So-called suspended tom holders are very popular on higher-end sets; these holders attach to the rim or to the tuning rods, not to the shell, thus suspending the drum and avoiding resonance-killing direct-to-shell contact.

Drum Tip

Setting up your kit on a large throw rug or piece of carpet is the best way to keep equipment from sliding away when you're playing.

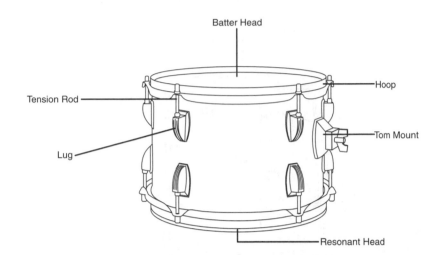

Batter Head

Tension Rod

Lug

Hoop

Tom Mount

Resonant Head

Your set's tenor voice—the small tom.

Tama's Star-Cast Mounting System—note how the holder attaches to the hoop, not the shell.

(Photo courtesy of Tama)

Where small toms are mounted directly in front of you, large toms are mounted off to your side. They're also larger than small toms, typically with diameters of 14 inches, 16 inches, or even 18 inches. If you go with a single large tom, you'll probably want a 14-inch × 16-inch or 16-inch × 16-inch model; you can add a second large tom either one size larger or one size smaller, if you like.

Where small toms are typically hung from a stand or a bass drum–mounted tom holder, large toms are, more often than not, fitted with three legs—thus explaining why large toms are often called floor toms. A newer trend is to suspend large toms from a stand, just as you do your small toms. If you go this route, you'll probably go with shallower shells in so-called "fast" sizes—12 inches × 14 inches or 14 inches × 16 inches.

Drum Note

Just because a drummer has a second floor tom doesn't mean that it will get a lot of use. **Buddy Rich** was famous for using his second floor tom as a towel and soft drink holder!

On the floor and to your right—the large tom.

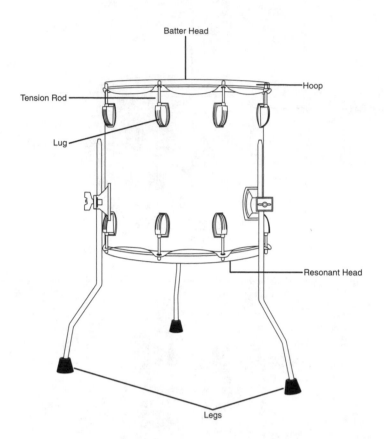

Drum Tip

If you do much traveling or gigging with your drums, you'll probably want to invest in a good set of drum cases. You can choose from cloth or fiber drum bags, or heavy-duty, hard-shell fiberglass cases. I like the more-expensive hard-shell cases (combined with some sort of inner lining to pad the drum and protect it from scratches) because of their better protection from drops and dings, but any protection is better than no protection. When you invest a lot of money in a good set of drums, it only makes sense to invest a little more to protect them!

Choosing Stands and Pedals

To put all this equipment in its place, you'll need a variety of stands and pedals. Stands are necessary to hold cymbals, snare drums, tom-toms, and anything else that doesn't sit directly on the floor. Most drummers end up with the following stands in their kit:

➤ A snare drum stand, which holds the snare in a type of "bucket" between your legs.

➤ Cymbal stands, in either straight or "boom" designs. (Boom stands use an angled section to place a cymbal closer in than is possible with a straight stand.)

➤ A hi-hat stand, which holds the two hi-hat cymbals you play with your left foot.

➤ Tom-tom stands, which hold small or large toms.

➤ Multi-stands, which combine two or more standard stand functions. (For example, Drum Workshop makes multi-stands that hold two toms and a cymbal boom—very space-efficient!)

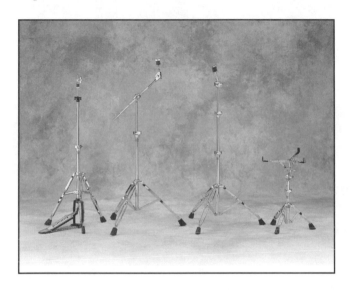

Double-braced stands from Ludwig—from left to right: hi-hat, boom cymbal, regular cymbal, and snare drum stands.

(Photo courtesy of Ludwig Drum Co.)

If you're tough on your kit—if you do a lot of traveling or if you play very loud and hard—consider buying heavy-duty double-braced stands. The legs of these stands have two bracing pieces instead of the standard single brace, and they typically have wider bases for increased sturdiness. You should also look for stands with memory locks to help you accurately position each stand in the exact same fashion every time you set up.

Even though you need cymbal stands and a hi-hat, the most important piece of hardware in your kit is probably your bass drum pedal. This pedal—played with your right foot, if you have a typical right-handed setup—moves a beater that strikes the batter head of your bass drum. Good pedals are not only quiet and reliable, but they also let drummers with a fast right foot execute both fast and subtle bass drum strokes.

While most every drum manufacturer offers at least one type of bass drum pedal, the industry's most popular pedals come from Drum Workshop. DW's chain-driven pedals are sturdy, reliable, and fast—just what every drummer is looking for!

Finally, you'll need something to sit on. A drummer's chair is called a throne (hey, you're the king of the band!); make sure you pick one that's both comfortable (for those long, hard gigs) and sturdy. You don't want your hind quarters to fall asleep midway through a set—nor do you want the center pole to thrust through the seat under stress! (Ouch!)

Drum Workshop's popular chain-drive bass drum pedal—the most-used pedal in the business.

(Photo courtesy of Drum Workshop, Inc.)

Drum Tip

If you have a double bass drum setup, you'll need two bass drum pedals. You can get a dual-bass effect from a single bass drum by using a double bass pedal, which uses two pedals (one positioned by your hi-hat) to drive two bass drum beaters on a single bass drum.

Choosing Cymbals

A drumset is more than just drums—it also contains several cymbals of various types. Cymbals are made from spun or hammered brass and are available in a mind-staggering number of different sizes and weights.

Every set should have at least one of these three basic types of cymbals:

➤ **Ride.** This is a larger, heavier cymbal—typically in the 20-inch diameter range—on which you play a straight-eighth backing pattern. A good ride cymbal has a relatively clean *attack* with a defined stick "ping," without a lot of built-up overtones or "wash."

➤ **Crash.** These are smaller, thinner cymbals—typically in the 16-inch to 18-inch range—that you hit hard to accentuate important points in the music. A good crash cymbal has a defined attack without being too overpowering.

➤ **Hi-hat.** This is a pair of cymbals—typically 14 inches in diameter—that you click together with your left foot via a hi-hat pedal. You can strike the hi-hat either closed (clicked together) or open (left slightly open, for more of a splashy sound).

You'll also find various special-effect cymbals, such as splash cymbals (small, thin, and splashy-sounding), sizzle cymbals (a ride cymbal with rivets, for a sustained "sizzling" sound), china cymbals (thin cymbals with an inverted edge that you play upside down for a "trashy" ride or crash sound), and swish cymbals (big chinas with rivets). These special-effect cymbals, while nice, are not necessary—especially in a beginning setup.

As the following diagram details, a basic setup might have five cymbals—a 20-inch ride cymbal, two crash cymbals (16 inches and 18 inches), and a hi-hat.

When you're shopping for cymbals, you'll be confronted with a brain-numbing variety from several major manufacturers, chief among them Sabian, Zildjian, and Paiste. While I'll provide a few tips for smart cymbal shopping, the best way to find the right cymbal is by ear, so bring a stick and start hitting!

First, identify the type of cymbal you want. If you want a ride cymbal, stick to the rides—don't try to use a big crash cymbal as a ride, because you won't be happy with the results.

Next, look for the right size. Generally, the larger the cymbal, the deeper the pitch. So, if you want a high-pitched cymbal, go for a smaller diameter; if you want a deep pitch, go for a larger cymbal. Ride cymbals are also larger cymbals than crashes—crashes are typically in the 16-inch to 18-inch diagonal range, whereas rides are typically 20 inches and larger.

Drum Word

Attack is the initial sound made when you hit a drum or cymbal—as opposed to the ring or "after tone." A so-called "clean" or "defined" attack produces a clearly distinguished sound, where a "muddy" or "mushy" attack tends to blend more into the general mix.

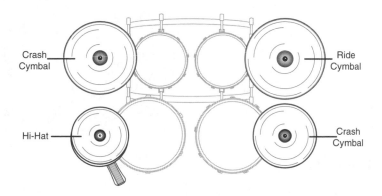

A typical cymbal setup—with two crash cymbals, a ride cymbal, and a hi-hat.

Now you can look at cymbal thickness. In general, thinner cymbals have a faster attack and a quicker decay (and a brighter sound), while thicker cymbals have more overtones and a longer, louder ring (and a darker sound).

In general, brighter, higher-pitched cymbals tend to have a little more projection and cut through loud mixes very well. However, brighter cymbals can also be a little overwhelming, especially in lower-volume situations. If you want to blend in well with the rest of your band—especially at lower volume levels—choose a lower-pitched cymbal.

Drum Tip

When auditioning cymbals, make sure that you use the same sticks you use when you're actually playing. Cymbals sound a lot different when hit with a thick stick than with a thin stick—and wood tips sound much different than nylon tips on a ride cymbal.

Rock, country, and R&B drummers tend to gravitate toward brighter cymbals, such as Sabian's AA or AAX series or Zildjian's A or A Custom series. Many jazz drummers prefer darker, hand-hammered cymbals, such as Sabian's HH series or Zildjian's K and K Custom series. You shouldn't feel bound by tradition, however; pick the cymbals that sound best to your ears for the music you play.

If you're just starting out, look for some of the prepackaged cymbal sets from Sabian, Zildjian, and other companies. These sets package cymbals with matching tonalities, typically including a ride cymbal, a crash cymbal, and a hi-hat at an affordable price. You can find a variety of entry-level cymbal sets in the $100 to $300 range (look for Sabian's B8 series or Zildjian's ZBT series), as well as higher-quality packages at higher price points.

One of Sabian's prepackaged Performance Sets—with a 20-inch ride cymbal, a 16-inch crash, and a 14-inch hi-hat.

(Photo courtesy of Sabian)

Hit It: Choosing the Right Sticks

If you think you have a lot of different cymbals to choose from, wait until you see the large variety of drum sticks available. Manufacturers such as Pro-Mark, Zildjian, and Vic Firth make literally hundreds of different types of sticks, all with slightly different lengths, diameters, tapers, and beads.

The end of the stick that you hit with is called the bead. You can find sticks with all different types and shapes of beads; some are round, some are oval, some are more pointy. In addition, you can buy sticks with either wood or nylon beads. Nylon-tip sticks tend to produce a brighter sound on cymbals and also last a little longer since they don't chip. On the other hand, many drummers don't like the bright pinginess of nylon tips, preferring the warmer sound of a wood tip. It's your choice.

The opposite end of the stick is called the butt. (No cracks, okay?) A stick is typically straight from the butt to the shoulder, and then tapers down to the bead. Different sticks have different taper angles and shoulder lengths. Again, it's your choice.

Choosing the right drumstick is a very personal decision. If you play a lot of soft music or jazz, you may want a thinner, lighter stick. If you play a lot of heavy rock, you may want a thicker, heavier stick with a big, round bead. In either case, you still have dozens of different models to choose from, and the models aren't named or numbered in a way to help you make your choice. In fact, sticks with the same number aren't necessarily the same from one manufacturer to another. And not all sticks are numbered—some are "signature" sticks named after a particular endorser. It's all very confusing!

Drum Note

I've known some jazz drummers who so dislike a bright ping on their ride cymbals that they actually soak the beads of new drumsticks in water for several days to produce the "mushiest" sound imaginable!

Bead   Shoulder   Butt

All sticks look pretty much like this—but they're all different!

That said, if you're just starting out, consider using a slightly larger and heavier stick, such as a 2A or 2B. For good all-around drumset playing, it's hard to beat a 5A or 5B. For softer jazz or symphonic playing, consider a 7A or 8A. (Better yet, ask your teacher what kind of stick he or she recommends.)

When selecting a stick, look for a good-quality hardwood with the grain running uniformly from butt to bead. The kind of wood you choose will affect the feel, balance, sound, and durability of the stick. Most sticks today are made of American hickory, which has a good combination of strength and weight. Other popular woods include oak, maple, birch, and beech.

Drum Tip

While the "standard" drum stick numbering system is anything but standard—and one manufacturer's 5A might be lighter or heavier than the same stick from a different manufacturer—there is some small amount of logic applied to the numbering of the most-popular models. In general, the higher the number, the smaller the stick. So a 2A is heavier than a 5A, while a 7A is lighter than either. (This doesn't apply to manufacturer-specific numbers, however, so you can't easily tell where a Pro-Mark 747 or 808 fits in the lineup.)

You should definitely try the sticks before you buy them, even if you've bought that particular type of stick before. Tap the sticks each on a solid surface to hear the pitch and to "feel" the wood; avoid sticks that feel or sound hollow. Make sure that both sticks in a pair are the same weight; you want a matching pair. Roll the sticks to make sure that they're straight; you don't want to be playing a pair of bananas.

The bottom line is that you should choose a size that fits well in your hand—both in diameter and in length—and that works well for the types of music you play. Don't choose a particular type of stick just because your friends use it or because a famous drummer endorses it; your hands aren't the same as theirs.

Meet Mr. Drum Dealer: Choosing Where to Buy

Now that you know what to buy, where should you buy it?

You can normally find drums for sale at four different types of dealers:

➤ **Full-service music store.** These mom and pop–type music stores carry all types of instruments, including drums. While I always like buying from moms and pops, unless Mom or Pop (or one of their kids) is a drummer, you might find a limited selection and limited knowledge on the part of store staff. Still, if the staff and selection is good, this is a good place to buy.

➤ **Chain music superstore.** Large national music-store chains, such as Sam Ash, Guitar Center, and MARS, have showrooms as big as some warehouses. You'll typically find large selections and good prices—and some chain-specific models in selected instances. Not all drum manufacturers sell to these superstores, however, especially when you're talking high-end and custom sets. The quality of staff is variable as well; some locations have great drummers on staff while others don't. Check out the stores in your area before you buy.

➤ **Catalog or Internet-based retailer.** Direct-to-consumer eCommerce is the next big thing, so direct drum dealers are popping up all over the place. If you know exactly what you want, buying online or through a catalog can sometimes save you money— as long as you don't forget the shipping costs! However, you won't get a lot of personal service online, and there's no way to play a set over the Internet, so this type of dealer isn't for everyone.

Drum Note

Know that not every drum dealer sells drums from every manufacturer. If you have your heart set on a specific brand of drums, your dealer choices may be limited.

➤ **Drum-only dealer.** What can I say—I love drum shops! I like walking into a store that's all drums and nothing but drums, that's staffed by drummers, that offers drum lessons from its own staff in the rear of the store, that has a huge selection of drums and cymbals, and that actually lets you play the drums in the store. A good drum shop will not only sell you your drums, but it also will service them and help you keep them in tip-top shape. You can also find a good selection of used and vintage drums at most drum shops, as well as a variety of custom and semi-custom drums. In short, I always recommend that you check out your local drum dealer when you're looking for a new set—it's a good bet that you'll find good merchandise and great service there!

Advice from a Pro: A Drum Dealer Talks About Buying Drums

Speaking of drum shops, I thought I'd ask my local drum dealer for thoughts on what beginning drummers should look for when they're shopping for their first drums. My local drum shop is the Drum Center of Indianapolis, and the guy who sits behind the counter (and pays the bills!) is Harry Cangany. (He's also a vintage drum expert, a frequent contributor to *Modern Drummer* magazine, and the author of *The Great American Drums (and the Companies That Made Them)*, available wherever drum books are sold.)

Mike Miller (MM): Do you find that kids just starting out go right to a drumset, or do they start with a snare drum first?

Harry Cangany (HC): Children being children, they want everything. They want the drums and they want the cymbals, and that may be a terrible first place to start. So we fall back and ask, "What does your drum teacher say?" A lot of times it's "Start with a snare drum and see if you like it—and if you like it, come in and we'll build a set around it."

MM: When somebody comes into your store looking for his or her first set of drums, what do you recommend looking at?

HC: There's never one answer, but let me give you some of the parameters.

Certainly, one parameter is always budget. A starter set of five drums and the hardware that goes with it is probably going to be in the $300 to $800 range, with $300 being absolute 100 percent Taiwan.

The sound of a drum depends on what it's made out of and basically where it's made. Maple is the wood of choice, but it's also the most expensive. In Japan and Taiwan, they don't have maple, so they have to come to the United States to get maple, or use a cheaper wood, like mahogany.

The other thing that I think is crucially important is the minimum number of tuning lugs on each drum. On our bass drums, even our least-expensive bass drum, we require eight. There are some models that have six, and they're just not going to tune as well—even though a six-lug bass drum will cost less than an eight-lug bass drum.

When you get to the mounted tom-toms—typically a 12 and a 13 mounted on the bass drum—there the minimum number of lugs is 6. There are a number of manufacturers who make five-lug toms, and they're harder to tune. Plus, a five-hole hoop, if it gets broken, is the most difficult thing in the world to get fixed, because it's not normal. There are even some companies who have 5 lugs on a floor tom—a 16-inch floor tom. Again, six is the minimum.

So, when you're dealing with the $300 range, an okay set is a red, black, or white plastic-covered, Philippine mahogany-shelled drum, with plated zinc metal on it. Of course, one of these sets is really designed to be the same as a BIC pen. It's going to last a certain amount of time, and then it's not going to be around any longer because it's going to have been beaten to death.

Drum Note

When you're in the central Indiana area, you can visit the Drum Center of Indianapolis at 5874 E. 71st Street. You can also order from the Drum Center via phone (317-594-8989) or over the Internet (www.drumcenter. com)—just tell them I sent you!

MM: I bought my first set around 1970, and back then Japanese sets were the low end—they were names like Apollo and Polaris. (My first set was a red-sparkle four-piece Polaris.) How good are the beginning sets today compared to the beginning sets back then?

HC: Back when you started, and certainly when I started, the beginning sets would have a lot of flash—you'd see blue sparkle and gold sparkle and green sparkle and red sparkle. Now you see flat black, flat red, flat white, and sometimes blue. That's it.

We tend to have thinner shells now, without reinforcement hoops. In the 1960s, when the imported stuff really started, the shells were thicker and needed reinforcement hoops. Now, with better technology (in some cases) and to keep costs down (in others), most manufacturers of low- to middle-cost drums use shells without reinforcement hoops.

In addition, the art of metalwork and plating is much better now. It's not only better manufacturing processes with better raw materials, but also the stands are better to hold it all together. They just are. Some of that is just 20 years of doing it.

The drums today are also deeper. The tom-toms are 2 inches deeper than they were back then, so a 12 is now a 10×12, and a 13 is an 11×13. That's pretty much the norm. A normal 5-piece set is a 22-inch bass drum, a 12-inch, a 13-inch, a 16-inch floor tom, and a snare drum. Beginning sets typically have one cymbal stand, a hi-hat stand, a bass drum pedal, and a snare stand, and they're all prepackaged—and manufacturers make a zillion of them. That's the typical lowest-cost drumset.

MM: So today's entry-level sets run $300 to $800. Can you get a brand name for that?

HC: As you get higher up that ladder, you're going to start getting brand names. The lower end has no name that Mom or Dad or the kids may know. Sometimes it's the name of the distributor—that's where CB700 came from: That was the name of the distributor that had them made in Taiwan. Sunlite and Peace are two other big low-end brands.

Right above those, Ludwig has its least-expensive sets, and Drum Workshop has just come out with its least-expensive sets. Ludwig and Drum Workshop don't make them themselves; they have them made for them and the sets are badged to say Accent by Ludwig or Pacific by Drum Workshop. The Ludwig set is in the high $300s, and the companies are mass-producing them in factories in Taiwan.

By the time you get in the $500-and-up range, you start seeing brand names where the companies are making their own drums—Mapex, Pearl, and Tama.

MM: So someone is into this $500 to $600 range, let's say. Do they have the cymbals on top of that?

HC: Right. The cymbal companies decided that they wanted to be like Chevrolet and have six or seven different models. Chevy wants to start you with the Metro and work you all the way up to the Corvette, and so do Zildjian, Sabian, and Paiste. They're trying to get people to start with their lowest-cost cymbals and work up to their higher-cost models.

A number of cymbals are available now in packages for kids starting out. In a single box, you'll get a ride cymbal and hi-hat, or a ride cymbal, a crash cymbal, and hi-hat.

Which low-end drumset you get determines which cymbals you get. The lowest-cost, low-end sets have only one cymbal stand. By the time you get to Pearl or Tama, you get two cymbal stands. So then you can either buy another cymbal or buy the box that has both the ride and the crash cymbals.

MM: What do those packages run?

HC: Depending on whose you get, you can get starter cymbals and a hi-hat for under $50 total. You go up to about $200 to $250 for a ride, a crash, and a hi-hat.

MM: Basically, everything included, you can get by for under $1,000?

HC: Yes, even getting a set from a big-name company, you might be right at $1,000. And that's 80 percent of the market. Eighty percent of the market is buying a starter set because 80 percent of the market is the 14- to 20-year-old just getting started or replacing his or her original starter set and getting a better starter set.

MM: How good are the snare drums in these beginning kits?

HC: The lowest-cost beginning kits have six-lug, zinc-plated, steel-shell snare drums—which, again, are BIC pens. They're okay to get you going, but at some point you're going to want an 8-lug or 10-lug snare drum. When you get to a Pearl or a Tama, they're okay by then, but they're still not as good as the next series up.

Every step you go up that ladder, the manufacturers really improve everything—they improve the hardware, they improve the spurs, they improve the finish, they improve the snare drum. That's until you get to the point where you're at the pro level and everything's the best it can be.

MM: For somebody coming in and buying his or her first drums, what's the most common mistake they tend to make?

HC: As consumers, we tend to buy with our eyes as much as we buy with anything. A kid can look at something and just be really shot with it, but it may not be the right choice. For example, a lacquer set is pretty impractical when you're a 12-year-old kid because you're going to have other kids around you; you're going to get scratches and chips and so forth on the drums. But it may be absolutely beautiful, so he pesters his mom and dad, and they get him that set.

On the other hand, talent will win out, and you rise to the level of the instrument. There are drums, and there are *instruments*. The cheap sets are disposable drums, like BIC pens, but when you get to a certain level, such as Drum Workshop and other brands like that, those are instruments. When those are in the hands of somebody, that person rises to the occasion and practices more.

MM: Is there any other advice you'd give to somebody just starting out?

HC: Warranty is important, and I think always buying a brand name is key. The closer somebody gets to $1,000, that person has a lot of choices, with some excellent brands out there. What you see in that price range are Pearl, Tama, Ludwig, and Mapex, really fighting hook, line, and sinker. So, the closer you get to $1,000, you get something good with a warranty, and if you have a name brand, you have resale value.

The Bottom Line: How Much Should You Spend?

Now that you're armed with all the information you need to choose the right drums for your needs, how much will you have to spend for this perfect set of drums?

Let's start at the low end and work up—and price drums and cymbals separately.

Putting Together an Entry-Level Set

If you're searching for a low-priced starter kit, it's easy to find a five-piece set (with a snare stand, a hi-hat, a bass drum pedal, and a single cymbal stand) in the $300 to $500 range. At the very low end of this range (sometimes called the "sub-entry" level), you'll more likely be looking at a set from a "no-name" manufacturer such as CB, Peace, or Sunlite. When you get closer to $500, you get into low-end series from name manufacturers, such as Ludwig's Accent series, Pearl's Forum line, Tama's Swingstar drums, Mapex's V series, and the Pacific line by Drum Workshop.

If you want an entry-level set from a name-brand manufacturer, be prepared to spend between $500 and $800. These sets—sometimes called "student-level" sets—include Tama's Rockstar line, Pearl's Export series, Yamaha's Stage Custom series, Mapex's M series, and Ludwig's Rocker line.

A quality entry-level set from Mapex's V series— priced around $500 for drums and hardware.

(Photo printed with permission by Mapex USA, Inc.)

In the sub-$800 price range, you'll likely get shells of mahogany, basswood, or some other low-end wood (until you get upward of $600, the shells probably won't be maple—or at least not *exclusively* maple), single-brace stands, a bass drum-mounted tom holder (probably not a suspended mount), and fairly standard heads (and not always from Remo or other name-brand manufacturers). Your finish choices will probably be limited to a single color or a small number of colors, typically in a solid color or a stain. You, also, won't likely have any options in terms of drum sizes or equipment variations.

You'll want to complement this set with an entry-level cymbal package from Zildjian, Sabian, or Meinl. Look for a package with a 14-inch high-hat, a 20-inch ride cymbal, and a 16-inch crash cymbal. (This means that you might have to purchase an additional cymbal stand, since most entry-level kits come with just a single stand.) You can find cymbal packages that fit this bill in the $100 to $200 range.

Add a drum throne ($75 or so), and you can have a brand-new set for as little as $500— although budgeting closer to $1,000 will give you a *lot* better quality, in terms of both sound and durability.

When you're shopping for an entry-level set, look for sets with better wood shells (all-maple plies are best), more lugs on the drums (six on the toms, eight on the snare and the bass drum), and sturdier hardware (suspension mounts for the toms and double-braced stands— if you can find them). Also ask the dealer about the heads on the drums; if the set comes with cheap or inappropriate heads, ask for an upgrade to a good set of Remo Ambassadors or Emperors, which can improve your sound considerably.

Building a Semi-Pro Kit

When you move beyond the entry-level sets into the middle of a manufacturer's line (priced between $1,000 and $2,500), you have a lot more options available to you. Mid-range sets—often billed as "semi-pro" or intermediate—typically give you better-sounding drums, more durable hardware, better-looking finishes, and a lot more choices than you get with entry-level kits. In fact, many manufacturers let you "custom select" just what drums and hardware you want in your kit, so you don't have to settle for an "off-the-shelf" combination if you don't want to. (Naturally, you'll have to special-order any nonstandard kits, while you can probably drive home a standard kit from your dealer's floor today.)

Let's look at a typical midrange kit. Ludwig's Rocker Pro/Classic Birch line is a good solid value, with seven-ply birch and Italian poplar shells and sturdy hardware. The kit pictured here, a five-piecer with power-sized toms (10 inches × 12 inches, 11 inches × 13 inches, and 16 inches × 16 inches), sells in the $1,500 range. By the time you add a decent set of cymbals (figure $400 to $500 for a hi-hat, a ride cymbal, and a crash cymbal) and a good throne, you're out close to $2,000—and have a set that sounds pretty good and should hold up well under most playing conditions.

A midrange six-piece kit from Ludwig's Rocker Pro/Classic Birch series.

(Photo courtesy of Ludwig Drum Co.)

Popular midrange sets include Pearl's Session series; Tama's Artstar series; Ludwig's Rocker Pros; the Workshop series from Drum Workshop; and Yamaha's various Custom series.

Spending the Bucks for a High-End Professional Set

Of course, all manufacturers have their featured lines: drums with exotic shell elements and extra-heavy-duty hardware and stands. These drums—like Tama's Starclassic Maple series, Pearl's Masterworks line, Mapex's Orion series, and Ludwig's Classic series—typically feature high-quality, visually appealing finishes, carry fairly hefty price tags ($2,500 and up), and might need to be special-ordered from the manufacturer.

At the high end of the high end is Drum Workshop, a company that pretty much custom manufactures every drum it makes. You can order DW drums in almost limitless combinations of finishes, sizes, and hardware—and even choose from traditional chrome, brass, or black rims and lugs. The DW set shown here is a double-bass set with four toms, all-maple shells, and a beautiful custom Tobacco Burst satin oil finish. You'll pay $4,000 or more for a set like this from DW or other high-end companies, but you'll have one first-class instrument that can last you a lifetime.

A high-end double-bass set from the custom specialists at Drum Workshop.

(Photo courtesy of Drum Workshop, Inc.)

The Least You Need to Know

➤ Decent entry-level sets can be found in the $300 to $800 range (without cymbals, but with basic hardware). Semi-pro sets have better-sounding drums and heavier-duty hardware, and sell in the $1,000 to $2,500 range. Professional and custom sets can cost from $2,500 to $5,000 (and up!) but offer fancier finishes, a wider selection of shell types and sizes, plenty of custom options, and the best hardware and mounts available.

➤ Thinner shells, suspension mounts, and quality woods (such as maple and birch) produce better sound.

➤ The big five drum manufacturers are Pearl, Ludwig, Tama, Mapex, and Drum Workshop.

➤ Today's typical drumset is a five-piece setup, with a snare drum, a bass drum, two small toms, and a large tom. The most basic cymbal setup is a ride cymbal, one or two crash cymbals, and a hi-hat.

➤ When you're shopping for a set of drums, make sure that you visit your local drum shop. You'll most often find a large selection of both new and used drums, as well as friendly and knowledgeable service from real drummers!

Chapter 3

Plugging In: Using Electronic Drums and Drum Machines

In This Chapter

➤ How electronic drums work

➤ How to tell the different types of electronic drums

➤ Why you might want an electronic drum kit

➤ How to add electronics to a standard acoustic drumset

The drums most people know are made of wood shells and plastic heads; when you hit them with a stick, they produce a *thud* that sounds just like a drum hit with a stick. (What else would you expect?) In today's high-tech world, however, pretty much anything you can do acoustically can also be done electronically, using digital recording and playback techniques. The merger of digital electronics with acoustic drums is the electronic drum—something both a little more and a little less than a traditional drumset.

I Play the Body Electric: Electronic Drum Kits

Electronic drums have been around since the late 1970s. Those early electronic kits featured arm-damaging hard rubber pads and generated synthesized bleeps and bloops that sounded more like something out of *Star Trek* than anything ever produced by an acoustic drum. The novelty of synthesized sounds soon wore off, to be supplanted by digitally recorded sounds—so-called samples of traditional acoustic sounds. Today's electronic drum kits use digital samples of great-sounding acoustic drums loaded onto a memory chip and triggered by the striking of an external pad. When you hit the pad, the sound of the sampled drum or cymbal is generated, just as if you were playing the original acoustic kit.

That's in theory, of course. In reality, sampled sounds never sound perfectly identical to their acoustic counterpart, and playing on a rubber pad isn't quite the same as playing on a real drum. Still, electronic drums provide a wider variety of sounds than you can produce with a single acoustic kit, and they let you play loud through an amplifier or soft through a set of headphones. They're also a lot more compact than acoustic drums, making them ideal for the gigging musician who hates to lug around a bunch of heavy wood drums.

Drum Word

MIDI stands for **musical instrument digital interface** and is a computer protocol for passing audio information digitally from one device to another.

How Electronic Drums Work

Most electronic drum systems work with *MIDI,* which is a technology for recreating sounds and music via computers. When you hit an electronic pad (or send an impulse through a trigger device—such as a small microphone—connected to an acoustic drum), an electronic signal is sent to your electronic kit's trigger module. This module is the "brain" behind an electronic kit, holding all the electronics and computer programming necessary to interpret the trigger signals and generate appropriate sounds.

When the trigger module receives a trigger signal, it analyzes the signal to determine whether it's a real drum hit. (The "smarter" modules filter out weak signals in an attempt to eliminate accidental or false triggers.) Depending on how the pad was hit and how hard you hit it (and, in some cases, *where* on the pad you hit), the trigger module assigns a number and velocity value to the "note event." (For example, if you hit a snare pad really hard, the trigger module might send a message of "note on, note number 38 on channel 1, velocity of 127." Don't even ask what all this means—it's all handled behind the scenes by the trigger module's built-in computer.)

This note event is then used to play a specific note—with predetermined pitch, volume, and duration—that is generated by the onboard synthesizer or plugged from the library of digitally sampled sounds. This note is run through an amplifier (or a set of headphones), and—voilà!—you hear the sound. You can assign any sound to any pad; you can even make your "drumset" sound like a chorus of car horns if you have those sounds programmed into your trigger module's electronic library!

Drop Out, Plug In: Different Types of Electronic Drums

The typical electronic kit looks kind of like a drumset without any shells—all you see are the "heads." In the case of many electronic kits, the "heads" are actually rubber pads, often sized smaller than a traditional drumhead. Hitting a rubber pad doesn't feel the same as hitting a normal drumhead, but that's one of the trade-offs involved with electronic drums. On the other hand, some sets enable you to assign different sounds to different areas of the pad, so you can generate multiple sounds from a single pad.

Other electronic kits feature what look like minidrums. These "acoustic-headed" pads have real drumheads (or, in some cases, a head-like mesh material), so hitting them is much like hitting a regular drum. These "acoustic" electronic kits appeal to drummers who want to retain a traditional feel while benefiting from access to all the electronic and digitally sampled sounds.

You can find electronic kits from a variety of manufacturers, including ddrum, Yamaha, and Roland. You'll want to compare the feel of the trigger pads (rubber or acoustic), determine whether the pads mount on standard drum hardware or require their own special mounting brackets, examine how easy the drum module is to program and use, and find out how many and what sounds are included with the system's sound library. (You should also ask how many additional sounds are available, and how you get those extra sounds into the unit—typically via CD or computer disk.)

An electronic kit that feels like an acoustic kit—Roland's V-Drums.

(Photo courtesy of Roland Corporation U.S.)

Another variation on the acoustic-feeling electronic kit, from ddrum.

(Photo courtesy of Armadillo Enterprises)

The Pros and Cons of Electronic Drums

Should you replace your acoustic drums with an electronic kit—or supplement your drum-set with electronics? On the plus side, electronic drums can reproduce any sound imaginable (including nondrum sounds) and enable you to quickly and easily change the sound of

Drum Note

Electronic drums will probably cost a bit more than a comparable set of acoustic drums. While some basic kits can be had for under $1,000, the really good kits can run $3,000 or more.

your kit to suit a particular song. They're also easy to haul around, set up, and tear down, which might appeal to some working drummers.

On the minus side, no matter how good they are, electronic drums never sound or feel quite like a good set of acoustic drums. The good ones are also a little more expensive than a comparable acoustic kit—and they require some amount of technical competency to work.

So, should you go electronic? My advice for beginning drummers is not to worry about electronic drums—and certainly don't replace your acoustic set with an electronic kit. As you move into the semi-pro and professional ranges, then you might want to consider augmenting your traditional drums with some electronics. Even then, however, it isn't truly necessary; most pro drummers get by just fine with their all-acoustic kit!

Drum Note

There are several other ways to create electronic drum sounds. Drum machines let you program in your own rhythms (using pads or buttons) and play them back with built-in samples and synthesized sounds; they're a great way for nondrummers to create drum parts or for drummers to create complex parts that might not be playable otherwise. (Just listen to the machine-created bass drum parts in a lot of dance music, such as Christina Aguilera's debut album—you can't play this stuff normally!)

Additionally, computerized sequencers let you create a sequence of drum patterns and then play them back for recording or live playing. Sequencers are great for adding extra percussion parts when you're on a live gig by yourself; just program the sequencers beforehand and press the Play button when it's time to run through the song live!

Pull the Trigger: Making Your Acoustic Drums Electric

If you don't want to replace your current drumset with an electronic kit, there's another way to access all those synthesized and sampled sounds available with electronic kits. All you have to do is put "triggers" on your acoustic drums and feed those triggers into an electronic drum module.

A trigger is like a mini microphone that attaches to a drum's shell or head and senses the vibrations made when you hit the drum. These vibrations trigger an electronic signal, which is then sent to the electronic brain in the trigger module. The trigger module then accesses preassigned sounds in its sound library, and an electronic sound is generated via a speaker or headphones. So, when you hit a drum that has a trigger attached, you get not only the sound of the drum itself, but also an electronically triggered sound from your drum module.

Many pro drummers like blending acoustic and processed electronic drum sounds. Sometimes the electronics are used to "fatten" a traditional drum sound by overlaying a more complex sound over the original sound; in other instances, a completely different sound is generated electronically and is fed into the mixing board for recording. (You might use an old yucky-sounding snare drum to trigger a digital sample of a classic Ludwig Black Beauty, for example.)

Drum Tip

Since triggers are relatively inexpensive—less than $50 a trigger—they're also viable alternatives to expensive drum mikes. Of course, you still have to invest in an expensive trigger module, but you might be able to get by for a lot less than you would with a traditional mike setup.

The Least You Need to Know

➤ Electronic drums use a trigger event (a hit on a pad or the vibrations picked up from a drum trigger) to send a signal to an electronic brain, called a trigger module.

➤ The trigger module translates the triggered signal into a specific note, using synthesized and sampled sounds stored in the kit's electronic sound library.

➤ The output from an electronic kit must be sent through an amplifier or a set of headphones; when you play through headphones, you can practice your drums noiselessly.

➤ Pads for electronic kits are either hard rubber or "acoustic heads," which resemble small traditional drums.

➤ You can also use your current acoustic kit to generate electronic sounds by attaching triggers to each drum and running the triggers through a freestanding trigger module.

Chapter 4

Bongos and Claves and Vibes, Oh My!: The Rest of the Percussion Family

---

In This Chapter

➤ Popular Latin percussion instruments—including congas, bongos, and timbales

➤ Other ethnic percussion—including tablas and talking drums

➤ Symphonic percussion—including gongs and timpani

➤ Melodic percussion—including marimbas and vibes

Before we dive headfirst into snare drums and drumsets and mainstream drumming, it's good to have a background in the rest of the percussion family—especially if you ever intend to do any symphonic gigs or play as a percussionist with another drummer. While there's not enough space here to go into playing techniques (heck, you can spend years studying any of these instruments!), you'll at least become a little familiar with some of the other instruments you're apt to encounter.

Laying Down a Latin Groove

Probably the most common auxiliary percussion instruments come from Latin America. In pure Latin music, however, many of these percussion instruments are likely to be more prominent than the drumset!

In most popular and jazz music, Latin percussion is used to add color and help keep the beat. It's easy to find an album that features some sort of Latin percussion, but if you want to get a real earful, pick up just about anything by Santana. Carlos Santana has always prominently featured all sorts of Latin percussion on his albums; it's an unmistakable sound!

Conga drums are essential to any Latin groove. Congas are deep-shelled wood or fiberglass drums, often with calfskin heads, that you play with your hands. You generate different sounds by hitting the head in different places and with different parts of your hand. A conga player typically uses two or more congas of different sizes mounted on stands, and often surrounded by an array of other Latin percussion instruments.

Congas—such as these LP Salsa congas—are essential to any Latin groove.

(Photo courtesy of LP Music Group)

Drum Note

Far and away the largest manufacturer of Latin and ethnic percussion instruments is the LP Music Group. LP produces several different lines of instruments for different levels of players— the LP line for experienced players, the Matador line for semi-pros, and the CP line for students and beginners. You can find LP instruments at most drum shops and music stores, or on the Web at www.lpmusic.com.

Bongos are kind of like small congas. Bongos come in pairs (a large one and a small one joined together), are very shallow, and are much higher in pitch than congas. You play bongos in pretty much the same way you play congas, using your hands and fingers to get different sounds from the drums. Traditionally, bongos are played sitting down, held between your knees, although in today's multipercussion environment, it's more common to see bongos mounted on a stand for easier access.

Where congas and bongos are played with your hands, timbales are played with sticks. The drums themselves are steel or brass with either calf or plastic heads, tuned rather tight; timbale sticks are thinner than normal drumsticks, with two butt ends and no bead. Where congas and bongos are used to keep a beat, timbales are also used for fills, accents, and color. You'll also find timbale players surrounding themselves with cowbells, woodblocks, crash cymbals, and other instruments they can use to add punch to the music.

Latin percussion is about more than drums, of course. When you want an authentic "click" sound for a bossa nova or a mambo (think "Girl from Impanema" here) and playing a rim click on your snare just won't cut it, then you have to pull out a set of claves. Claves are two small wooden rods that you strike together to get a highly resonant "click" sound and play in a repeating rhythm. (Somewhat confusingly, the rhythm you play with a clave is also called a clave.)

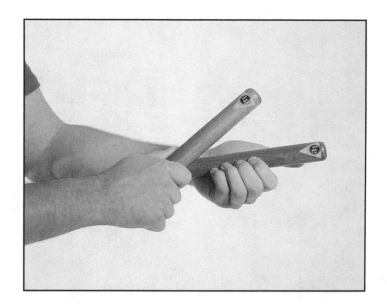

Use claves to produce an authentic Latin "click."

(Photo courtesy of LP Music Group)

When you want a "ch-ch-ch" or "sh-sh-sh" sound—the Latin equivalent of a closed hi-hat—then you turn to any number of shakable instruments. Among the most common are maracas (two small, hollow pods filled with steel balls or seeds), shekeres (a large, hollow gourd wrapped in a net of beads), and shakers (any hollow wood or metallic cylinder filled with steel or plastic balls).

This only scratches the surface of available Latin percussion instruments. There isn't enough space here to talk about guiros, cabasas, castanets, or any number of interesting and great-sounding instruments—you're on your own from here!

Groove to a World Beat

Latin America is only one part of the world that produces unique percussion instruments. Every region has its own native instruments because every musical culture has its own types of drums!

In Africa, for example, you'll find a lot of interesting and essential instruments. The talking drum, for instance, lets you keep a beat while changing the pitch of the drum—in effect, making the drum "talk."

In India and the Middle East, the instruments are a bit more sophisticated—as is the music, which often incorporates wildly complex time signatures. Perhaps the most well-known Indian instrument is the tabla, which is the rhythmic staple of most traditional and popular Indian music. Tablas typically are played in pairs, and players use their hands not only to strike the drums but also to manipulate the heads to produce different pitches and sounds.

In India, tabla players are the local equivalent of rock star drummers!

(Photo courtesy of LP Music Group)

Where Do They Get Such Wonderful Toys?

You don't have to go outside the United States to find interesting and useful small percussion instruments. Many of these smaller instruments—often called "toys" because of their size—are used to spice up a variety of different kinds of music.

For example, where would popular music be without the tambourine? (For one thing, the littlest kid in the Partridge Family wouldn't have anything to do!) Whether played on two and four or shaken on every eighth or sixteenth note, a tambourine can add a little extra color to just about any song.

Drum Tip

Most tambourines used for today's popular music come with jingles and no heads, while so-called "concert" tambourines come with calfskin or plastic heads. The heads often produce a ring that is unsuitable for popular music, but they allow symphonic musicians to produce a distinctive tambourine "roll" by wetting the thumb, pressing it into the edge of the head, and then rapidly moving it around the circumference of the instrument, making the jingles rattle in turn. This is a much different sound than just shaking the tambourine rapidly—and is fast becoming a lost art.

Other popular percussion instruments include woodblocks, cowbells (technically a Latin percussion instrument), and sleigh bells. In fact, just about anything shakable or hittable can be a percussion instrument. For example, listen to "God Only Knows" from The Beach Boys' *Pet Sounds* album, and you'll hear studio great Hal Blaine playing empty orange drink bottles—and they sound great!

Hey Mr. Tambourine Man—play a song for me!

(Photo courtesy of LP Music Group)

Orchestrate Your Way to the Top

If you go into symphonic drumming, you'll encounter a whole other group of instruments. Yes, you'll find snare drums and bass drums and cymbals, but you'll also find triangles, gongs, and timpani.

Of this bunch, the timpani is probably the most important new instrument in the concert percussionist's repertoire. Sometimes called "kettledrums," timpani are very large copper-shelled drums with plastic or calfskin heads. What makes timpani different from any other drum you've ever played is that timpani can be tuned to precise musical notes. (Normal drums can't be tuned to a fixed pitch.) So, you can tune one timpani (a setup typically has two or more drums) to B-flat and another to D-sharp and play a little melody! You tune timpani with a foot pedal that tightens or loosens the head; timpani mallets have wooden or metal handles and soft felt heads.

A full set of tunable timpani from Musser.

(Photo courtesy of Ludwig Musser)

Some Percussion Is Melodic

Percussion instruments are defined as things that you hit. While most things you hit go *crack* or *crash* or *boing* (with a single pitch or note), there are some percussion instruments that are actually melodic. All melodic percussion instruments look a little like a piano keyboard, with the same "key" layout, but instead of keys, they use wood or metal bars.

In symphony orchestras, you'll likely see a marimba, which is a very large instrument with highly resonant rosewood bars. You play a marimba with mallets (often two in each hand) that have heads made of either rubber or string wound around a rubber or wood center.

A xylophone is kind of a junior marimba, with smaller (and higher-pitched) wood bars, typically played with harder mallets. On the softer side of the family is the vibraphone (often called "vibes"), which features metal bars and is played with softer mallets. You can hear vibes on a lot of popular and jazz recordings; look for anything by Gary Burton or Milt Jackson (and the Modern Jazz Quartet) if you want to hear some great vibe playing.

The Least You Need to Know

➤ Percussionists often use instruments other than traditional drumsets to help keep the beat and add color to music.

➤ Congas, bongos, and timbales are popular Latin percussion instruments used in all sorts of popular music.

➤ The most-heard percussion instrument in an orchestra is typically the timpani, which can be tuned to actual musical pitches.

➤ When you want to play a real melody on a percussion instrument, pick up your mallets and turn to a marimba, a xylophone, or a vibraphone.

Chapter 5

Heads, Shells, and Lugs: Tuning and Caring for Your Drums

> ### In This Chapter
>
> ➤ How to clean your drums and cymbals
>
> ➤ What parts to carry with you on a gig—just in case
>
> ➤ How to tune your drums
>
> ➤ How to change heads and what kind of heads to use

When you take your new drumset home from the store, unpack it, and set it up, those drums sound *awesome*. But after you've been playing them for a while—especially if you've been using them on gigs—those wonderful new drums start to sound a little ... well, a little less new.

The longer you have your drums, the more you have to take care of them. You need to clean them, repair things that break, change heads from time to time, and do whatever else is necessary to keep them in tune. This is standard operating procedure for any drummer, and this chapter shows you what you have to do to keep your not-quite-new drums sounding brand new.

Time for a Cleaning: Keeping Your Set in Tip-Top Condition

Basic drum care is really as simple as keeping your drums, cymbals, and stands clean and in good working condition. (This also involves replacing worn-out drumheads, which is discussed later in this chapter.) If you make a habit out of cleaning your set regularly, it won't be much of a bother, and it will save you a lot of grief later.

Drum Tip

I recommend doing basic cleaning once a week—just pick a day and time, and spend a half-hour or so doing the basic tasks. More intense cleaning doesn't have to be done quite as often; once a month is fine for the "strip 'em and clean 'em" routine.

Drum Don't

If you use a chrome cleaner on your set, make sure to follow the directions on the label. Do not use a chrome cleaner while hardware is still attached to the drum—the chrome cleaner can actually damage wood shells!

Drum Don't

If your cymbals have a "brilliant" finish, make sure you pick a cymbal cleaner specially formulated for this type of cymbal. Using a regular cleaner on a brilliant finish can damage the finish.

Cleaning Your Drums

Cleaning your toms, bass drum, and snare drum should be a regular affair—just like dusting your house. (You *do* dust your house, don't you?)

Take a clean, soft cloth—as soft as you can find—and carefully rub down all your shells, lugs, and rims. Try to wipe out any accumulated dust from that little area where the head meets the rim; use a small brush to clean out the crack, if necessary.

If your kit has a lacquer finish, you can use a high-quality, nonabrasive, no-wax furniture polish to put a little shine on the shells. You don't want to do this on nonwood shells or on shells with a plastic wrap finish, though. If you have a wrapped covering, you can use Windex to polish up the shells—but make sure you don't leave any streaks.

For a more thorough cleaning, you'll want to disassemble each of your drums. This means not only removing the heads, but also removing the lugs and any other mounted hardware. When you're down to the naked shells, go through your normal cleaning routine—only now you can work on any gunk that was wedged around or behind the lugs.

While you have your drums disassembled, take the opportunity to clean up your lugs and other hardware. Use a high-quality chrome-cleaning compound—like that found in most automotive supply stores—to put a shine on all your chrome parts.

Cleaning Your Cymbals

Basic cymbal cleaning is a lot like basic drum cleaning. Just use a soft, clean cloth to wipe down your cymbals once a week or whenever you're tearing down from a gig.

You should also perform a more strenuous cleaning and polishing on a less-frequent basis. Once a month or so, you should head over to your local drum shop and buy a bottle of Brite Stuff or one of the many other cymbal cleaners. (You can also use Comet or other commercial cleansers to scrape through really built-up gunk, although these chemicals may be too abrasive and cause damage to some cymbals.)

Before you polish a cymbal, spread out some old newspapers or towels so you don't get old cymbal gunk on your clean carpet or wood floor. (Trust me on this one; I still have "cymbal spots" in my spare bedroom from a particularly intense and ill-prepared cleaning session several years ago.) Now apply the cymbal cleaner per the label's instructions, and use a soft, clean cloth—and a lot of elbow grease—to wipe off the cleaner and apply a nice shine. Heed the directions to clean only a small area at a time; if you tackle too large an area, the cleaner may dry on the cymbal before you get a chance to wipe it off.

Once you've finished a cymbal, grab a clean cloth and go over the cymbal one more time. Use a lot of pressure to get rid of any remaining residue, and you'll end up with one shiny, great-looking cymbal.

Drum Note

Clean cymbals sound different from dirty cymbals. All the sticky residue that builds up on a cymbal actually affects the cymbal's tone—and, to a lesser degree, its sustain. Some drummers like the bright, shimmery sound of a clean cymbal; others like the darker, slightly trashy sound of a dirty old cymbal. If you're one of those who likes all the overtones that build up as you use a cymbal—kind of like the way the flavors build up in an old cooking pot over time—then you don't need to worry about polishing your cymbals; a quick wipe with a soft cloth is the right method for you.

Cleaning Your Stands and Pedals

You clean your stands and pedals the same way you clean the hardware attached to your drum shells. For casual cleaning, wipe them down with a soft, clean cloth. For more serious cleaning, use a commercial chrome cleaner—and disassemble each stand before you start. You can also apply a thin coat of Vaseline to the surface of your stands, let it sit for a day or two, and then buff it off; this will help prevent pitting and rusting.

Drum Tip

Cymbals really benefit from preventive maintenance and careful handling. You should always wipe down your cymbals before you pack them up and make sure the cymbals don't rub against each other in transit by inserting a towel or plastic bag in between them. If you do a lot of packing and unpacking, you should invest in a good-quality cymbal case as well.

When you're setting up your kit, make sure you have the cymbals mounted properly. Always check the cymbal sleeves, felts, and washers to make sure they're in good condition and not too worn away from use. (If the felts or sleeves are worn, the cymbal may rub up against the bare metal of the stand and slowly carve a new groove inside the hole of the cymbal.)

When you set up and tear down, always handle your cymbals by the edge. This keeps you from getting oil from your hands in the grooves up the cymbal. (You can always wear gloves during set up/tear down, although this might be a tad excessive.)

Your bass drum and hi-hat pedals need a little extra preventive maintenance. All moving parts should be periodically oiled, per the manufacturers' instructions, to keep things properly lubricated. Make sure you wipe off excess oil when you're done to keep the oil from getting on your drums or heads.

Make Like a Boy Scout—and Be Prepared!

It's always a good idea to carry a few spare parts when you're at a gig or on the road—just in case. I like to carry extra cymbal felts, sleeves, and washers since it's so easy to lose these during setup or teardown.

In addition, if you have a strap-driven bass drum pedal, carry an extra strap with you. I learned this lesson when I was in junior high school, taking drum lessons from a senior named Roger Fouch, who was the drummer in the high school's jazz band. I was watching Roger play with the band at a Sunday afternoon concert, and right in the middle of "Lucretia MacEvil," I saw a look of surprise on his face—and noticed a total absence of bass drum sound. The strap on Roger's bass drum pedal had snapped, leaving him without the use of his bass drum for the last half of the concert; if he'd had a spare strap, he could have quickly made a replacement and been back and kicking for the next song.

Of course, you can't prepare for *all* contingencies. When I was in college, my original Fibes tom-tom mount broke while I was playing a friend's recital, sending my two small toms tumbling forward in the middle of a song. I had to play the last two tunes with my toms resting precariously on top of my bass drum—and then head out the next day to get a new tom mount installed on my kit. I don't know of any drummers who carry an extra tom holder with them on gigs, though, so a catastrophe like this probably can't be avoided.

You *can,* however, carry extra heads for each of your drums, as well as a spare set of snares. Pros sometimes carry extra snare drums so that they (or their *drum tech*) can switch drums in and out if a snare head breaks.

The bottom line: Be prepared. If something can break, it probably will—and in the middle of a tune!

Perfect Pitch Not Required: Tuning Your Drums

Every musical instrument needs to be kept in tune. Guitarists tune their guitars, pianists tune their pianos (well, they hire piano tuners to do this, but you get the point …), and drummers tune their drums. You tune your drums because the heads settle down onto the shells over time or because every time you whack a drum its head loosens slightly or because you want to get a different sound out of a drum. Drummers who play loud and hard may need to retune their kit several times during a gig; even if you have a lighter touch, you may need to touch up the tuning every few weeks.

Drum Tip

If you find your drums squeaking or rattling, you can probably fix the problem by "packing" your lugs. Remove your lugs from your drums and then stuff the inside of the lugs with either pipe insulation or plain cotton balls. When you put your lugs back on your drums, you'll find that all the noise is gone! (Note that some high-end drum manufacturers, such as Drum Workshop, pack their lugs at the factory as a matter of course.)

Drum Word

A **drum tech** (or technician) is a person who maintains, tunes, sets up, and tears down drumsets for professional drummers. These guys know how to take care of drums and how to tune them—well and quickly. They're real pros, performing a highly valuable job for touring drummers.

Tuning a drum is an involved process because it includes several different elements:

➤ Batter (top) head tension

➤ Resonant (bottom) head tension

➤ Relationship between the tension of the top and bottom heads

➤ Type of head

➤ Type of shell

➤ Muffling of a head or shell's natural ring

When you tune a head, you're tuning for pitch (higher or lower), for tone (deep or bright), for projection, and for ring (resonant or muffled). To get the right combination of qualities, you have to work with both heads and, in some cases, some form of muffling.

Choosing the Right Heads

Every drum has at least one head and probably two. (You can have single-headed toms and bass drums—which produce a very dry, punchy sound—like the "pudding" drum sounds that were popular back in the mid-1970s.) The head you hit is called the batter head; the head you don't hit is called the resonant head. (You can also call them top and bottom heads, unless you play your drums while standing upside down!)

The drum head is where the sound of the drum starts. Which type of head you choose—and how you tune the head—is as important to the sound as the drum's shell and overall construction. In fact, some experts say that 85 percent of the sound produced by a drum comes from the heads—so you can see where the wrong head choice can really muck up your sound!

Drum heads today are typically made of Mylar, a type of plastic. Back in the early days of drumming, heads were made of calfskin—but skin heads are notoriously susceptible to changes in humidity and require constant retuning. Plastic heads are more constant in tone and more tolerant of today's typical playing conditions.

Drum Note

Shell depth and diameter also affect the tuning of a drum. The depth of a shell affects the warmth and resonance of the drum, as well as the drum's volume and articulation. (A deeper drum increases volume and power; a shallower drum creates a shorter tone and a faster response.) The shell's diameter directly affects the pitch of the drum. (Larger diameter equals lower pitch.)

The big head companies today are Remo, Evans, Aquarian, and Ludwig. Most of these companies make heads in several different weights and types:

➤ **Single-ply thin.** With a single-ply head, there is only one layer of Mylar. The very thinnest heads, such as Remo Diplomats, are best suited for bottom-only use—they're extra resonant but not very durable.

➤ **Single-ply unmuffled.** Single-ply heads have a sharp attack and a good amount of ring, but they aren't as durable as double-play heads if you're playing really loud and hard. Single-ply unmuffled heads, such as Remo Ambassadors and Evans G1s, are good all-around heads and are preferred for most recording and close-miked situations.

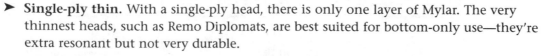

➤ **Double-ply.** Double-ply heads, such as Remo Emperors or Evans G2s, have two layers of Mylar. This thicker construction makes them dryer (less ring), diminishes the attack, and makes them more durable, which is important to hard rock drummers.

➤ **Muffled.** These are heavier heads that produce a more mellow sound with less sustain, typically due to some sort of built-in muffling device. These heads, such as Remo Pinstripes or Evans Genera HDs, are very dry, with very little—if any—ring.

➤ **Hydraulic.** These heads, which contain a thin layer of oil between two layers of plastic, are the fattest, "thumpiest" heads available, and they're also extremely durable. If you like this sound, check out Evans Hydraulic models; this company made its reputation manufacturing high-quality hydraulic heads.

You can also choose between coated and uncoated heads. Coated heads have a rough texture that muffles a drum's overtones, to a small degree. You want a coated head on your snare drum if you ever play with brushes; for your toms, which you don't play with brushes, you probably want the unmuffled sound of uncoated heads.

Changing Heads

If a head is way out of tune—and can't be put back into tune, no matter how hard you try—then you probably need to replace that head. In addition, heads go "dead" over time and need to be replaced on a regular basis, no matter how hard you hit them.

How often should you change your heads? It all depends on how hard and how often you play—and how tight you crank up the head tensioning. Here are some signs that you may need to change a head:

➤ The coating begins to wear off a coated head.

➤ You see one or more dents in a head.

➤ The head, when removed from the drum, appears caved in or stretched out.

➤ You can't tune the drum properly—especially noticeable with low-pitched tuning.

➤ The head buzzes when hit.

➤ The head has a hole in it. (Duh!)

That said, the following table offers some general head-changing guidelines for hard-working drummers; if you're not playing several hours every day, you can wait longer between head changes.

Recommended Time Between Head Changes

Head	Change This Often
Snare drum batter	Once a month
Snare drum bottom	Every three months
Bass drum batter	Every three to six months
Bass drum front	Once a year
Tom-tom batter	Every three to six months
Tom-tom bottom	Once a year

When you have to change a head, follow these steps:

1. Remove the old head.

2. With the old head removed, use this opportunity to clean the inside of your drum. Pay particular attention to dirt and dust around the edge of the shell.

3. Position the new head on the shell, and press down slightly to fit it on the shell.

4. Place the rim on the head.

5. Screw each tension rod into place, finger-tight.

6. With your drum key, tighten each tension rod a full turn.

7. "Seat" the head on the shell by pressing hard around the rim. You may hear some pops and crackles; this is natural as the head adjusts itself to the bearing edge of your drum.

8. Finish tuning the drum, as discussed later in this chapter.

Because the head will continue to form-fit itself to the shell, you may need to retune a new head several hours after you've changed it.

How to Tune a Wild Drum

The general approach to tuning a drum is the same across your entire set, whether you're tuning a tom, a bass drum, or a snare drum. (Snare drums do have some unique tuning considerations, which are discussed later in this chapter.)

The top (batter) head controls attack and ring, while the bottom head controls resonance, sustain, overtones, and *timbre*. This means that tuning the bottom head properly is every bit as important as tuning the top head.

When you tune a drum, you use a *drum key* to adjust the tension rods that hold the rim to the shell. These tension rods screw into the lugs on the outside of the shell; the more you tighten them, the higher the pitch of the head becomes.

There is a set order in which you should adjust your tension rods—*don't* go from one to the next in a clockwise or counterclockwise fashion! You need to apply tension to the drum head evenly, which means going back and forth across the head as shown in the following diagrams:

Start by tightening the tension rod at position one; don't tighten it all the way, just a couple of turns. (This is because you want to keep an even tension across the drum head, which you can't do if one lug is supertight and the others are superloose.) Now move to position two and give that tension rod the same number of turns; do the same with the remaining lugs, in order.

Drum Don't

If a drum is tuned wrong or is improperly seated the first time a head is mounted, you'll likely do damage to the head. Avoid potential damage by making sure that tension is equal across all the lugs before you take a stick to the head.

Drum Word

Timbre is the overall tonal character of the drum—not to be confused with pitch, which is the fundamental note of the drum. Saying that a drum is "bright" or "warm" or "woody" is referring to its timbre.

Drum Word

A **drum key** is a small tool typically in the shape of a "T" that fits over the end of a tension rod. You use your drum key to loosen or tighten the tension rods, thus tuning the head down or up.

*Proper tuning order for a
six-lug drum.*

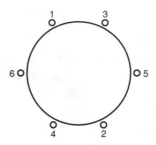

*Proper tuning order for
an eight-lug drum.*

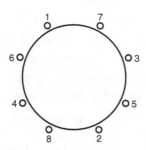

*Proper tuning order for a
10-lug drum.*

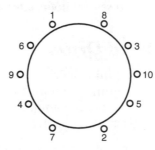

Now you're back at position one. Tighten this rod a little tighter, and then move around the lugs again, applying a little extra tension each time around. Keep this up until the head is free of wrinkles and a very low tone is produced when you hit the head.

Continue tightening the rods (in order), a little bit at a time—no more than a quarter turn each time. From time to time, you should tap the head next to each tension rod and tighten or loosen each rod so that the tones are all the same all around the drum. (When drummers say that a drum "is in tune with itself," they mean that the head is equally tensioned all the way around.)

Repeat this procedure until the head has the desired pitch. Give the head another set of taps around the edges to make sure the tuning is even, and then you're done—with that head. If you use double-headed drums, you'll need to repeat this procedure with the bottom head.

When you're tuning the bottom head, you not only have to tune it to itself, but you also have to tune it relative to the top head. You can tune each head to the same pitch; you can tune the bottom head lower than the top; or you can tune the bottom head higher than the top. There's no one way to do this; you'll need to experiment with different tunings on each of your drums to find the method you like best.

Drum Note

While most drummers use two-headed drums, you'll occasionally see a kit with a single-headed bass drum and toms. Historically, there was a single-headed craze that ran from the mid-1960s to the mid-1970s, driven by a desire for a very dry tom sound in the studio. (For a good example of this hypermuffled sound, listen to **Ringo Starr**'s drums on The Beatles' *Abbey Road* album; he used single-headed toms with cloth towels draped over the heads to achieve what some called a "pudding" sound.) Even today, many studio drummers use single-headed toms and bass drums for a dry sound when recording.

A two-headed drum develops a resonance within the drum and between the heads. A single-headed drum lacks this resonance, thus sounding dryer and less ringy. If you want a very dry sound, I'd recommend trying traditional muffling first, then moving to a two-ply or hydraulic head, and then—if you want even less ring—removing your bottom heads. Some recording engineers like working with the simpler sound of a tightly miked single-headed drum; they don't have to deal with a lot of ring or overtones, and they can do a lot of "touching up" via equalization and sound enhancement from the mixing board.

Once you have one drum in tune, you get to tune the other drums in your kit. You'll want to tune the drums to each other so that the smaller drums have a higher pitch than the larger ones. You get to choose the difference in pitch between the drums; when you're tuning toms, consider tuning them either a third or a fourth apart.

Know that there is no right or wrong way to tune your drums; every drummer does it slightly differently. In general, however, if you tune a drum too tight, the pitch will sound unnaturally high and the tone will be "choked." If you tune a drum too low, the tone will start to disappear completely, and you'll produce a "flappy" sound. You'll need to be somewhere in the "sweet spot" for each drum, and then use your own ears from there.

How to Muffle a Ringy Drum

Drums ring. They just do. Between the resonance of the shell and the resonance of each of the heads, you get a sound that goes on and on.

Some drummers like their drums to ring. Other drummers want a dryer sound with less ring. If you want to reduce the ring of a drum, you have to muffle the drum.

Drum Note

As a drummer, you probably don't know—and don't need to know—what different pitch intervals are. Ask someone who plays piano or guitar to play a major third or a fourth, and listen to the difference between the two notes; this is a specific interval, and you may want to tune your drums so that they play that same interval when struck.

Drum Tip

One of the most common drum-tuning mistakes is to listen to the way a drum sounds in your practice room and muffle the drum so that it sounds dry when you're playing by yourself. If you do this, your drums will lack projection when you're playing with other instruments. You see, the natural ring of a drum blends in with the sound of other instruments and adds to the depth of tone and the projection of the drum. In other words, if your drums sound dry by themselves, they'll sound *too dry* when you're playing with a band.

Recognizing this, you want to tune your drums so that they have some amount of ring. In fact, a drum that sounds a little too ringy when played by itself will probably sound just right when played with a band. To test this, have somebody else play your drums during your band's sound check, and listen to how your drums sound from the audience. I guarantee that you'll hear a different sound than you do when you're sitting behind your kit!

The lesson is to muffle sparingly, if at all. The ring you hear in your practice room turns into something good when you're up on stage!

Drum Tip

One of the best guides to tuning your drums is Professor Sound's Drum Tuning Bible, found on the Web at www.drumweb.com/ profsound.shtml.

One way to reduce drum ring is to loosen the batter head a quarter to a half turn. Another way is to either increase or decrease the pitch of the bottom head so that it's different from the pitch of the top head. Either of these approaches produces a slightly dryer, funkier sound.

The next thing to try is a different batter head. If you're using a single-ply head, switch to a double-ply head or even a Remo Pinstripe or CS head—the one with the big dot in the middle. If you want even less ring, go all the way to an Evans Hydraulic head; these puppies don't have much ring at all!

If you still have unwanted ring—or don't like the tone of these types of heads—then it's time to turn to some external muffling techniques, including these:

➤ Put a strip of duct tape on your batter head. You can experiment with different lengths of tape and with different positions for the tape on your head. You can even layer multiple strips for a heavier muffle.

➤ Tape a tissue or napkin to the rim of your drum, and let it lay loose on your batter head. Again, experiment with different thicknesses and positions.

➤ Use a commercial muffling device, like those that look like Mylar "O" rings. (You can also make your own muffling rings by cutting up an old drumhead.) Some of these come with multiple rings of different sizes; you can layer multiple rings on top of each other to increase or decrease the muffling effect.

➤ An older technique, which some drummers dismiss as dated, is to cut a long strip of felt and mount it underneath the batter head. Experiment both ways and with different widths of felt.

➤ To muffle a bass drum, try putting a pillow inside the drum—*not* touching the heads. (Drum Workshop makes a professional drum muffler that resembles a pillow; it works in the same fashion.)

These are only some of the ways to muffle a drum. I can remember my first drum teacher muffling a very ringy Ludwig snare drum by placing his wallet on the head—and it worked! (You need to have the right combination of cash and credit cards in the wallet, however ....)

The important thing to remember is that too much muffling is bad. If you take all the ring out of a drum, you may as well be whacking on a table top. It's the ring that makes a drum sound like a drum—a little ring is a good thing!

Tuning Your Snare

Tuning a snare drum is different than tuning a tom or a bass drum in that you have one extra element to consider—the metal snares that stretch across the bottom of the drum. Not only do you have to deal with tuning the snares, but you also have to work a little extra magic with the bottom head—which, on a snare drum, is called the snare head.

Most of the time you want to tune the snare head tighter than the batter head. This will produce a crisp sound and minimize unwanted buzz from the snares.

You can also adjust the drum's crispness by tune-tuning the tension knob on the snare strainer, which loosens or tightens the metal snares themselves. Loosen the tension knob too much, and the snares will start to rattle; tighten it too much, and the snares start to choke up. In between these two extremes is a wide tonal range, from "fat" to "crisp."

Here are some tips for achieving specific snare drum sounds:

➤ For a fat and "wet" sound, tune the snare head as low as possible, while leaving the batter head fairly tight.

➤ For a controlled and cutting crack, tune the snare head two or three tones higher than the batter head.

➤ For a highly resonant, almost ringy, sound, tune the snare and batter heads almost identical in pitch, or tune the snare head just slightly higher than the batter head.

Drum Tip

If you're tuning for a particular type of sound, make sure you're using the right heads for the job. Thinner heads will produce more resonance, more ring, and a brighter sound. Two-ply heads will have less ring and a darker sound. Hydraulic heads (which have a thin layer of oil between two layers of plastic) have a very wet kind of thud with very little ring. To learn more about choosing heads, see Chapter 2, "Before You Play, You Have to Pay: Buying Your First Drums."

After you get your snare drum perfectly tuned, chances are good that you'll run into a problem unique to snare drums—sympathetic vibrations. This is the buzz that is generated when your snares vibrate when a particular pitch is played on one of your other drums or by an–other instrument. There are several things you can try to get rid of this buzz, including ...

➤ Readjust the tuning of your snares or your snare head. (The problem with this method is that it interferes with the overall tuning scheme of your kit.)

➤ Loosen slightly the four tension rods on either side of the snares on your snare head.

➤ Position a playing card or a tissue or shoelace between the snares and the snare head. (While this may get rid of the buzz, it will probably also muffle the snares to an undesirable degree.)

My experience is that you'll probably always have some degree of sympathetic snare buzz—but in a live situation, it will probably get lost in the overall mix. It's more of a problem in a studio situation, and that's where some of the extreme solutions (like sticking something between the snares and the snare head) might be necessary.

Tuning a Tom

While the general guidelines for drum tuning apply to both small and large toms, there are some tom-specific tuning guidelines to note:

➤ For a fatter sound, tune the resonant head lower than the batter head.

➤ For a more resonant or ringy sound, tune the batter and resonant heads almost identical in pitch.

➤ For an extremely wet, thuddy sound, use a hydraulic batter head.

➤ To reduce ring, tune the resonant head slightly higher than the batter head.

➤ To pull as much volume as possible out of a two-ply or hydraulic batter head, use a thin single-ply resonant head on the bottom of the drum.

➤ To reduce undue overtones and sustain while maintaining an aggressive attack, combine a single-ply batter head with a muffled resonant head.

➤ For a slightly darker (yet still resonant) tom sound, switch to ebony heads on both sides of the drum.

Tuning Your Bass Drum

The combination of heads you use on your bass drum will dramatically affect the drum's sound. The following table details the sound produced by various head combinations.

Bass Drum Head Combinations

Sound	Batter Head	Front Head
Open tone, highly resonant, ringy	Single-ply unmuffled	Single-ply unmuffled
Strong attack, open tone, diminished but lingering overtones	Single-ply muffled	Single-ply unmuffled
Strong attack, dense but focused sound, controlled overtones	Single-ply muffled	Single-ply muffled
Strong attack, controlled overtones	Single-ply muffled	Two-ply
Punchy, focused, no overtones	Two-ply or hydraulic	Two-ply

In addition, there are a number of tricks you can use to achieve particular bass drum sounds. Here are some things to note:

➤ A higher-pitched tuning produces an overall punchier sound.

➤ For an even punchier sound, tune the front head higher than the batter head.

➤ For a fat sound, tune the front head as low as it will go without becoming "flappy."

➤ Reduce overtones by placing a blanket or pillow inside the drum—or by using a felt strip across the batter head.

➤ Cut a small hole in your bottom head to reduce ring; make sure the hole is off-center and eight inches or less in diameter.

➤ Produce more resonance by adjusting your spurs to push the drum as far off the ground as possible.

With all these variations possible, drum tuning is more of an art than it is a science. The thing to do is to try as many different tuning combinations as possible, then pick the combination that sounds best for your specific style and situation.

Drum Tip

One way to cut a perfectly round hole in your bass drum's front head is to use a knife to cut around the edge of a small eight-inch splash cymbal. Another way is to heat a coffeepot, then press the bottom of the coffeepot against the drum head—melting a corresponding hole in the head.

The Least You Need to Know

➤ Once a week you should "dust" your drums and cymbals with a soft cloth.

➤ Once a month you should take your drums apart and give them a thorough cleaning; at the same time, you should polish your cymbals.

➤ Tuning drums is more of an art than a science, although there is a specific order to follow when tightening tension rods.

➤ Muffling can be accomplished with duct tape, felt strips, or Mylar "O" rings—although most drummers tend to overmuffle their drums.

➤ When you change a drum head, make sure you "seat" it tightly before tuning.

Chapter 6

A Brief History of Time: Drummers to Listen To

In This Chapter

➤ The best big-band drummers

➤ The drummer who single-handedly sold thousands of Ludwig drumsets

➤ Rock's best groove masters

➤ The studio drummers who defined the sound of rock and roll

Every drummer has his or her influences, other drummers who've helped shape a drummer's style or technique or who served as the inspiration for an aspiring drummer. This chapter is all about *my* influences—drummers who inspired me and who I think any beginning drummer should listen to.

Take note: This chapter reflects my personal tastes and influences. No doubt I'm leaving off dozens of other important drummers—possibly including some of your own favorites. I apologize if I didn't include your favorite drummer, but, as I said, this is *my* list. When you write your own book, you can make your own list!

Straight-Ahead Stylists: Great Jazz Drummers

I've always thought that big-band drumming was the most demanding—and most *fun*—type of drumming there is. A big-band drummer has to have complete command of dynamics (very loud to very soft), time signatures (a fair amount of 3/4, 5/4, and 7/4 creeps into the repertoire), and just plain groove—plus, you have to be both a sensitive accompanist *and* a showy soloist. It's no surprise, then, that some of my favorite—and history's most important—have been big-band drummers.

Arguably, the most influential big-band drummer of all time was **Gene Krupa.** He certainly wasn't the first drummer to hit the skins behind a big band, but he was, at the time, the most popular. It may be hard to imagine this now, but Gene's popularity as a sideman in the 1940s was greater than that of our superstar drummers today; fans filled clubs and concert halls just to hear a Gene Krupa drum solo.

And what solos they were. Perhaps the most famous drum solo of all time is "Sing Sing Sing"; Gene's driving beat on the large toms might be the most imitated bit of drumming ever. (If imitation is the sincerest form of flattery, then **Sandy Nelson**'s "Let There Be Drums" and **Cozy Cole**'s "Topsy II" are very flattering homages to Krupa's ground-breaking work.) But Gene's influence goes well beyond flashy solos; this guy could drive a big band harder and farther than just about any drummer before or since.

Gene Krupa getting wild at the height of his big-band popularity—dig the crazy angle on that snare drum!

(Photo courtesy of Harry Cangany)

Of course, when you're talking about powerful drumming, you have to talk about **Buddy Rich.** Now this was one powerful cat! Although Buddy had an ego the size of a small planet (excuse me—a *large* planet!), he put that ego to work in a unique show-stopping style. His big-band work mesmerizes; no one matches Buddy Rich when it comes to power and flair and just plain drive. His solos on "Channel One Suite" and "West Side Story" are mind-boggling in their speed, power, and sheer technique; to this day I know few drummers who can play the notes that Buddy played.

I had the good fortune to catch Buddy in concert a few times in the early 1970s, and once, was seated directly off to his right, close enough to touch his two large toms. (Not that I would have touched them, of course—Buddy was *very* particular about his equipment!) What impressed me about his playing that night was not his dazzling technique (as impressive as it was) on the loud and fast numbers, but rather his control and sensitivity on the softer tunes. He probably played a quarter of that gig with brushes, and his taste surprised me. (He also had masterful brushes technique—very precise and controlled.)

Throughout much of his career, Buddy played a five-piece Slingerland set, very similar to the one pioneered by Gene Krupa. This set featured just one small tom, with the fifth drum being a second floor tom.

Drum Note

Most big-band drummers haven't played *exclusively* with big bands. For example, Gene Krupa is equally well known for his small-group work, including his own quartet and The Benny Goodman Trio and Quartet.

(Buddy typically used this second floor tom to hold his drink and a towel—a very useful piece of equipment!) The kit also had a ride cymbal sprouting from the bass drum, positioned very low and tight to the right; two crash cymbals, one to the left and one to the right, both tilted almost horizontal; and a small splash cymbal, also mounted on the bass drum. This Krupa/Rich-style kit was influential in its own right; I can't tell you how many big-band drummers I've seen with similar or identical outfits.

Buddy Rich doing what he does best on his trademark five-piece kit.

(Photo courtesy of Harry Cangany)

Big band isn't the only type of jazz, of course; small-group drummers like **Art Blakey, Elvin Jones**, and **Jack DeJohnette** have influenced several generations of drummers. My favorite small-group drummer is **Joe Morello**, who did his most popular work with The Dave Brubeck Quartet in the late 1950s and early 1960s. You really couldn't tell it from his recorded work—he wasn't much of a showboat—but Joe had *incredible* technique. For example, he could play a buzz roll with one hand without breaking a sweat. (I *still* don't know how he did that!)

Joe Morello's greatest claim to fame, however, was his impeccable taste and his ability to play in a variety of odd times. His signature work, "Take Five," was actually a pop hit when it was first released. (Imagine that—a jazz tune with a drum solo in an odd time signature hitting the pop charts!) The drum solo on "Take Five" was all about taste; he started simple and tight, gradually loosening up and playing very complex counter-rhythms. It's hard enough to play a simple beat in 5/4, let alone play such an intelligent solo—and keep it swinging. To this day, "Take Five" is my favorite drum solo of all time.

"Take Five" wasn't the only odd-time tune that allowed Joe to shine. Many drummers prefer his 5/4 solo on "Castillian Drums" to his "Take Five" solo, and he also finessed his "way through 9/8 in "Blue Rondo a la Turk" and 7/4 in "Unsquare Dance." Joe was also a master of the jazz waltz, as evidenced by his playing on "Kathy's Waltz."

Joe Morello is more than a great drumset player; he's also a terrific instructor. His *New Directions in Rhythm* (now out of print, unfortunately) was one of the first drumset method books I used when I was learning the drums, and to this day it influences my cymbal work when I'm playing in 3/4. (Just let your right hand play 2-2-2 over a two-bar phrase—it's a great groove!) Today, his *Master Studies* is one of the most-recommended method books in the drum community.

During the 1960s, jazz started to evolve. The chord changes became more sophisticated, and the rhythms became more complex. Some of the most influential new jazz sounds came from Miles Davis, and *In a Silent Way* and *Bitches Brew* helped prepare the music world for even more radical changes to come. The drummers on these albums—particularly **Tony Williams**—bridged the gap between cool jazz and jazz fusion, with a sound that was fresh and daring at the time.

The next evolution in jazz was a revolution. Jazz fusion melded jazz sensibilities with a progressive rock beat, creating a sound that traditional jazzers hated but intelligent rockers loved. The influential fusion bands—including the Mahavishnu Orchestra, Weather Report, and Return to Forever—were marked by dazzling musicianship and some of the best drummers of the day. Perhaps the best fusion drummer was **Billy Cobham**, master of the huge drum double-bass kits and dazzling single-stroke rolls around the toms. Billy could put down an incredibly complex groove, while at the same time executing fills and solos that caused most drummers to drop their jaws in astonishment. If you don't believe me, check out his seminal work on the Mahavishnu Orchestra's *Birds of Fire* and on his own *Spectrum;* on the latter, listen to "Quadrant 4" and "Snoopy's Search/Red Baron" for impeccable groovemanship and technique.

Drum Note

If you want to go CD shopping, Appendix B, "Drum Records: Recommended Listening," includes a fairly large list of important works from the drummers discussed in this chapter. In addition, you should check out the *Let There Be Drums!* CDs (three discs in all, one each for the 1960s, 1970s, and 1980s), compiled by **Max Weinberg** and distributed by Rhino Records. Mighty Max does a great job of picking songs with the best and most influential drum parts of their time—including several songs that might have flown in under your personal radar!

Drum Starrs: Great Rock Drummers

Most drummers of my generation and after were more influenced by rock drummers than by jazz drummers—and the single most influential rock drummer of all time was **Ringo Starr**. Not that Ringo had the best technique (he didn't) or played kick-ass drum solos (he didn't), but rather because he was the beat behind the biggest rock band of all time. When The Beatles first appeared on the *Ed Sullivan Show*, tens of thousands of teenagers decided to form their own garage bands, sending thousands of wannabe drummers to their local music stores to buy black oyster pearl four-piece Ludwig kits just like the one Ringo played. That kit—both in configuration and in color—was arguably the most popular single drum kit of all time.

The guy who inspired a million drummers— Ringo Starr and his famous four-piece Ludwig kit.

(Photo courtesy of author's personal collection)

Had Ringo been just an average drummer his influence might have stopped there. But the reality is that Ringo was an extremely solid drummer, and brilliantly inventive in his own way. Again, this creativity wasn't manifested in bursts of technique, but rather in interesting and unexpected approaches to various songs. Even some of the earliest Beatles tunes found Ringo eschewing the traditional cymbals-and-snare approach for a more measured groove. When you fast-forward to *Abbey Road,* you find Ringo not only navigating rather complex Lennon/McCartney song structures, but also using his drums and cymbals in non-traditional fashion. Even Ringo's sole recorded drum solo, on "The End," is impressive in its simplicity. I think every drummer can learn something about role and restraint from listening to the fourth Beatle.

Where Ringo and **Charlie Watts** of The Rolling Stones showed remarkable restraint, other rock drummers were pushing the envelope in the other direction. One of the most extreme drummers of all time was wild man **Keith Moon** of The Who. Keith really didn't know the definition of the word *restraint,* and his playing was typified by roundhouse fills and constant cymbal crashing. It was an exciting style and perfectly fit The Who's pared-down power-trio sound—he filled whatever gaps might have been present between John Entwistle's solid bass and Peter Townsend's windmill power chords. In his own way, Keith Moon set the precedent for Billy Cobham's slightly more controlled blazing round-the-set fills.

If you wanted a slightly more tasteful sound, all you had to do was listen for a Rascals' tune on the radio. Drummer **Dino Danelli** is an often-overlooked influence in mid-1960s rock drumming whose versatile, tasteful, and enthusiastic work propelled hit after hit for The Rascals. Just listened to his tasteful jazz-waltz on the 3/4 "How Can I Be Sure," his near-big-band approach to "Girl Like You," his straight-ahead rock beat on "People Got to Be Free," or his imaginative breaks on "Too Many Fish in the Sea," and you'll understand what I mean. Dino was also known for what he *didn't* play; there's not a single sound from a drumset in "Groovin'," just congas and tambourine—very tasteful. I never tire of Dino's drumming or those great Rascals' hits.

Dino Danelli's playing was almost jazzlike at times, which leads to my next two favorite drummers. **Bobby Colomby** was the drummer for Blood, Sweat & Tears, one of the first and best examples of the short-lived jazz-rock groups of the late 1960s and early 1970s. Bobby brought a jazz sensibility to rock and roll and was as apt to break into a straight-ahead jazz groove as he was to get down and dirty with a rock beat.

My favorite drum fill of all time was in "Spinning Wheel," where Bobby played sort of a five-stroke roll with two extra taps, with a kind of controlled retard—all in a two-beat fill. (Other drummers share my admiration for this fill; Buddy Rich once said that this fill was "perfect" and couldn't have been done in better taste.)

The other major jazz-rock group was Chicago, at least in the early years. **Danny Seraphine** was Bobby Colomby's counterpart and competitor, but he approached jazz-rock more from the rock side of things. He was known more for a driving, imaginative beat, such as that found on "Beginnings," "25 or 6 to 4" (just check out that bass drum!), and "Make Me Smile"—part of the epic "Suite for a Girl from Buchanan" on the *Chicago II* album.

If you want to hear some of the best rock fills ever, you can turn to session heavyweights **Russ Kunkel** and **Andy Newmark**. Russ's heavy but controlled style can be found on numerous albums from Carole King, Jackson Browne, Bob Dylan, Dan Fogelberg, Linda Ronstadt, and others. Interestingly, his most famous fill was accomplished with brushes on toms on James Taylor's hit "Fire and Rain"; it's the epitome of taste and playing what's right for the song.

Andy Newmark was known for his big tom sounds on albums from John Lennon, George Benson, Rod Stewart, David Bowie, George Harrison, and others—even though he used a simple four-piece kit most of the time. Listen to the fills in Carly Simon's "Anticipation," and try to figure out how he got those sounds from two tom-toms!

Most rock drumming is all about groove, and some of the more interesting grooves have come from the inspired mind and limbs of **Steve Gadd**. Steve is a jazzer in rock land, and it shows in his complex and imaginative playing. For the best of Gadd, listen to Paul Simon's "Fifty Ways to Leave Your Lover"; I had to watch him live (on *Saturday Night Live*) to figure out how he accomplished that beat. His most famous work, however, was on the title track of Steely Dan's *Aja*. Marvel at the sophistication of the mid-song solo—which was recorded in just two takes!

Another great groove master was the late **Jeff Porcaro**. Jeff was a studio cat who played on many, many albums, although he's most known for his work with Toto. For the ultimate in smooth and sophisticated grooves, listen to Toto's "Rosanna" or Boz Skaggs' "Lowdown." Jeff was a master in taking what could have been a simple beat and turning it into something truly transcendent.

Any discussion of sophisticated rock drummers would have to include **Stewart Copeland**. During his stint with the Police (and later throughout a solo career and much film and TV show scoring), Stewart fused several different styles to create a sound that was truly unique. Listen to any Police album, and you'll hear bits of rock, reggae, jazz, and classical—all played with impeccable taste and stunning technique. His wide-open toms and high, crisp snare influenced a generation of drummers to switch from the more muffled "pudding" tuning prevalent in the 1970s.

Finally, from today's crop of drummers, I'm partial to **Kenny Aronoff.** Whether you listen to his rock-solid work with John Mellencamp or any of his voluminous studio work for dozens of other artists, Kenny exudes intelligence, taste, and feel. (Ironically, Kenny and I went to Indiana University at the same time in the late 1970s, and I knew him then as a fusion drummer with incredible speed and technique; he was able to change his style completely to meet the much different needs of Mellencamp's band.)

Drum Note

Learn what Kenny has to say to beginning drummers in Chapter 25, "Parting Advice from One of Today's Hottest Drummers: An Interview with Kenny Aronoff."

Groove Masters: Great Studio Drummers

Kenny Aronoff is unique today in that he combines powerful live playing with the flexibility to back a variety of other artists in the studio. In today's musical environment, most artists use the same musicians onstage and in the studio, but it wasn't always that way. Back in the 1960s and 1970s, the majority of studio work was done by a handful of specialists, studio musicians skilled in getting the right sound on records—fast.

So when it comes down to truly influential drummers, you have to look at the cats who put down the tracks that defined the rock and roll sound. These studio drummers, who played backing tracks for hundreds of different rock and pop groups, created the sounds and the beats that all rock and pop drummers play today.

The undisputed king of studio drummers was **Hal Blaine.** Unofficial leader of the "Wrecking Crew," the group of ace Los Angeles studio musicians in the 1960s, Hal played on more number-one songs than any other musician in history. His list of credits could literally fill up all the pages of this book and includes artists like Elvis Presley, Phil Spector, The Beach Boys, The Monkees, The Grass Roots, Simon and Garfunkel, The Association, Petula Clark, The Byrds, The Mamas and The Papas, The Tijuana Brass, Neil Diamond, The Carpenters, America, John Denver, The Fifth Dimension, Tommy Roe, Jan and Dean, Roy Orbison, and Frank Sinatra. Suffice it to say that if you listen to any 10 hit songs from the 1960s or early 1970s, Hal Blaine is probably playing on four or five of them.

The great thing about Hal is that he played exactly what the song needed—no more and no less. Listen closely to many of the classic Beach Boys and Phil Spector cuts, and you'll find that Hal rarely, if ever, used cymbals; you won't find a lot of traditional ride patterns or hi-hat or ride cymbal—just heavy bass drum and snare drum. Then again, if the song called for it, he went all out; Tommy Roe's "Dizzy" demonstrates Hal's incredible technique. Hal Blaine is best known, however, for his impeccable groove; listen to "Wedding Bell Blues" or "California Dreamin'" or "Wouldn't It Be Nice," and you'll hear some of the best drumming ever recorded.

When you listen to those great hits recorded in the L.A. studios back in the 1960s, if Hal Blaine wasn't playing drums, **Earl Palmer** was. Earl and Hal were the two top drumslingers in the studio scene, and Earl's 1960s credits read a lot like Hal's, with hits recorded for Phil Spector, Ray Charles, Frank Sinatra, Bobby Vee, Bobby Darin, Jan and Dean, Andy Williams, Sam Cooke, The Righteous Brothers (including "You've Lost That Lovin' Feeling"), The Ronettes, Sonny and Cher, Neal Hefti (the theme from the *Batman* TV series), Ike and Tina Turner, and The Monkees.

Earl's greater influence, however, came before he moved to California, during his early days in New Orleans. It was there, in the mid-1950s, that Earl and other local musicians truly defined the sound and the beat that we now call rock and roll. Earl Palmer was *the* drummer on seminal rock and roll hits such as "My Blue Heaven" and "I'm Walkin'" for Fats

Drum Note

You can learn more about Hal Blaine and the L.A. studio scene from Hal's book, *Hal Blaine and the Wrecking Crew*, available at your favorite bookstore. You can also read an interview with Hal in Chapter 7, "King of the Studio: An Interview with Drumming Legend Hal Blaine."

Drum Note

To learn more about Earl Palmer's remarkable career, read *Backbeat: The Earl Palmer Story*, available at bookstores everywhere.

Domino, and "Tutti Frutti," "The Girl Can't Help It, "Long Tall Sally," "Lucille," and "Good Golly Miss Molly" for Little Richard—some of the first rock records *ever*. Earl single-handedly took the more swinging boogie-woogie beat and evolved it into the straight-eighths rock beat we know today.

Another seminal studio drummer was **Benny Benjamin**, the main drummer for Motown. That Motown beat—"the sound of young America"—was a product of Benny and bassist James Jamerson. Listen to any Motown hit, and you'll hear Benny's enormous influence on the music of our times.

At the same time that Benny Benjamin was working his magic in the motor city, two cats a bit south of Detroit were creating a laid-back soul sound. **Al Jackson Jr.** and **Roger Hawkins** were the main studio drummers in Memphis and Muscle Shoals, respectively. Al Jackson was the drummer for Booker T. and the MG's, and backed artists like Al Green, Otis Redding, Sam and Dave, and Wilson Pickett. Listen for Al's perfectly restrained groove on "Green Onions," "Time Is Tight," "Soul Man," "Midnight Hour," and "Dock of the Bay."

Roger Hawkins was the soulful sound behind R&B stars like Aretha Franklin, Bobby Womack, and Percy Sledge, as well as a wide variety of other artists, such as Paul Simon, Boz Skaggs, and the Oak Ridge Boys. You can hear his sweet groove on "When a Man Loves a Woman," "Respect," and "Chain of Fools."

These studio cats are the unsung heroes of the drum world. The next time you hear one of their records, listen hard and take notes; you'll be listening to a legend.

Musical Chameleons: TV Drummers

Special mention should be made of the drummers you see on your television sets week after week and night after night; these cats are so visible that they can't help but be influences. I'm talking about the drummers you see on late-night talk shows and on weekly variety shows.

Perhaps the first "TV star" drummer was **Bobby Rosengarden**, leader of the *Tonight Show* band early in Johnny Carson's tenure. He was followed on the *Tonight Show* by the more visible **Ed Shaughnessy**, of the mutton-chop sideburns and double-bass setup. Both of these drummers have impressive big-band chops, and gave the studio audiences some real treats when they played live through the commercial breaks. (We missed most of the music at home—we had to watch the commercials instead!)

Today's TV drummers are a versatile lot: Switching from rock to country to jazz in a single show isn't unusual. **Anton Fig** of *Late Show with David Letterman* has the taste and chops for the job, and he is often seen backing all-star bands around New York City when his schedule allows. **Max Weinberg** of *Late Night with Conan O'Brien* is better known for his "day job" as Bruce Springsteen's drummer in the E Street Band, even though he shows impressive jazz and R&B chops on Conan's show. **Marvin "Smitty" Smith** fills the Rosengarden/ Shaughnessy shoes on Jay Leno's *Tonight Show* and acquits himself quite well. And **Shawn Pelton**, long-time drummer on *Saturday Night Live* (and fellow Indiana University grad), is also a well-known New York session drummer, having recorded with Celine Dion, Bruce Springsteen, Billy Joel, and Shawn Colvin.

The bottom line: If you want to catch some of today's best—and most versatile—drummers, watch a little late-night TV!

The Least You Need to Know

➤ Drummers Gene Krupa and Buddy Rich epitomized the powerful, exciting big-band drumming of the 1940s through the 1960s, while Joe Morello was the master of small-group jazz, especially in odd time signatures.

➤ The sound of rock and pop music was defined in the recording studios of the 1950s and 1960s by drum legends like Earl Palmer, Hal Blaine, and Benny Benjamin.

➤ Ringo Starr, with his four-piece Ludwig kit, inspired a generation of teenagers to become rock drummers, while Steve Gadd and Jeff Porcaro brought rock drumming to a new level of sophistication in the 1970s and 1980s.

➤ Today's most influential and versatile drummers are the guys who play for late-night talk shows—Anton Fig, Max Weinberg, and Marvin "Smitty" Smith.

Chapter 7

King of the Studio: An Interview with Drumming Legend Hal Blaine

---

In This Chapter

➤ How Hal Blaine got started playing drums

➤ Why Hal was such a great studio drummer

➤ What the L.A. studio scene was like in the 1960s

➤ What advice Hal has for beginning drummers

Hal Blaine is a legend. As the top Los Angeles studio drummer in the 1960s and early 1970s, he played on more than 8,000 different tracks for hundreds and hundreds of different musicians. His list of hits is staggering, and it's almost impossible to listen to an oldies radio station for more than 10 minutes without hearing a Hal Blaine song.

In March 2000, Hal was one of the first five "sidemen" inducted into the Rock and Roll Hall of Fame. (One of the other inductees was Hal's long-time friend and rival, Earl Palmer.) While officially "retired," Hal continues to play an occasional live date with pianist Sam Ocampo, and he has recently played on albums by Mark Wilson (www.goldenbullet.com) and Lorin Hart (home.earthlink.net/~lorinhart/).

Interestingly, Hal's accomplishments extend beyond drumming. He wrote the book *Hal Blaine and the Wrecking Crew,* which chronicles his career and the golden era of studio playing; you can find it at your local bookstore or online at Amazon.com. Hal is also a bit of a comedian ("What do you call a guy who hangs around with musicians? A drummer."), and he recorded the comedy album *Buh-Doom!* which is available at 1-800-221-DISC (1-800-221-3472) or online through Amazon.com or CDNOW.

What Makes a Drummer Great

I have to admit, I'm an unabashed fan of Hal Blaine. To my regret, I was too young (and too self-involved) to be aware of Hal during his heyday, but I have come to appreciate him greatly in the years since. (Wisdom and maturity come with age, apparently—something else I've only recently learned!)

What is so great about Hal Blaine? First, you have sheer quantity. Name any 10 hit singles from the early 1960s through the mid-1970s, and chances are that Hal played on three or four of them. When Dick Clark featured Hal on his *Rock, Roll, and Remember* radio program, he essentially played his normal song list—because when you play a list of Hal's records, you're playing the top hits of the era.

The second great thing about Hal Blaine is the variety of styles he had to play—and master. How many drummers do you know who could play for both Frank Sinatra and The Mamas and The Papas—and play the right kind of drums for each? When you read the list of artists Hal played for, and then consider how different these artists sounded, you really appreciate his versatility.

Beyond this versatility is Hal's creativity, his ability to play just the right part for whatever song he was playing on. Sometimes that meant playing full-out, as on The Fifth Dimension's "Aquarius/Let the Sun Shine." Sometimes that meant playing a Buddy Holly–like tom-tom riff, as on Tommy Roe's "Dizzy." Sometimes that meant playing nothing but bass drum and snare drum, as on The Ronettes' "Be My Baby." Sometimes it meant playing something *other* than drums, as on The Beach Boys' "God Only Knows."

(By the way, in spite of the huge Octaplus tom setup he used in later years, Hal was a master of *not* playing cymbals or toms, if that was what the song called for. Just listen to The Beach Boys' *Pet Sounds;* I don't think there's a single cymbal or hi-hat struck through the whole album.)

The point is, Hal played what was right for the song—and then put his own mark on it. You can always tell when you're listening to a Hal Blaine drum part, no matter what style it's in. Even though Hal's part on The Grass Roots' "Midnight Confessions" is completely different from his part on Sonny and Cher's "I Got You Babe," you still know that it's Hal Blaine on drums. He played for the song, but was still Hal Blaine; his personality always came through.

Not that there aren't typical "Hal Blaine moments." Back when he was cutting records with Phil Spector, Hal typically played just bass drum and snare (sometimes snare and large tom hit together) throughout most of the song, with no cymbals or hi-hats, just to cut through Spector's heavily produced "wall of sound." When the end of the song came, however— what musicians call the "out chorus"—Hal would cut loose like a man possessed, with thundering rolls around the toms and all sorts of amazing licks while the song was fading out. When you listen to these records, listen closely for Hal's trademark lick, a quarter-note triplet played on two toms simultaneously. You'll hear this lick on numerous songs (The Crystals' "Da Doo Ron Ron" and The Ronettes' "Be My Baby" are good examples), and it's vintage Hal. (**Max Weinberg** once wrote about how he would occasionally throw that lick into one or another of Bruce Springsteen's songs; every time he played the lick, Bruce would yell out "Hal Blaine!" in joyful recognition.)

I can point out many other examples of prime Hal. Toward the end of Simon and Garfunkel's majestic "Bridge Over Troubled Water," Hal played the backbeat with tire chains— just one of many times when he knew that something different was called for. Any of the classic Phil Spector "wall of sound" recordings also show off Hal at his best; to get it all in one blast, spring for the *Back to Mono* box set, which includes the legendary *A Christmas Gift for You* album, which may be Hal's best recorded work. Finally, to get a taste for how Hal's drum parts developed in the studio, check out the boxed set of The Beach Boys' *Pet Sounds* album; the four CDs in this set include lots of live in-the-studio takes and in-between-take recordings, providing a rare look at a masterpiece in the making.

If you want to listen to more of the "best of Blaine," I recommend you check out his tasteful fills on any of the Carpenters' hit singles, especially "Close to You"; his dynamic big-band-like backup on Petula Clark's "My Love"; his solid grooves on a plethora of Fifth Dimension tunes, particularly "Up, Up, and Away" and "Wedding Bell Blues"; his incredible versatility navigating different styles and tempos on Richard Harris's "MacArthur Park"; and his driving snare drum on The Mamas and The Papas' "California Dreamin'" and "Monday, Monday."

Hal Blaine—along with **Earl Palmer**, **Benny Benjamin**, **Roger Hawkins**, **Al Jackson Jr.**, and other studio contemporaries—truly created the drum sound of a generation. Hal did it with flair, with humor, with impeccable technique, and with his own unique style. That's why I'm a Hal Blaine fan—and why I *always* turn up the radio when one of his songs is playing.

The Hal Blaine Interview

As I was writing this book, I had the good fortune to talk to Hal Blaine about his career, his opinions on today's music industry, and his advice for beginning drummers. I found him charming and extremely entertaining, full of great stories and great advice; any drummer can learn something from this master.

(Thanks to Josh Touchton at Mapex USA, Inc. for helping to set up this interview.)

Hal Blaine—the most-recorded drummer in history.

Mike Miller (MM): I want to start out by congratulating you on your induction into the Rock and Roll Hall of Fame.

Hal Blaine (HB): That was fun.

MM: It's good to see you and **Earl Palmer** and the studio guys finally getting some recognition.

HB: I know, I know, and they cut it all out of the TV thing, which is really a pity. Earl was just livid. Personally, I couldn't care less. It was 20 years ago, great. Seriously, who in the hell cares? The Rock and Roll Hall of Fame, you know, it's nice, and that's fine, and good-bye.

The one that I was very interested in was Bill Gates's former partner, Paul Allen. He put this museum together in Seattle called the Experience Music Project. They came down here with a film crew and filmed me. They're going to have film running for as long as the museum is open each day—people like myself, different artists, different musicians, talking about music. The crew that came in here blew me away! They were the guys that just got the Oscar for *Titanic!*

MM: Well, Paul Allen can afford to hire the best. (laughs)

HB: Evidently! I didn't realize that he's a guitar player. Plain and simple. A very *wealthy* guitar player. (laughs)

MM: A big Jimi Hendrix fan, I hear.

HB: Yeah, well it was originally going to be called the Jimi Hendrix Experience, but then it became the Experience Music Project. They're supposedly doing a magnificent job.

MM: Hal, one thing that every beginning drummer is fascinated by is how other guys got started. How did *you* get started playing the drums?

HB: Well, I had a couple of relatives who were drummers: a female, who was with an all-female orchestra, and a cousin, Bill, who was a drummer in some little band, and a brother-in-law who was a great trumpet player. So I was kind of around music growing up.

When I was a kid, my dad used to take me to work every Saturday at the State Theater in Hartford, Connecticut, and I would watch absolutely every band, every singer, every dance act—absolutely everything. And I got hooked on drums, being a showoff. You know, drummers are showoffs, and they get all the toys to play and hit. A guitar player has one guitar and a piano player has one piano, but a drummer has all this stuff to play. We're built-in showoffs, and I guess we need attention. That's how it works. My sister bought me my first little set of drums, and you start bangin' on 'em.

MM: How old were you when you got your first set?

HB: Oh, I was about 11 or 12. I used to set them up on the front porch; we lived on the second floor. After school, with the kids coming home from school, I'd be up there banging my drums, getting the attention.

MM: When you were first starting off, were you taking lessons?

HB: No, I was the only Jewish kid in an all-Catholic drum and bugle corps, which was kind of a funny thing. The priest used to see me peeking through the bars, watching the guys play and march and everything. Finally, he came over to talk to me one time, and I told him I was a drummer. I wasn't a real drummer, but I was a drummer. So he invited me in, and I got to play march music with the guys and march with the guys. It was really a lot of fun.

You know, one thing leads to another that way. Eventually we moved to California, and when I was in high school, I got in some little bands. I had my own little band and played around San Bernardino and up in the mountains of Lake Arrowhead and Big Bear Lake. You know, we used to play a job for $5 and a free chicken dinner. For real.

That's kind of the way it starts. I went through the service, played USO shows, played Army bands, got out of the service, came home from Korea. I met some nice people in San Bernardino who wanted my band in this new nightclub that was opening up.

One of the top disc jockeys, Bill Bellman (he was known as Bill the Bellman), asked me if I could come into the radio station sometime. They had a studio, and he was a songwriter. He wanted to do demos, and he just happened to be a friend of mine. I'd go into the studio with him and several other San Bernardino musicians—great musicians. All black, by the way—most of my early days were playing with black musicians, it was just one of those things that happened. Anyway, we got to do all these demos with Bill the Bellman, which led to eventually being in Hollywood and doing demos for all the big songwriters, which led to "These guys that did the demos—we better get them for the record."

So I'd had a certain amount of studio time behind me and studio experience when I really got my first big break and started working with Tommy Sands, who was a teenage idol in those days, and Sam Cooke. Sam Cooke was a major, major artist, and, of course, that led to Phil Spector, and the rest is history.

MM: If somebody were aiming for studio playing today, how would they go about it?

HB: First of all, studios are not like they used to be. Every kid has a garage studio today. They make their own demos. They have their own computer that plays their own drums and their own horns and their own violins and everything. The synthesizers that do all of that, the sampling that has been done through the years—there used to be companies advertising that they had me sampled, and Shelly Manne sampled, and various drummers, various other artists. You could buy those samples, and you could have me playing an entire track to no music—you write your own music to it, that type of thing.

So today it's a different thing. Today, if you go in live—well, there's not a lot of live recording going on anymore, like we used to do with Frank Sinatra, Dean Martin, and those kind of people that sang live. With The Beach Boys, we did live instrumental tracks, but they would go in and do their voices later. The same with Jan and Dean, and The Monkees, and The Partridge Family, and all those groups. I mean, I can't tell you how many television pilots I did, from *The Brady Bunch* and on and on and on. We did everybody, because we were the new kids in town that knew what the words "rock and roll" meant.

And it was just crude, it was just a backbeat. There was nothing to rock and roll; it was nothing—but to the old established guys it was a dirty word. Rock and roll was just "dirty black music, and we're not gonna play that." So when rock and roll started to infiltrate the television shows, movies, commercials, and records, of course, whenever they were gonna do something, they said, "Call those rock and roll guys." Well, that was us. That was the Wrecking Crew.

The reason they called us the Wrecking Crew—that was a phrase really that I kind of coined—was because we were working with a lot of these old established musicians who'd been in the studios for 30 years, and they used to look at us; here we were in Levis and T-shirts, and smoking cigarettes—no drugs—and these guys would look at us, in their three-piece suits, and they'd say, "These kids are gonna wreck the business." So we became the Wrecking Crew, and it got so that producers would call my secretary and say, "We need that Wrecking Crew for so and so," and she'd just book the dates. I mean, we were booked three months, four months in advance, sometimes.

MM: And you'd be playing, what, three dates a day?

HB: Probably a minimum of three dates a day, sometimes four, up to seven.

MM: Pretty much the same cats playing?

HB: It was me and a nucleus of rhythm players, you know, bass players and guitar players. Later, they would bring in their own strings, their own horns, that kind of stuff—if they were gonna do that.

Drum Note

Hal's long-time drum tech is Rick Faucher, a legend in his own right. Over the years, Rick has worked with Hal, Jim Keltner, and many other L.A. studio drummers.

I'd do rock and roll records in the beginning. You can listen to Sam Cooke's "Another Saturday Night"—I think it was H. P. Barnum who was the arranger. Those were the kind of records that we were doing that the old established guys were saying, "That music is terrible, it's filthy, it's awful, it's not music." They had no idea—and within a year they were begging us to work with them. After all, I became the big contractor, and a lot of us became leaders, and these guys had their noses up our asses. At the beginning they hated us and then all of a sudden they loved us because we had work.

MM: When I was a kid, I remember reading an article in *Life* or *Look* or one of those magazines about a drummer—later on I realized it was you—that everybody wanted the Hal Blaine sound to make a hit record, and if they couldn't book you, they'd book your drums.

HB: It wasn't that they couldn't get me, but if somebody was doing a date with their own group and they wanted my sound, they would ask if they could rent one of my sets for their drummer. I had about a dozen sets of drums then. I had a guy that took care of my drums exclusively, and he still is—this is his thirty-sixth or thirty-seventh year with me, taking care of my drums. And he would, you know, deliver the drums and set them up for whoever and then pick them up after the session.

Drum Note

Hal's groundbreaking set of eight tunable concert toms were eventually popularized as Octaplus toms from Ludwig.

The rental was putting me on the contract, which today, of course, has managed to give me my pension from the union. Because with every job we did, it was an employer's pension, and I did so much work, obviously, in those days, and built up that pension.

MM: What kind of set were you playing back then?

HB: I had a little four-piece set. I started out with Ludwig, then I had some Rogers, then I went with Pearl.

In the early 1960s, I designed a set that completely changed the drum world. We went from a little three- or four-piece set of drums; I built a set of drums with an octave of tom-toms so that I could make those long filling rolls rather than just one or two or three tom-toms.

MM: Who made that set for you—was that Ludwig?

HB: No, no, no. I stupidly gave it to them. I was a Ludwig drummer, and they were thrilled. I introduced that set—my set of drums—on an Ed Sullivan special, and every drum company in the world within three months was putting out that set of drums. Like a fool, I never patented anything; I didn't get a design patent or an actual patent. When I do clinics today, one of the first things I do is talk about that if you come up with any design or anything, you get yourself a design patent, which is the easiest thing in the world—it costs you nothing.

There's a little item out there called the ching-a-ring. Well, I made a ching-a-ring out of a tambourine, probably in 1959. I was using that on my hi-hat—I still have the original tambourines here that I was using; I should have put a design patent out on 'em—and before you know it, companies are making ching-a-rings.

MM: You're playing Mapex drums now, right?

HB: I'm playing Mapex drums, and they've turned out to be *incredible* drums. They are just terrific. They're all maple, hence the name Mapex—everything has an "ex" after it, for excellence. Their hardware, the foot pedals, everything they make—just beautiful stuff. I never needed it as heavy as it is today, but for today's kids that are just beating the s**t out of their drums, you really can't beat Mapex. I mean, they're all making good drums, but I think Mapex has it way over the companies where you pick their drums up, and it's like, nothing. The difference is when you start picking up DW and Tama and Mapex.

Now, Mapex is the biggest seller in South America; all the drummers in South America play Mapex. I get letters from Argentina, from Brazil, from drummers around the world, from Turkey—it's wild. And they know who I am, which is kind of nice.

MM: I'm amazed, listening to the old recordings, how many of the songs really didn't have traditional drums or traditional drum beats on them. I think back to a lot of the stuff with The Beach Boys, like the song that you played the orange drink bottles on.

HB: That was just a matter of percussion sounds, coming up with different sounds. I remember playing my snow-tire chains on "Bridge Over Troubled Water."

MM: Great sound.

HB: Perhaps it was my creativity. I wanted to know what the song was about, and wherever it led me, that's where I would come up with a certain sound that they wanted.

MM: One thing I find is that a lot of drummers just play too much. When do you know when *not* to play?

HB: Well, you know, that comes with experience, learning that less is more. That one good knock in the right place is worth a million sixteenth notes.

Kids today don't listen. I'm amazed—when I go into a studio today, if I go into a studio that I haven't been playing in for some time, where the guys don't know me, everybody has headsets, and the engineer says to me, "Hal, what do you want in your headsets?" And I say, I just want a little bit of everybody and just a touch of the singer, and no drums. They say, "No drums?" That's right. I don't want any drums in my headset. "Why is that?" Well, I don't have to play with *me,* I have to play with six or seven or eight guys out there. If everybody listens a little bit to everybody, you'll play together. But these guitar players get in, and they say, "I wanna hear my guitar, turn me up, turn me up"—it's crazy. All of a sudden they're playing with themselves. They're not listening to anybody else.

They just don't make music today the way we used to make music. Now maybe each generation has said that, but it's the truth. There'll never be another golden era like the 1960s and 1970s and part of the 1980s. It has all changed. I mean, you can't understand the lyrics today, these kids screaming. These drummers who are using baseball bats for drumsticks. I mean, it's hysterical.

When guys look at me, when they see the Hal Blaine signature stick, they say, "My goodness, how can you play with that little light stick?" I say, first of all, I got microphones on me. I don't have to play loud. I play what I feel. I play dynamics. Now if they want me playing really heavy, I'll just turn the sticks over and use the butt ends—it really doesn't matter. I don't need the sticks that these guys are using—they're building muscles and they're getting cramps and they're hurting their fingers and they're getting deaf.

MM: I'm still amazed by the versatility you guys had back then.

HB: Yeah. In the morning I'd play on some rock and roll record, then I'd be doing Barbra Streisand records, some of the most beautiful music in the world, and then three hours later I'd be in playing a Latin session. I mean, it just went on and on and on. It's amazing to me, and I guess amazing to a lot of people, that we could do that. It was wild, but we were guys who, at that time, had that experience, and we could do it.

MM: It was an amazing era, and great stuff came out of it. They don't make 'em like that anymore.

HB: I know. They really don't. It's really a shame, but, you know, it'll come around again. I remember the big bands, and I was a big-band drummer—that was my meat. I was with Count Basie, I was working with lots of big bands. It was wonderful, and I loved it. But the big bands were getting crazier and crazier, the arrangements were getting wilder, the chords were more dissonant, where it really wasn't pleasant to the ear—even to the ears of the musicians! It finally wound up with Stan Kenton playing all this wild music—I mean, it was wild! Then all of a sudden this guy came along with a quiet little trio to Capitol Records, and turned the whole recording business upside down. His name was Nat King Cole. Quiet, little wonderful music.

So people who were really getting enough of the Stan Kentons and these wild bands who were just blowing their brains out, all of a sudden Nat King Cole came along, and you could hear every word. It was impeccable, and his music was beautiful.

One of the saddest parts of my career was, after he died, going in and putting drums on all his stuff. He had a fine drummer, **Lee Young**, but Lee played quiet little brushes; you never knew he was there. Dave Cavanaugh, who was one of the big producers of the time, a great arranger at Capitol, decided to update and put some real drums on Nat's stuff. So I spent, I don't know, a week or so, everybody crying in the studio listening to Nat on tape, talking in between takes, and so forth. Really very, very sad. Very sad.

All this music that we're listening to today that's so crazy—but people are coming along, like this chick Diana Krall, she's playing very quietly. I think she's eventually going to turn the tables around where everybody starts coming out with kind of a quiet version of songs.

MM: I've always seen a trend more toward simplicity, over time.

HB: Oh, absolutely! Less is more. It's one of the things you learn.

MM: When MTV had all those "unplugged" concerts, that was kind of that trend. Take the electronics away, strip down the instrumentation, and see what it sounds like.

HB: Right. That's one of the wild things about David Grisman. He has this wonderful company, and he's made over 30, 35 albums. We've done records with Jerry Garcia and various people, but acoustically. He will not have anything electric on his records. You listen to these albums, they're magnificent. And he sells a lot of albums, a lot of albums.

MM: You worked with John Denver for a long time, right?

HB: Working with John Denver is the perfect example of how we used to build a song. John would sing the song; we would all produce our own parts. When we were ready to make it, we would yell into the booth to wake up the producer, who was sleeping there or doing a crossword puzzle, and we would make a record. I had 10 major hits with him, 10 major albums through those years.

MM: You've done studio drumming, you've done live drumming, you were on the road with John Denver. For a beginning drummer, what's the difference between doing studio and being on the road?

HB: The difference is when you're working a live performance, you're getting immediate response to what you're doing. People are screaming, and they love what you're doing. People are listening with their *eyes*. You become more of a showman when you're on stage.

People listening to records—when you're in the studio, you're playing music. You don't have to show off, so to speak. You don't have to raise your arms a little higher than normal and things like that, the little tricks you learn—you know, how to jump up out of your seat on the very end of the song—those kind of things that you do onstage.

Another difference is that you can have an awful lot of fun on the road because when the show is over at night, you know that you're going to get a good night's sleep and have a nice breakfast in the morning. Especially the John Denver show. We never carried a bag; our bags where all numbered, they were always in your hotel room whenever you arrived. I mean, it was just the most incredible job, probably ever, in show biz. And everybody made money.

Nowadays, as you know, all you have to do is look at VH1 to see where are they now. You know, these guys are homeless and living in the streets, and they made millions and they put it up their nose or in their arms. Of course, now that they realize how foolish they were, they want to start the band over again. It doesn't work. Today, the demographics of record buyers are from 11 to about 24 years old. They don't want old people anymore. They want young kids; they want little gorgeous chicks. You see this on MTV and VH1 when they're doing videos. It's just the way it is. It's hard to understand the songs because everybody's playing as loud as they can, and the singers are not really trained singers—they're people just out of high school or whatever, and they're screaming. They're just hollering, and you don't know what the heck they're saying.

But, I'm not a young kid anymore. You know, if I was a young kid in high school, and that was the trend, and we were all 15-year-olds, maybe I'd be going along with that.

I know that there are an awful lot of fine musicians out there, and they're all trying hard; they're studying hard. I try to tell drummers they've got to know how to read music. How do you expect to walk in and sit down with maybe a 60-piece orchestra when they put a part in front of you? You know, it's the old joke—how do you get a drummer to quiet down? Put music in front of him. (laughs)

MM: When you do your clinics and you talk to the drummers, what mistakes do you see beginning drummers making?

HB: The first thing is, they don't want to study. They just want to get in and play music. They want to play their favorite rock and roll song that they've heard 2,000 times on the radio or on their CD player at home, and now they're a drummer because they're playing exactly what the drummer played on the record. They think that's all they have to do, and they start these garage bands and they play cover songs. But how in the hell can they possibly be creative and play their own songs?

You know, it's easier to hit the lotto than hit the jackpot with a group. There are 10 million groups out there, and record companies don't sign groups anymore today. I shouldn't say that—sometimes they do. But if you have a band today, and you write songs—let's say 12 or 14 songs—and you record them—they're not bad, you know, halfway-decent commercial—you can get them burned on CDs for next to nothing. You can have them packaged for next to nothing. And every time you go out and play somewhere, you sell your own CDs.

Now, I know, from heads of record companies, that they watch some of these sales. I know there was one big group, Smashing Pumpkins or Hootie and the Blowfish, all of a sudden there was some group that was selling something like 30,000 records almost every two months. Well, that's when a record company takes notice. They'll go in and offer them a lot of money to put the record on *their* label.

It's not like the old days. It's not like you went in, you worked on a record in the studios, and so forth. It just doesn't work that way today. That's why it's such a long shot for a drummer to really make it.

I think the last guy to really start to happen, along with me and after me, was **Jim Keltner.** Fine drummer. Fine, fine drummer. You know, he'll even tell you, I was the guy that started recommending him for work. Even Jim, now he's out on the road today with Crosby, Stills, Nash & Young. He's out there because he's making more money on the road than he's ever known in the studio. Studios are just not happening anymore. If you're going to be a sideman, so to speak, you have to be with a group that's out there making it, and making money.

It's such a long shot today, it's a shame.

Aside from popular music, there are a lot of musicians, who are fine, fine musicians; they study classical music all their lives, and they go into a symphony orchestra. Well, a violinist can always find work because they use 20, 30, or 40 violins in a symphony orchestra. And if it's not this town, it's the next town or the next town.

But a drummer—there's only one drummer in a band. If you're lucky enough to get into that band, whatever it is, whether it be pop or classical, you're very fortunate to have a job.

I hate to discourage guys, but damn it, it's a fact of life!

MM: It's a tough industry—like you said, there's only one drummer in a band. But I've been surprised at how noncompetitive—how friendly and cooperative—most of the people in the drumming community are.

HB: That's true. Drummers are all friends. I mean, when we, the so-called rock and roll Wrecking Crew, came along, we were all guys working in nightclubs, making a hundred bucks a week. All of a sudden we're making a thousand dollars a day. Now that's one hell of a leap! Like falling into a vat of chocolate. And you gotta be friends.

One of the things I used to tell the guys when I was contracting was, "If you smile, you stay around a while. If you pout, you're out!" Because a lot of guys would walk in, look at their music, and say "Eh, the same s**t today," or "What kind of s**t are we playing today?" Well, the microphones are on and producers hear that, then they'll come to me and say, "I don't want that guy around here! I want guys who *want* to play on my records."

So that's one of the things I used to tell the guys. So everybody was friendly. Everybody loved one another. There were no arguments, there were no fights. Fortunately, during our era, there were no drugs. Rarely were there drugs.

The Mamas and The Papas were a different story. They had lots of drugs. Coming out of The Mamas and The Papas, Michelle Phillips, who became quite a great actress—she does a lot of movies, she recently married an old buddy of mine who's a plastic surgeon—she's the only one, really, who didn't do drugs. The rest of them, you know, Denny was always drunk, jumping out of windows and breaking his legs. John Phillips had a liver transplant, and now he's drinking again. Cass, of course, unfortunately passed away.

I look at all these groups, there's something like 175 groups that I worked with, did their records, and there may only be a couple of guys still out there. Freddy Cannon goes out once in a while to do something. Gary Lewis still goes out to do something once in a while. He's one of the few guys that won't admit that I played drums on his records. I played on his records, I played on his father's records, I was doing movies with his father. I mean, it's ridiculous—I've got pictures of him sitting in the studio, you know, fooling around with *my* drums! He's the only guy who said, oh no, he played his own drums on his own records. Total BS.

I do need to say, when it came to The Monkees, for an example, they really did play music, but they didn't make their own records. Now I remember one night, there was this big, big thing that hit Hollywood: The Monkees do not make their own records. I mean, it was the scandal of scandals.

MM: But nobody made their own records back then ....

HB: That was common knowledge, but not necessarily to the general public. To the kids, all of a sudden this thing came up—The Monkees do not make their own records. So, in order to straighten that out, they took The Monkees, and they had them in the little Studio C at RCA one night. Coincidentally, *we* were in Studio A making Monkees records. Closed session, nobody could get in there. In Studio C, all the press, all the media was there, all the TV guys with their cameras, taking pictures of The Monkees playing music, and singing. (laughs) So, that kind of took care of that.

A lot of guys are constantly asking me, *still,* didn't it bother Dennis Wilson that you made the records with The Beach Boys? Well, Dennis *loved* that I made the records because he could be out surfing and motorcycling and boating and you know, nothing but chicks and boozing and getting in car crashes. (laughs) That was Dennis. The proof of the pudding is when he made his own album, he hired me. (laughs) He really didn't mind.

There was only one drummer that did. When I did The Byrds, that was the only drummer that pissed and bitched and moaned, and Terry Melcher, the producer, had to tell him to shut up and sit the f**k down! (laughs) Anyway, they were thrilled at the end, because right out of the box came "Mr. Tambourine Man."

MM: Of all the people you played with, is there anybody you wanted to play with that you didn't get to?

HB: There are many people, obviously; there were lots of people in those days that I did not get to work with. But they were mostly people who had their own group and had good musicians and went in and made their own records.

MM: It seems that the ones you weren't playing on, **Earl Palmer** was.

HB: Right! Exactly. I was just gonna say, "You've Lost That Lovin' Feeling." I was always Phil Spector's drummer, so Earl got to do that when I was in England, and it was a big hit. I mean, it was Phil Spector producing. Everything he did was a big hit.

MM: What drummers do you listen to today—who do you like?

HB: There are some fine drummers out there. I have friends like **Gregg Bissonette**—very, very fine drummer. **Kenny Aronoff**, who I see with so many groups, knows just how to play—like I said, less is more. Of course, Nashville discovered drums about 15 years ago, so **Paul Leim** and those guys are down there, and country music has become rock and roll, and they're just playing what we were all playing in Hollywood, and they're doing a great job.

MM: What advice would you give to a new drummer just starting out?

HB: Study. You know like they say, location, location, location? Study, study, study. Practice, practice, practice. Because practice makes perfect. You're not gonna get anywhere if you haven't studied because you walk into a band and they throw that music in front of you—how in the hell are you going to play a song? Unless you happen to know it backward. Now what if it's a brand-new song?

What is music? Music is only a roadmap. You start here and you end here, but in between there may be some stops and starts and left turns and right turns, and so forth. That's all music is. Everyone is reading the same part; that's so that everyone—whether it's a five-piece band or a thousand-piece band—everybody starts at the same downbeat and ends at the same place.

It's only a roadmap, and if you can read English, you can read music. I've heard guys say, "I don't want to have to read notes because it'll hurt my soul." Well, that's such BS, absolute BS. If you can read the newspaper or a comic book, you can read music. It's no different. You learn to read in groups.

When you first started to learn to read English, you were reading, "the," "man," "dog," "cat," "c-a-t." Music is no different. When you first learn it, you're learning your one-e-and-ahs and two-e-and-ahs and so forth, but before you know it, you're reading in groups. Now when you read a newspaper, you don't think about the word "the," "can," "run," "cat," "go," "stop." You don't think about those things. You're automatically reading them. Once you start reading music you learn to read in groups. Bop bop, bop bop, dadadadadot, dadadadadot. Once you've practiced it and studied it, you don't think, "one-e-and-ah two, one-and two-and"—you don't think that way; you think in groups. So you automatically do it without thinking about it.

Once in a while you run into a figure that an arranger has written that's really difficult, and you go back to the old, "Let's see now, this is one-and two-and-ah three-and four-and one-and." You spell it out and then you've got it. But if you don't know those basics, you can't do that.

Drum Note

The score to *The Carpetbaggers* was written and arranged by award-winning composer Elmer Bernstein, who has created the soundtracks for hundreds of Hollywood films from 1951 to today.

The hardest thing I ever did was a movie called *The Carpetbaggers* with an incredible arranger who writes some of the most difficult music in movies. He writes a lot of stuff in six. I walked into this session—why I even got hired, I don't know. But I walked in and the percussionist saw me, and I didn't know this percussionist. He was an older guy, and he was one of those guys that read fly specks. I mean, he played all these marimba and xylophone parts on all the cartoons, for years. One of the great, great guys—terrific guy. He saw me looking through the music and sweating. He came over and put his arm around me and said, "Look, there's no problem. We run into something here, we just talk it out. Nobody has to know." And it was beautiful, and it came out great! It would go from six to three to four to two to one, unbelievable stuff. And it worked out fine.

So, if I hadn't had some kind of basic training, I could have never done that in a million years. That's all it is.

The advice that I give kids is that you *must* learn how to read music. Because then you become a part of the joke, you know. What did the drummer say on his very first professional job? "Would you like fries with that order?" (laughs) What does a drummer say when he knocks on your door at night? "Domino's!" You know, you're either gonna be a drummer or you're gonna work in a fast-food joint, and that's all there is to it.

There are so many things that I try to explain to kids when I do clinics. When you drive a car, if you remember when you first started driving, maybe you were 12 or 13, and you were learning; you couldn't wait until you were 16. Finally you're driving, and now you're scared to death; you're shaking all over, you're looking ahead, you're trying to see a light, remember to step on the brake, step on the gas, turn on your signals .... Well, within three or four months, you're now looking at people, you're waving to people, you're listening to the radio, you're not thinking because you're automatically seeing that light coming up that's green or red; you're automatically stepping on the brake or the gas or turning on the street you're supposed to turn on. You don't think about it. You're not saying to yourself, "I'm going to turn here and then I'll step on the brake and then I'll turn ...." You don't think that way.

Drum Note

For more information about Hal Blaine—past, present, and future—check out his Web site at www.halblaine.com.

Reading music is the same way. You don't think about it; you're just doing it. You're playing those licks—they're just in groups. Every time you see those triplets, dadada dadada dadada, you know what they are. Not the *first* time, but by the fifteenth or twentieth time.

So, I guess that's my advice.

MM: That's great advice, Hal. Thanks for spending the time talking.

HB: My pleasure.

The Least You Need to Know

➤ Hal Blaine is the most-recorded musician in history, playing on more than 8,000 different tunes—including dozens of number-one and Grammy-winning hits in the 1960s and 1970s.

➤ Hal is a firm believer that less is more: One good knock in the right place is worth a million sixteenth notes.

➤ To Hal, the biggest mistake beginning drummers make is not wanting to study.

➤ Hal's advice for beginning drummers is to study, practice, and learn how to read music.

Part 2
Bang the Drum Slowly: Snare Drum Basics

Start here to learn how to read music, how to hold your sticks, and how to play basic snare drum beats and the 26 drum rudiments. You'll learn quarter notes, eighth notes, and sixteenth notes—plus triplets and syncopation. You'll also learn how to play open rolls and closed rolls and how to put it all together for some really kickin' snare drum beats. Part 2 includes tons of exercises and snare drum solos—so you'll have lots of stuff to practice!

Chapter 8

Wholes, Halves, and Quarters: Notes and Notation

In This Chapter

➤ Counting your way through a song

➤ Introducing all the different notes—and rests—and explaining how to play them

➤ Figuring out tempo and dynamics

➤ Understanding navigation notation

If you read last chapter's interview with drum legend **Hal Blaine**, you know that Hal advises beginning drummers to learn how to read music. I happen to agree, so this chapter is all about learning to read.

Reading music isn't that hard, really. All you need to learn is a little basic math and how to count to four.

Taking the Measure of Things

Music is about counting. Listen to your favorite rock and roll song and feel the beat. (Go ahead, tap your foot—it's okay!) You'll feel the beats fall into groups of four—one two three four, one two three four. It's easy to hear because it's very natural.

Each group of four beats is called a *measure*. The first beat in a measure is counted as "one." The second beat is counted as "two." The third beat is counted as "three." The last beat is counted as "four." There is no "five"—if you count out "five," you've counted too far! Whenever you hit "four," the next beat is always "one."

Every time four beats go by—one two three four—another measure is completed. You put enough measures together—one two three four, one two three four—and you have a song.

When you're reading written music, a measure is indicated by bar lines on either side. As you can see in the following figure, the music itself is written on a *staff*; the lines and spaces on a staff can indicate either specific pitches (for piano, guitar, and other such music) or specific pieces of your drumset (for percussion music).

A standard staff and several measures.

Taking Note—of Notes

Every time you hit a drum, you're playing a note. There are different types of notes, with each note signifying a specific length of time—as measured by parts of a measure.

To better explain, we have to get into a little math. (Don't worry—there won't be any story problems!) You see, each note lasts a specific duration—and each duration reflects a ratio to another duration. As you can see from the following figure, each shorter note is precisely half the duration of the previous note. So, if you can divide and multiply by two, this should be fairly easy for you.

Whole Notes

The most basic note is called the *whole note.* A whole note is called a whole note because it lasts a whole measure. Since there are four beats in a measure, this means that a whole note lasts four beats. A whole note looks like a big empty circle, nice and "whole."

When you put a whole note in a measure, that's the only note that goes in that measure; no other notes will fit. When you play a whole note, you hit the drum once at the very beginning of the measure (on beat one), and then you don't hit it again in that measure because that one hit lasts a whole measure.

Drum Word

A **measure** is a container that holds a specific number of beats. In 4/4 time, a measure holds the equivalent of four quarter notes. The beginning and end of a measure are signified by bar lines.

It's simple math—each smaller note is exactly half of the previous note.

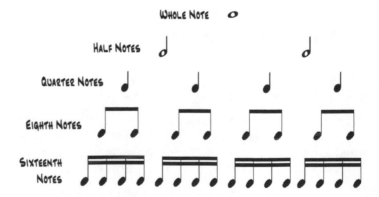

Half Notes

Since the whole note is the largest note, let's go down one size and look at the next smallest note. Remember that I said each shorter note is exactly half of the previous note? Let's apply a little math and divide a whole note by two to see what we get.

The next smallest note is called a *half note.* (It's half of a whole note—pretty simple, eh?) Since a whole note lasts a whole measure, a half note lasts a half measure. This means that a half note lasts *two beats,* which is half of the four-beat duration of a whole note. Put another way, you can put two half notes in a measure, since two half notes equal one whole note.

A half note looks like a whole note with a line next to it. The line is called a stem, by the way—and the stem can point up or down; either way is fine.

Quarter Notes

Let's keep going. If a half note is half of a whole note, what is half of a half note? Well, do your math, and when you divide ½ by 2, you get ¼. This means that half of a half note is a *quarter note.*

Since a half note lasts two beats, a quarter note—which is half that duration—lasts one beat. Put another way, you can fit four quarter notes in a measure, one to a beat.

When you tap your foot to the beat of a song, your foot is playing quarter notes. One two three four—each of those counts is a quarter note.

A quarter note looks like a half note with the *head* filled in.

Drum Note

Okay, time for the disclaimer: Not *all* measures have four beats. Some have three, some have five, and some have other amounts. However, since the vast majority of popular music has four beats, let's keep things simple here and talk about only four-beat measures. We'll talk about other time signatures later in this chapter and in Chapter 20, "Take Five: Playing in Odd Times."

Drum Word

A **staff** is a group of horizontal lines with spaces in between, with each line and each space signifying a specific pitch or (in the case of a drumset staff) a specific instrument. Which note is on which line or space is determined by the clef at the start of the staff; a five-line staff with a treble clef (the one that looks like an "&" sign) starts with the pitch E on the bottom line and goes up from there. Drum staffs, like those used in this book, typically assign a different drum or cymbal to each line or space; a roadmap to the staff assignment is typically given at the start of a piece of music.

Eighth Notes

Just like the scientists in *Fantastic Voyage* or Ray Palmer, the Atom, in DC Comics, notes just keep getting smaller. Again, we're operating on a two-to-one ratio, so let's take a quarter note and divide it in half. Doing the math, ¼ ÷ 2 = ⅛—so the next-smallest note is the *eighth note.*

Drum Note

There's no hidden meaning as to which direction a stem is pointing. Notes placed on the lower half of the staff typically have their stems pointing up, whereas notes placed on the upper half of the staff typically have their stems pointing down. It's a simple matter of putting the stem where you have the most free space!

Drum Word

A **head** is the big, round part of a note. The stem is always attached to the head.

Drum Word

A **flag** is the little doohickey dangling off the stem of eighth notes, sixteenth notes, and all smaller notes. The flag is always at the end of the stem, so if the stem is pointing up, the flag is above the note's head; if the stem is pointing down, the flag is below the head.

Just as there are four quarter notes in a measure ($4 \times \frac{1}{4} = 1$), each measure holds eight eighth notes ($8 \times \frac{1}{8} = 1$). Put another way, there are two eighth notes for every quarter note ($2 \times \frac{1}{8} = \frac{1}{4}$)—or two eighth notes for every beat.

An eighth note looks like a quarter note with a *flag* on it. If you have two or more eighth notes in a row, the flags may be joined together. (The flags don't have to be joined together; it's just that it's easier to read that way sometimes.)

Sixteenth Notes

Okay, you know where this is going. Half an eighth note is (do the math!) a *sixteenth note* ($\frac{1}{8} \div 2 = \frac{1}{16}$). There are 16 sixteenth notes in a measure ($16 \times \frac{1}{16} = 1$), or four sixteenth notes per one quarter-note beat ($4 \times \frac{1}{16} = \frac{1}{4}$).

A sixteenth note looks like a quarter note with *two* flags on it. As with the eighth note, if two or more sixteenth notes are next to each other, the flags may (or may not) be joined together.

Taking Count

While it's fairly easy to write down a series of notes (once you get the hang of it, that is!), how do you communicate notes and values to other musicians *verbally*? Do you go all mathematical and say things like "the fourteenth sixteenth note" or "the eighth note after the two sixteenth notes on beat four"?

There's a relatively easy method of signifying notes, and all it takes is the ability to count up to four. It starts fairly simple, in that each beat in a measure is counted as either one, two, three, or four. So if you're counting off four quarter notes, you count them as "one, two, three, four." If you want to talk about the fourth quarter note in a measure, you call it "four," as in "in the last measure, let's put an accent on four."

If the downbeat is always one, two, three, or four, what about the eighth notes that lie in between the beats? Simple—count them as "and," as in "one-and, two-and, three-and, four-and"—all very even. You'd talk about an eighth note like this: "Put a big punch into the 'and' after three."

This is pretty easy—but what about sixteenth notes? Here it gets a little tricky, but it'll seem natural once you get into it. Use the nonsense syllables "e" and "ah" to represent the sixteenth notes in between eighth notes. So if you're counting a group of straight sixteenth notes, you'd count "one-e-and-ah, two-e-and-ah, three-e-and-ah, four-e-and-ah," all nice and even. When you're talking about sixteenth notes, you'd say something like this: "The trumpet player is a little flat on the 'e' after four."

Drum Note

While we'll stop for now with sixteenth notes, there are lots of notes even smaller than that. Each successive note is half the value of the previous note and is indicated by an additional flag on the stem. For example, the thirty-second note is the next-smaller note after the sixteenth note, and it has three flags on its stem. After that is the sixty-fourth note, with four flags. In actuality, you won't run into too many notes smaller than the sixteenth note—except in rolls, which are discussed in Chapter 12, "The Big Bounce: Open and Closed Rolls."

Still not sure about this? Then examine the following figure, which shows how you'd count various groupings of notes.

ONE TWO THREE FOUR   ONE AND TWO AND THREE AND FOUR AND   ONE E AND AH TWO E AND AH THREE E AND AH FOUR E AND AH

It helps to count all the notes when you're just starting off.

This method of counting is important because when you're first starting out, it really helps to count your way through every measure of every exercise. When you count, it's easier to keep your place and to see where each note falls. So get in the habit of counting "one-e-and-ah, two-e-and-ah," until you become familiar with all this notation and can keep a steady beat.

Taking a Rest

If a note is something you hit, what do you call something you *don't* hit? In music, when you're not playing, you're resting—so any note you don't play is called a rest.

When you see four quarter notes, you hit your drum four times. When you see four quarter note rests, you *don't* hit your drum four times—that is, you rest over four beats.

Each type of note—whole note, half note, and so on—has a corresponding rest of the same duration. So you have a whole rest that lasts a whole measure, a half rest that lasts a half measure, and so on. Rests are used to indicate the spaces in between the notes and are just as important as the notes you play.

The following figure shows all the notes you've just learned and their corresponding rests.

More math—each note has its own rest of the same duration.

WHOLE	o	=
HALF	♩	=
QUARTER	♩	= ⸮
EIGHTH	♪	= ⸜
SIXTEENTH	♬	= ⸜

Taking a Note—and Dotting It

Sooner or later you'll run into something a little different—a note or a rest with a dot after it. When you run into a so-called dotted note, that note should have a longer duration than the normal version of that note—one and a half times longer, to be precise.

Here's where your math skills come back into play. Let's take a dotted quarter note as an example. A regular quarter note is worth a single beat. Take $1 \times 1\frac{1}{2}$, and you get $1\frac{1}{2}$ beats—so a dotted quarter note is worth $1\frac{1}{2}$ beats. You could also go about it by saying that a quarter note equals four sixteenth notes, and $4 \times 1\frac{1}{2} = 6$, and six sixteenth notes equal $1\frac{1}{2}$ quarter notes. However you do the math, it comes out the same.

Taking Two Notes—and Tying Them Together

Another way to make a note longer is to "tie" it to another note. A tie is a little rounded connector placed between two notes, and it essentially tells you to add the second note to the first note.

If you were playing a wind instrument, you would literally play the two tied notes together. For example, if two quarter notes were tied together, you'd blow through them for the equivalent of a half note.

You're not a wind player, however, so when you see two notes tied together, you hit the first note as normal, then *don't* hit the second note. So when you see two quarter notes tied together, you hit the first note, but don't hit the second.

Taking the Beat and Dividing by Three

There's another little oddity in music notation—and this one is very important. Everything we've done up to now has divided notes and beats by two. What happens, then, if you divide by something other than two?

The most common division other than two is dividing by three, and is called a triplet. When you see the number 3 over a group of three notes (or three rests—or any combination of three equal notes and rests), you know that those three notes have to fit into a space that would normally hold just two notes.

In the following example, you see a group of eighth-note triplets. Instead of playing two eighth notes on the fourth beat, you play three equal notes. Triplets have more of a rolling feel than straight eighths and are counted as "trip-eh-let."

The three notes of a triplet fit in the space of two regular notes.

Other common triplets are quarter-note triplets (where three of them are spaced over two beats) and sixteenth-note triplets (three in the space of a single eighth note).

Taking Time—Signatures

Up to this point, we've assumed that all measures have four beats, and that each beat equals a quarter note. That's a pretty good assumption because rock and roll, soul, jazz, country, reggae, and other popular forms of music usually use this four-beat form. However, not all music follows this same form.

Written music uses something called a time signature to signify how many beats are in a measure and what kind of note is used for the basic beat. A time signature looks kind of like a fraction, with one number sitting on top of another number. The top number indicates how many beats in a measure, and the bottom number indicates the note value of the basic beat.

Let's take our standard four-quarter-notes-to-a-measure form. Since we have four beats in a measure, the top number in the time signature is a four. Since the basic beat is a quarter note, the bottom number is a four (as in the 4 in 1/4). So the standard form we've been using is called "four four" (because of the 4 on top of the 4).

A variety of different time signatures—the number of beats is on top, and the type of note is on bottom.

If our measures had three beats instead of four and still used a quarter note for the beat, then you would have a 3/4 time signature. What if the basic beat wasn't a quarter note but was an eighth note—and there were six of them in a measure? That time signature, which is fairly common in jazz and orchestral music, is called "six eight," or 6/8.

When you're playing in an orchestra or a big band, *always* check the time signature before you start playing. It's always located at the start of the first staff of music, and it tells you exactly how to count!

Taking the Pulse

Now that you know how to figure out how many beats are in a measure, how do you know how *fast* to play those beats? The speed of a song—how fast the beat goes by—is called the tempo. A faster tempo means a faster beat; a slower tempo makes for a slower song.

Tempo can be indicated in one of two ways. The most accurate way is to indicate tempo as a certain number of beats per minute. This gives you a very precise speed for your song, especially when you use a *metronome*. You set your metronome to a specific number of

Drum Note

If a time signature changes in the middle of a song, a new time signature will be inserted at the point of change. This new time signature remains in effect through the rest of the song or until another new time signature is introduced.

beats per minute, and it tick-tocks back and forth at the proper speed. When you play along to the metronome, you're playing at exactly the right tempo.

The second way to indicate tempo, typically found in orchestral music, is through the use of traditional Italian musical terms. These terms correspond to general tempo ranges, as indicated in the following table.

Drum Word

A **metronome** is a device that precisely ticks off beat after beat at a specified tempo. Metronomes can be either old-fashioned, pendulum-type affairs or modern computerized devices that emit a type of electronic beat. When you're in a recording studio (or in some live playing situations), you might run into something called a "click track." A click track is nothing but an electronic metronome, typically played on a synthesized instrument, like an electronic woodblock or cowbell. When you play along to the click track—which is harder than it sounds—you play at a constant, precise tempo throughout the entire song.

Different Tempos

Tempo	Means ...
Grave	Very slow
Largo	Slow
Larghetto	A little faster than Largo
Adagio	Moderately slow
Andante	Moderate—a "walking" tempo
Andantino	A little faster than Andante
Allegretto	A little slower than Allegro
Allegro	Fast
Vivace	Lively
Presto	Very fast
Prestissimo	Very, very fast
Moderato	Moderate
Molto	Very

So when you see a score marked "Allegro," you know that it should be played fairly fast. If you see a piece marked "Largo," you know that the tempo should be fairly slow. This method isn't terribly precise, but it will get you in the ballpark.

You may also see a marking called a Ritardando (typically indicated as "Rit." or "Ritard."). When you see a Ritardando, that means you should gradually slow down the tempo.

If you see a little bird's eye over a note, that's called a fermata, or a "hold." It means to stop the beat and hold that note indefinitely (until the conductor tells you otherwise).

Taking It Up—and Taking It Down

You now know how to indicate how fast or how slow a song should be played. How do you indicate how loud or how soft you should play?

A song's dynamics indicate how loud or soft you should play. There is a set range of volume levels, from very soft (pianissimo) to very loud (fortissimo), as indicated in the following table.

Different Dynamics

Marking	Dynamic	Means ...
ppp	Pianississimo	Very, very soft
pp	Pianissimo	Very soft
p	Piano	Soft
mp	Mezzo Piano	Medium soft
mf	Mezzo Forte	Medium loud
f	Forte	Loud
ff	Fortissimo	Very loud
fff	Fortississimo	Very, very loud

The dynamic marking, just like the tempo marking, typically appears at the beginning of the song. If you don't see a dynamic marking, that means the song should be played at a medium volume.

Dynamics can and do change throughout the course of a song. When you see a new dynamic marking sitting all by itself, that means you abruptly change volume at that point. If you see a mark that looks like a giant "less than" sign (called a crescendo), that means you gradually increase the volume from your current level to the new level indicated at the end of the crescendo. If you see a mark that looks like a giant "greater than" sign (called a decrescendo), that means you gradually decrease the volume from your current level to the new level indicated at the end of the decrescendo.

Crescendos and decrescendos indicate gradual increases or decreases in volume.

If you need to hit a specific note harder than the other notes around it, you'll see an accent mark (>) over that note. When a note is accented, you simply play it louder than a normal note. If you see a marcato (^) over a note, that means to hit it extra hard—with a good firm crack!

Taking a Do-Over

As **Hal Blaine** said in the previous chapter, reading music is like reading a roadmap. To that end, there are various indications you'll see in a score that provide direction—to repeat a section or to jump to another section within the song.

When you're playing a long piece of music, various parts of the song might be indicated by numbers or by letters. For example, you might see the letter A at the beginning of the first verse, and the letter B at the beginning of the second verse, and the letter C at the start of the chorus. This way other musicians can tell you to start at a specific point in the song by saying "Start at letter B."

Alternately, the measures of a song might be numbered. If this is the case, you can say "Start at measure 16," and everyone will know what you mean.

A section of music that should be repeated is bordered by repeat marks. Unless otherwise noted, you repeat a section only once (that is, you play it twice), and then you move on to the next section.

REPEAT MARK   REPEAT MARK

When you see repeat marks, you should repeat the previous section—beginning with the opening repeat mark.

Drum Tip

If you get confused by all this navigation notation, don't hesitate to ask your conductor, teacher, or another player what a particular mark means. The last thing you want to do is to jump to the wrong section of the song—when the rest of the band is playing something completely different!

Sometimes you'll need to repeat a section but play a slightly different ending the second time through. When you see this in the score—called a first ending and a second ending—you play the first ending the first time through, and then when you repeat the section, you skip the first ending and play the second ending.

Another way to repeat a section of a song is to return to a section designated with a sign (called a Segno sign). When you see the notation "D.S. al Coda," you jump back to the Segno sign, play through until you see another sign, called a Coda, and then return to where you left off. If you see the notation "D.S. al Fine," you jump back to the Segno sign, play to the measure marked "Fine," and then stop.

A similar jump method is notated "D.C. al Coda" or "D.C. al Fine," where you jump to the beginning of the song and then follow through to the Coda or the end (Fine).

The Least You Need to Know

➤ Each measure in a song is comprised of a set number of beats; the number of beats and the basic note per beat are indicated by the song's time signature.

➤ Whole notes are worth four beats; half notes are worth two beats; quarter notes are worth a single beat; eighth notes are worth half a beat; and sixteenth notes are worth a quarter of a beat. Put another way, there are four sixteenth notes to a beat, two eighth notes to a beat, and one quarter note per beat.

➤ Each type of note has a corresponding rest of the same duration; a rest is a note that you *don't* play.

➤ Dotted notes or rests are worth $1\frac{1}{2}$ times the normal note or rest.

➤ How fast you play each beat is signified by the tempo of the song; tempo is noted in terms of beats per minute, or by traditional Italian music notation.

➤ How loud you play a song is signified by the song's dynamics, which are noted in traditional Italian music notation.

Chapter 9

Get a Grip: Holding Your Sticks

In This Chapter

➤ The right way to hold your sticks

➤ Matched grip versus traditional grip

➤ The proper drum stroke

It's time to pick up your sticks and start playing. Sound simple? It is—if you do it right. If you don't learn the right way to hold and use your sticks, you can end up expending a lot of excess energy and possibly damaging your hands or wrists. So learn the *right* way to play—from the very start!

Shake Hands with Your Sticks

There are actually two different approaches to holding your drumsticks. With matched grip, both your hands hold the sticks the same way; traditional grip requires you to hold your left hand differently from your right. Either of these grips is acceptable, although most drummers today tend to play with matched grip, which is a little better suited for around-the-toms drumset playing.

Make a Match: Learning Matched Grip

Matched grip is the most commonly used grip today. Since both your hands use an identical grip, it's easier to learn; this grip also makes it easier to reach over and play the right side of your drumset with your left hand.

Another advantage to matched grip is that it's pretty much how you'd grab the sticks instinctively. Reach out with your hand and grab the stick about a third of the way from the butt end. Grab it with your thumb and the first joint of your index finger, then close your other fingers loosely around the stick. Now turn your wrist so that the back of your hand is facing upward and the stick is angled inward at about a 45-degree angle.

Repeat this procedure with your other hand, and you've mastered the matched grip!

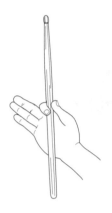

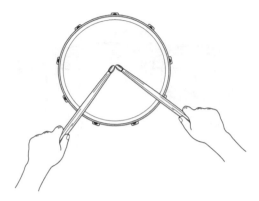

This is where you grasp the stick ...

... and this is how you hold the stick.

Positioning your hands with matched grip.

Drum Tip

Sticks come in all different shapes and sizes, and it's important to get the right stick for your hands and your playing needs. When you're first starting out, however, it's a good idea to use a slightly heavier stick than you'd use otherwise; it helps to build strength in your hands, much the way that swinging several baseball bats at once helps a batter prepare for a normal swing. For more information on choosing your sticks, see Chapter 2, "Before You Play, You Have to Pay: Buying Your First Drums."

Drum Note

Some drummers use a variation on matched grip called French grip, where the wrist is turned slightly so that your thumb is on top of the stick. This grip, popular with tympani players, depends more on finger control while promising faster speed.

Not Quite the Same: Learning Traditional Grip

With traditional grip, your right hand grips the stick in a matched grip, while your left hand uses a different grip. Some drummers claim more sensitivity, especially on their snare drum, when using traditional grip; you'll find more jazz drummers than rock drummers using this grip. In reality, however, traditional grip is no better or worse than matched grip—it's all a matter of which you grew up with!

To use traditional grip, remember that it's only your left hand that's different; use the grip described previously for your right hand. Turn your left hand so that your palm is facing up, and then slip the stick between your second and third fingers, and on through the pocket between your thumb and first finger. There should be about a third of the stick sticking out from the left side of your hand. The stick should rest on your third finger, held in place by your second finger.

Drum Note

Traditional grip originated with marching drummers of old who had to sling their drums over their shoulders. This put the drum at an angle, with the left side higher than the right. To properly strike the drumhead, drummers had to strike the drum differently with their left hand than with their right—and the traditional grip was born.

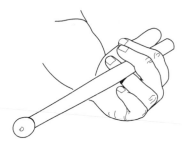

Holding the left stick in a traditional grip.

When you play traditional grip, your sticks should form a 90-degree angle on your drumhead. As you can see, your right hand is positioned palm down, while your left hand is palm up.

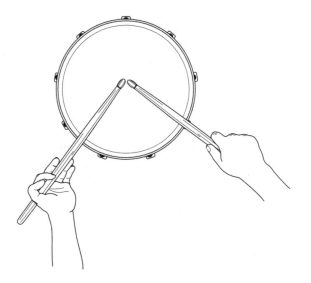

Positioning your hands with traditional grip.

Drum Tip

If you're playing snare drum only—especially in a concert band or orchestra—you'll be standing up. (You sit down to play only when you're playing your drumset.) When you're playing standing up, make sure you have a snare drum stand that is tall enough for your needs; since many snare stands are designed for drumset use, you may need to add an extension piece to get it high enough for you.

How high is high enough? Your snare drum should be positioned roughly at waist level. Depending on your style, you may position it a tad above or below your waist. If you're playing matched grip, the drum should be level horizontally. If you're playing traditional grip, you'll want to angle the drum downward slightly, from left to right.

Bang a Drum: Learning the Stroke

Whether you're playing matched grip or traditional grip, your right-hand stroke is always the same. (Your left hand, naturally, varies by grip.)

The proper matched-grip drum stroke is very simple. Position your stick parallel to the drumhead, with the bead of the stick about three inches off the surface. Now use your wrist (*not* your fingers or your arm!) to quickly snap the stick down to the center of the head and then immediately back up.

This "down-up" motion is your stroke. You should control the stroke in both directions and *not* allow the stick to bounce up of its own volition. It's important that you control the entire stroke; otherwise, you'll be bouncing all over the place and waiting for your stick to return to position.

Drum Don't

Your natural inclination may be to raise your stick just before you begin the downward stroke. This "up-down-up" stroke is extremely inefficient, can actually slow down your playing, and, when playing at faster tempos, is difficult to control. Work hard to perfect the "down-up" motion *without* an initial upstroke.

To make a stroke with your left hand in a traditional grip, you also start with the stick parallel to the head and about three inches off the head. Now use your left wrist to snap the stick down to the head and then back up. It's basically the same "down-up" motion as with matched grip, except that you're doing it by turning your wrist to the right, as opposed to moving your wrist down and then back up.

You can control the volume of your stroke in several ways. First, you can begin your stroke from a higher level; hitting the drum from 12 inches away produces a louder note than hitting it from an inch away. Second, you can apply more force to your downstroke; the harder you hit the drum, the louder the note.

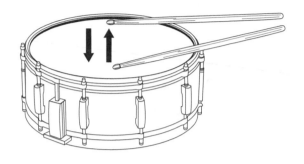

The perfect stroke—down and then up.

Drum Tip

When you progress to playing the full drumset, you'll find that there are subtle ways you can vary your grip and stroke. While the basic stroke remains the same, how you hold or move your sticks will produce different sounds for different types of music.

As you know, the basic drum stroke is made with your wrist. When you're playing a jazz rhythm on your ride cymbal—especially at fast tempos or low volume levels—you may want to make the stroke more with your fingers than your wrists. This produces a lighter sound and enables you to play a little faster on those uptempo jazz and bebop tunes.

When you're playing loud rock and roll, you may want to put a little more arm into your stroke—especially when crashing cymbals or playing a really heavy backbeat on the snare. By moving the fulcrum from your wrist to your elbow, you put more power behind the stroke and play louder, although with a little less speed.

For a slightly "chunkier" sound, you can try choking up on your sticks. This makes the stick more of an extension of your arm and forces you to play heavier into the drum—without necessarily increasing volume. One drummer who plays this way is **Levon Helm** of The Band; listen to "The Weight" or "Cripple Creek" to hear how this sounds.

When you practice your stroke, start off slowly and deliberately. Practice one hand at a time, and then put your hands together in alternating strokes. Once you have the stroke under control, try speeding up—either one hand at a time or alternating hands. As you play faster, take particular care to play the entire stroke and not let the bounce off the drum dictate the upstroke. Play down and then up with a sharp snap; avoid pressing the stick into the head. The motion, when viewed by an observer, should look like a whip cracking.

As you get comfortable hitting the drum, you can move ahead to the exercises in the next chapter (Chapter 10, "A One and a Two and a Three: Playing Your First Notes"). Remember as you work through all the exercises in this book—even the most complex ones—that your stroke should always be controlled and deliberate. It's hard work to do it right—especially at faster tempos—but the results are worth it!

The Least You Need to Know

➤ There are two ways to hold your sticks—matched grip and traditional grip. Most drummers today use matched grip.

➤ Hold the stick about a third of the way up from the butt, between your thumb and the first joint of your first finger.

➤ Use your wrist to strike the drum with a quick "down-up" motion, controlling both the downstroke and the upstroke; don't let the bounce off the head dictate the upstroke.

Chapter 10

A One and a Two and a Three: Playing Your First Notes

> **In This Chapter**
>
> ➤ Starting with quarter-note exercises
>
> ➤ Adding eighth notes and sixteenth notes
>
> ➤ Playing accents
>
> ➤ Playing your very first drum solo!

You know how to hold your sticks. You know how to stand (or sit) with your drum. You even know how to hit the drum.

Let's apply your newfound technique with your newfound ability to read music (which you learned back in Chapter 8, "Wholes, Halves, and Quarters: Notes and Notation"), and start playing the snare drum.

If you already have a drumset, you might be wondering why we're starting with just the snare drum instead of using the entire set. The answer is simple, really. It's easier to play one drum with two hands than it is to play five (or more!) drums with four different limbs. Do the math; playing a drumset is much more complicated than playing a snare drum. Once you master the fundamentals on the snare, *then* you can learn how to add the other drums in your setup.

Playing Quarters

As you recall from Chapter 8, a quarter note is equal to one beat. Each measure (in 4/4 time) has four beats, so there are four quarter notes in each measure.

Exercises 10.1 through 10.8 lead you through some basic quarter-note patterns. You should repeat each exercise several times before proceeding to the next pattern; it's okay to take a break between exercises.

Make sure you count your way through each exercise. (For the first several exercises, I've notated the "count" above each note, to help you with your counting.) It may seem dorky, but it's really helpful when you verbally count "one two three four" as you play through each measure.

Note that some of these exercises include quarter-note rests, which are notated with the "count" in parentheses. Obviously, when you see a rest, that's a beat you *don't* play—although you should still count your way through the rest.

When you play these exercises, pay close attention to the sticking. (The proper hand for each note is displayed under each note—R is for right, and L is for left.) Each exercise includes *two* stickings; play the exercise a few times with the first sticking, and then repeat the exercise with the alternate sticking. This way you'll strengthen both your hands and learn how to "lead" with either hand.

The important thing when playing these exercises is to play with a steady beat at a steady speed, or tempo. You want each beat to be equal to all the other beats—and each note to sound the same as all other notes. Strive to produce a consistent sound throughout each exercise by playing even, measured strokes with each hand. It's natural for notes played with one hand to sound different from notes played with the other, so this is something you'll have to work at overcoming.

Drum Note

You can listen to all the exercises and solos in this book online, at either the *Complete Idiot's Guide* Web site (www.idiotsguides.com) or at my personal Web site (www. molehillgroup.com/drums.htm). When you're learning how to play these exercises, it's nice to hear how they're *supposed* to sound!

Playing Eighths

Once you're comfortable playing quarter notes, you can move up to playing eighth notes. Remember that there are two eighth notes to every beat; you count them as "one-and two-and three-and four-and."

Exercises 10.9 through 10.16 combine quarter notes and eighth notes. It's important to play these at a tempo that you can easily navigate; you may need to start out slower than you did with the quarter-note exercises.

Notice that I included only one recommended sticking for each of these exercises. Once you've mastered this sticking, you should experiment with different stickings (like starting with the left hand instead of the right) to strengthen both your hands. Remember, the goal is to play each note in a consistent fashion so that all the notes sound the same.

Playing Sixteenths

Exercises 10.17 through 10.32 add sixteenth notes to the mix. These exercises incorporate quarter notes, eighth notes, and sixteenth notes, so you get a little bit of everything. (When you count sixteenth notes, say "one-e-and-ah two-e-and-ah three-e-and-ah four-e-and-ah.")

Playing Accents

For the first 32 exercises, you should strive to play each note at the same volume as all other notes; you want each exercise to sound even throughout. Starting with Exercise 10.33, however, you're introduced to the concept of accents.

An accent—indicated by a ">" over a note—indicates a note that should be played louder than the other notes. How much louder should you play an accent? This is a matter of taste and style, so I'll let your ears (and the ears of your drum teacher) be the judge.

To play an accent, simply hit the drum harder than you would normally. This means raising your stick slightly higher on the upstroke, and then striking downward with more force than you would normally.

You have to be careful, however, not to let an accented note slow you down. Beginning drummers sometimes tend to stumble over accents, thus interrupting the beat or inadvertently playing an accented note for slightly longer than it should be played. So even though you raise your stick slightly higher for an accent, you have to compensate for this and keep the underlying beat constant throughout.

Drum Solo: *Taking Back the Beat*

Enough of the exercises—let's get to the fun stuff! *Taking Back the Beat* is a drum solo that incorporates all you've learned about quarter notes, eighth notes, sixteenth notes, and accents. It even adds some new things to your repertoire, in the form of dynamics.

Let's walk through the dynamic changes in this solo. You start out in measure 1 at mf, which is medium loud. The first four measures are played at this volume, until you reach the two *pick-up notes* at the end of measure 4 leading into measure 5. Here, you ratchet the volume down to piano (soft) for the next four measures. Then, with the pick-up note at the end of measure 8 leading into measure 9, you increase the volume to f (loud). You stay loud for the next four measures, then head back down to mf (medium loud) for eight measures.

A big change-up occurs with the last four pick-up notes in measure 20, which should be played mp (medium soft). The next four measures continue medium soft, then you increase to mf (medium loud) for four measures. The final four measures of the song start medium soft (mp) and gradually increase (via a crescendo) to very, very loud (fff). The last four notes are very, very loud—and accented!—so you should whack the heck out of them!

Drum Word

A **pick-up note** is a note (or group of notes) appearing at the end of one measure that actually begins the musical phrase that starts in the following measure.

The Least You Need to Know

➤ When you practice an exercise, you should try to make every note consistent.

➤ Start each exercise at a tempo that enables you to play the entire exercise without stopping or slowing down.

➤ Remember to count each beat and each note; it helps you keep your place within the measure.

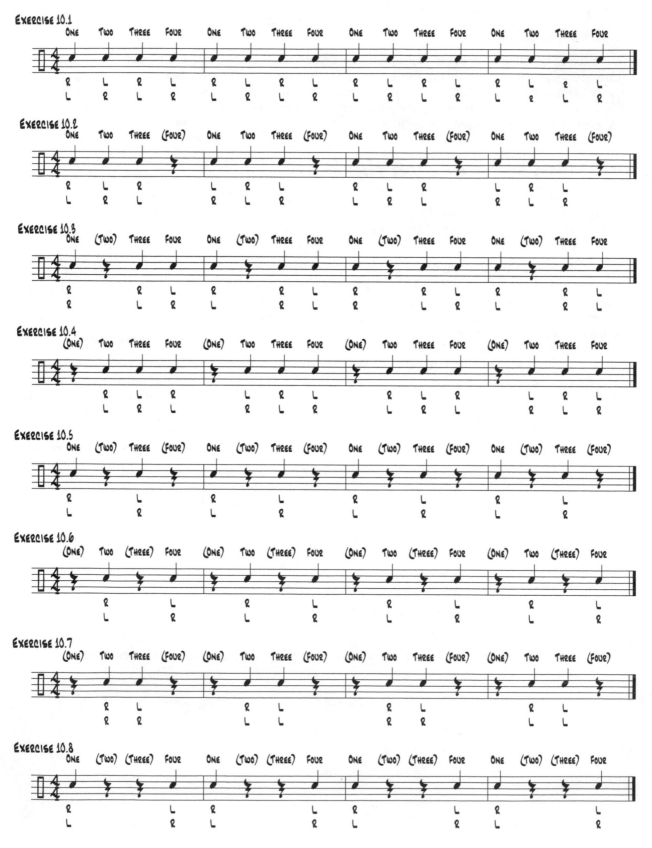

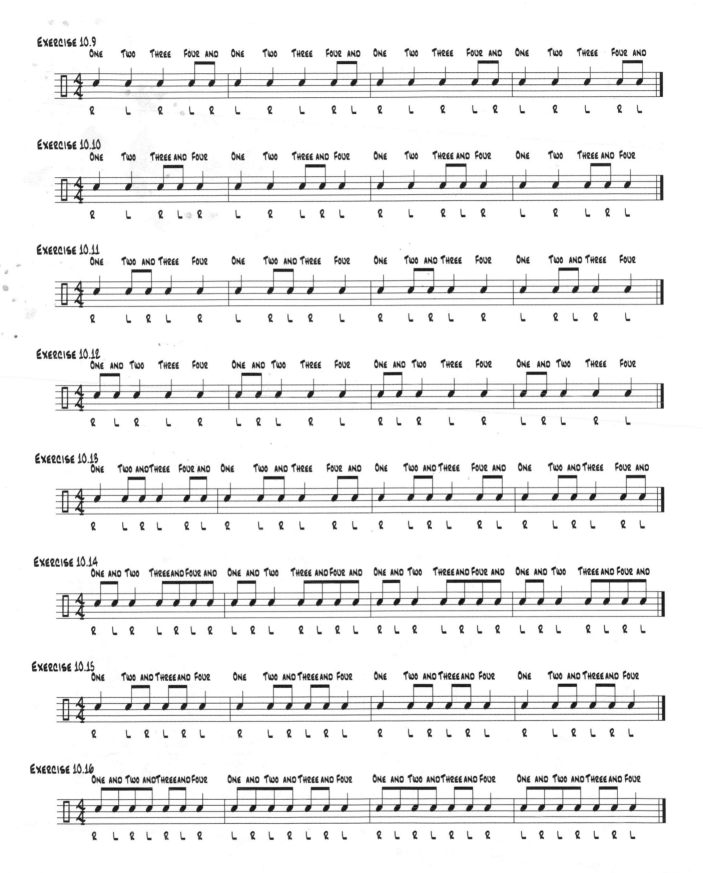

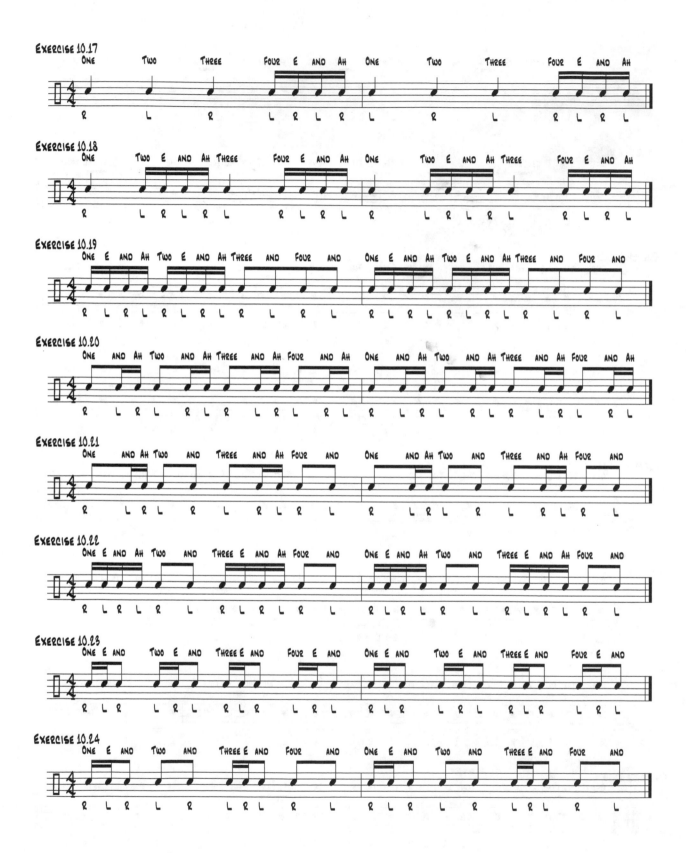

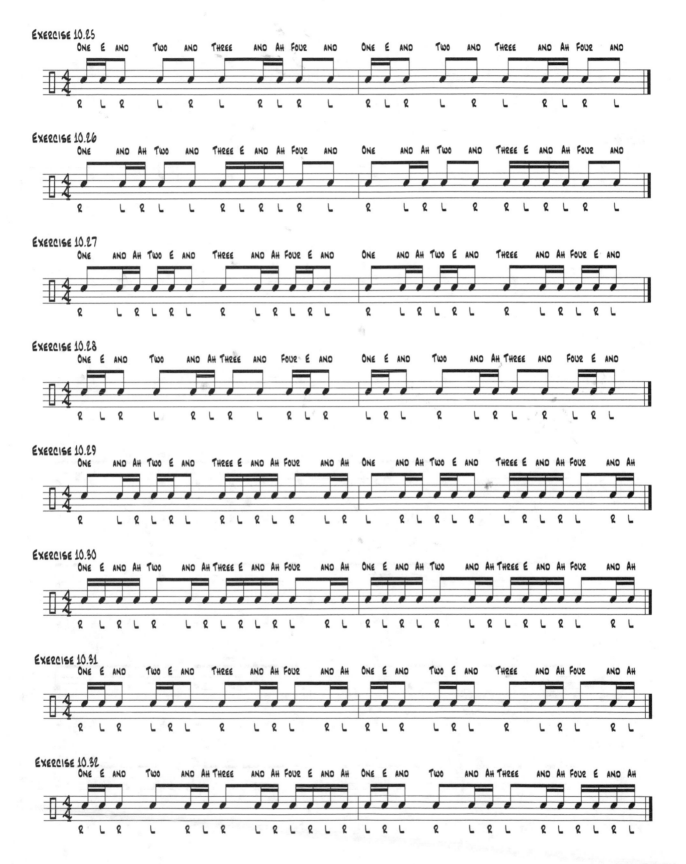

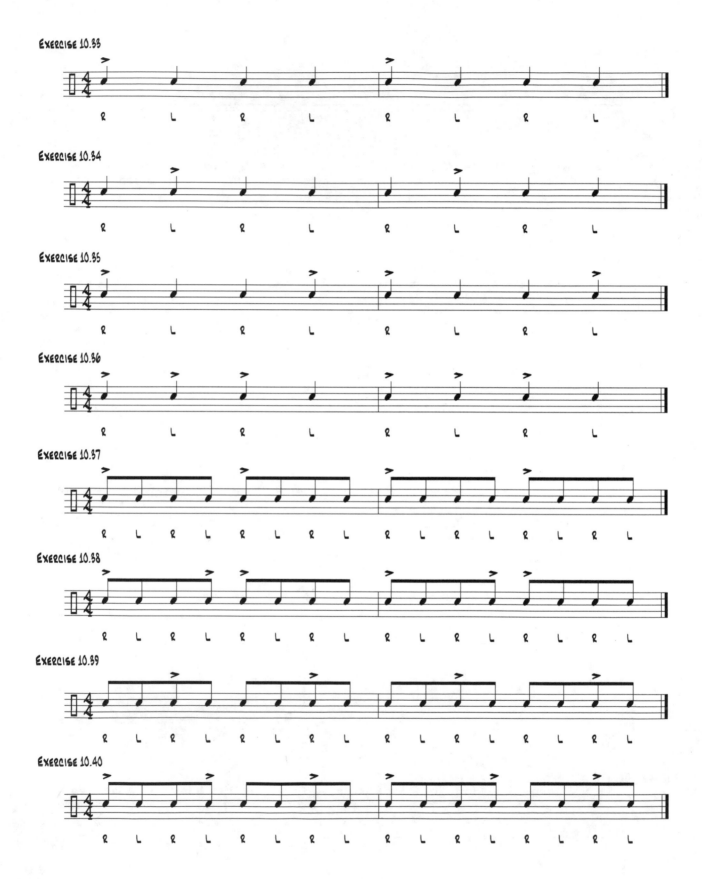

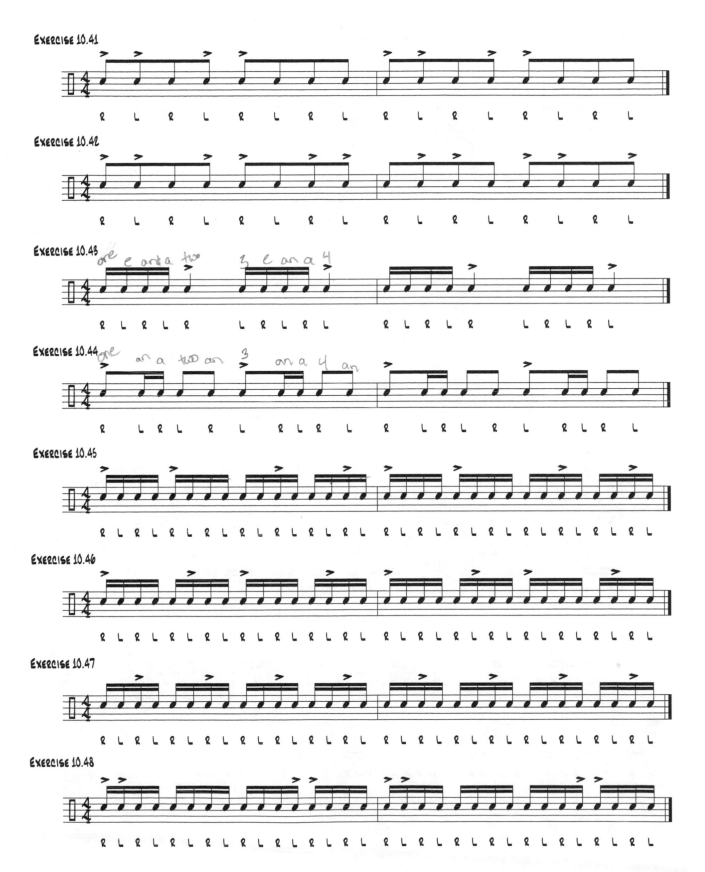

Playing Offbeat: Syncopated Rhythms and Triplets

In This Chapter

➤ Learn to play a syncopated rhythm

➤ Swing your way through groups of triplets

➤ Put it all together in a syncopated solo

So far you've played notes that are relatively straight. In fact, you can march to all the previous exercises; the emphasis is always on the downbeat, and the beat is always evenly divided.

More sophisticated music, however, sometimes puts the emphasis on a note other than the downbeat—and is sometimes divided into threes instead of twos or fours. Read on to learn how to play these sophisticated beats—with syncopation and triplets!

Skipping a Beat: Syncopation

Syncopation is when there's an emphasis in a place you're not expecting it—or when there isn't an emphasis where you *were* expecting it. This can be done by accenting something other than the downbeat—or by putting a rest on the downbeat. This type of change-up creates patterns that may sound "off" at first but ultimately have kind of a funky or jazzy feel.

Exercises 11.1 through 11.8 present syncopation using quarter notes and eighth notes. In these patterns you'll sometimes find the downbeat missing (via a rest), thus emphasizing the following upbeat. It's vitally important when playing these exercises that you *count* all the beats, even the missing ones, so that you don't get lost.

Exercises 11.9 through 11.16 introduce sixteenth-note syncopation. These patterns can be very difficult to play, so you probably want to dissect them carefully before you start playing. Count them out ("one-e-and-ah"), and note exactly where each note falls. You may even want to write four dots over each beat so that you can see the even subdivision and determine just where each note you play should be.

Here are some things to watch for as you play through this group of exercises:

➤ **Exercise 11.9** introduces the dotted-eighth/sixteenth-note pattern that is very common in shuffle and jazz grooves.

➤ **Exercises 11.12 and 11.13** combine the syncopation from Exercises 11.10 and 11.11 into new patterns.

➤ **Exercise 11.14** is pretty much all off-beat sixteenth notes—everything is on an "e" or an "ah."

➤ **Exercise 11.15** repeats a three-note pattern in an unexpected way.

Drum Don't

One common mistake when playing syncopated beats is to rush the notes, thus inadvertently speeding up the tempo. For this reason, you might want to practice with a metronome to force a steady beat. You might even want to set the metronome to play eighth notes so that you can keep your eighth notes and rests as even as possible; just set your metronome for twice the normal tempo, with each click representing half a beat.

Three for Two: Playing Triplets

As you learned back in Chapter 8, "Wholes, Halves, and Quarters: Notes and Notation," a triplet is a group of three notes that fit into where two notes normally fit. So, an eighth-note triplet replaces two normal eighth notes and is stretched over an entire beat.

Exercises 11.17 through 11.24 present eighth-note triplets and their variations. Look closely at Exercise 11.20, which compares similar "shuffle" patterns in triplets and in syncopated dotted-eighth/sixteenth notes. The triplet should have a "looser" feel than the "tighter" dotted-eighth/sixteenth note. (It's 3 vs. 4, remember.)

Also of interest is Exercise 11.21, which features a quarter-note triplet. This one's a little tricky in that you play three notes over four beats; another way to think of this is playing every other note of two eighth-note triplets.

Exercises 11.25 through 11.32 feature sixteenth-note triplets. Many drummers actually find these easier to play than eighth-note triplets! Just remember that the notes go by faster than straight sixteenths, so you may need to start at a slower tempo than normal.

A Syncopated Solo: *Freddie's Feet*

I've always thought of tap dancers as drummers without drumsets. They use their feet to create intricate rhythms that a drummer might normally create on a snare drum. Interestingly, many of the great drummers—including **Buddy Rich**, **Earl Palmer**, and **Steve Gadd**—were tap dancers when they were younger.

My list of favorite tap dancers is very long, but the one name that taps above the rest is Fred Astaire. Watch any of his great movies with Ginger Rogers, or any of his later movies on his own, and marvel not only at his dancing technique, but also at the heavily syncopated rhythms he creates when he tap dances. Fred Astaire danced to some great tunes and then improvised his own rhythm track on top of the tunes.

Drum Tip

One way to practice triplets is to play eighth-note triplets with one hand while playing straight eighth notes with the other hand. Make sure that both hands hit together on every downbeat!

This chapter's drum solo, *Freddie's Feet,* was inspired by the syncopated tap dancing of Fred Astaire. The rhythms in this solo are typical of what you'd hear in an Astaire tap dance number—lots of offbeat accents and playing *around* the beat. When you practice this solo, it's important not to rush the beat; you should always feel a steady, constant beat, even when the notes are flying everywhere *but* that beat! (It's also important to "ground" the syncopation—so take care to plant the quarter notes in measures 1, 3, 5, and 7 firmly on the beat for greater contrast with the subsequent off-beat accents.)

For kicks, you might want to play this solo along with an uptempo number by George Gerswhin or Irving Berlin; I had "Steppin' Out with My Baby" in mind as I was writing it. (If you do this, repeat the first 24 measures over and over to the form of the song; leave measures 25 to 28 for the finale.) This solo should have a slightly loose, kind of "jazzy" feel, and playing along with that type of song will help you get the right feel.

Note that throughout the solo you're "trading measures" with yourself. You'll find that you'll play a two-bar phrase and then "answer" that phrase with something similar but slightly different. For example, look at measures 5 through 8. Measures 5 and 6 are the "call," while measures 7 and 8 are the "response." In fact, measure 7 repeats measure 5 precisely, while measure 8 takes off in a slightly different direction. (This is a good technique to remember when playing drumset solos—it forces you into a consistent pattern.)

This pattern is broken at the very end of the solo, where a single pattern is repeated, each time softer than the last, in measures 25 and 26. This pattern is doubled in measure 27, as you increase the volume for the final volley in measure 28.

As with all previous solos, start slowly and gradually increase your tempo with practice. The goal here is consistency and feel—*not* speed! Just try to imagine Fred Astaire tapping his way through the solo, full of grace and control. If you can duplicate that feel on your snare drum, you're doing something right!

Drum Don't

When you're keeping the beat in a band, be careful about using too many syncopated rhythms. Listeners and dancers depend on you to keep a steady beat, and too much syncopation can trip them up!

Drum Note

Eighth-note triplets are quite common in jazz and shuffle beats.

The Least You Need to Know

➤ Syncopation is when you put the emphasis in an unexpected place.

➤ Triplets put three notes in the place of two.

➤ Syncopated patterns are like the rhythms improvised by tap dancers—and a syncopated drum solo is like a tap dance by Fred Astaire!

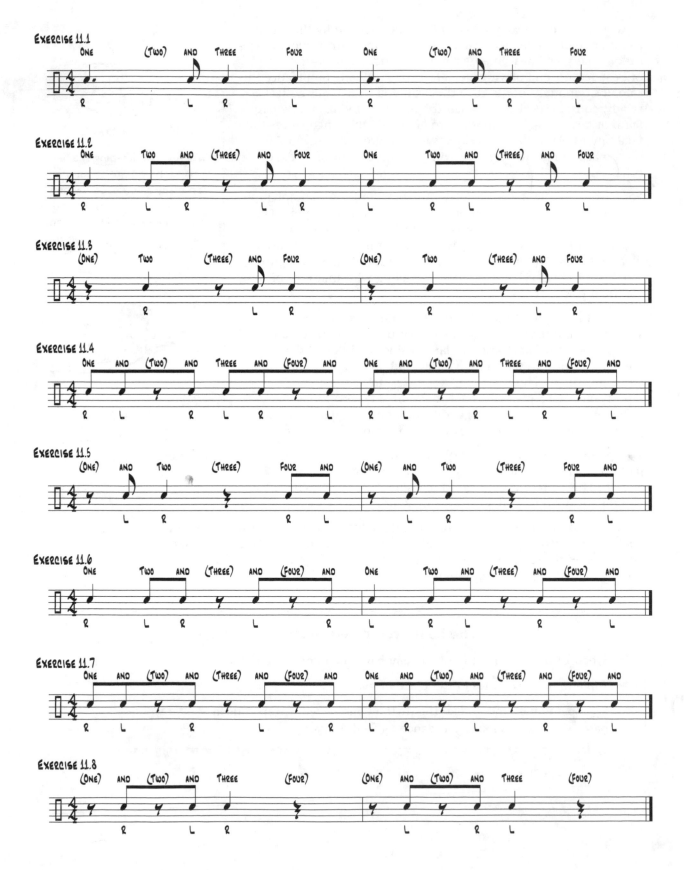

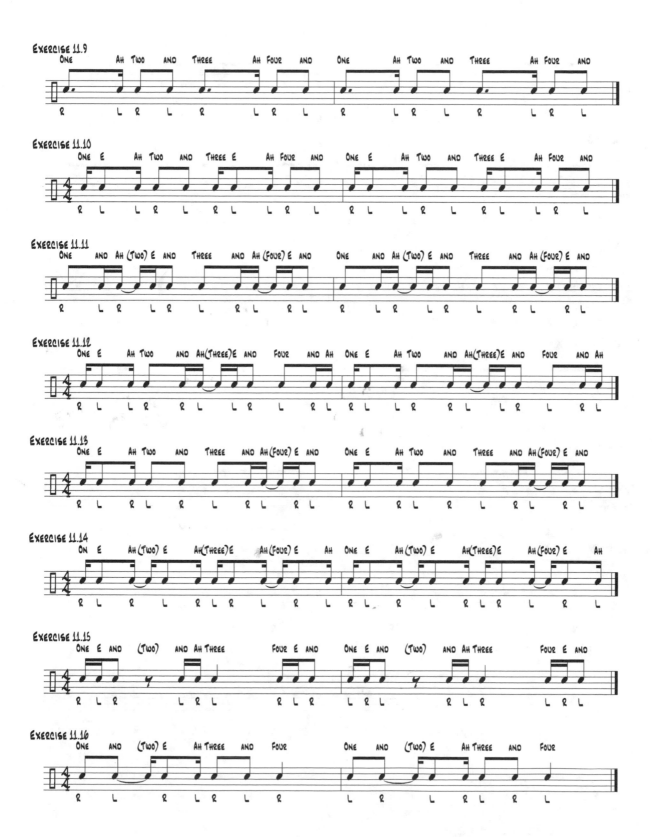

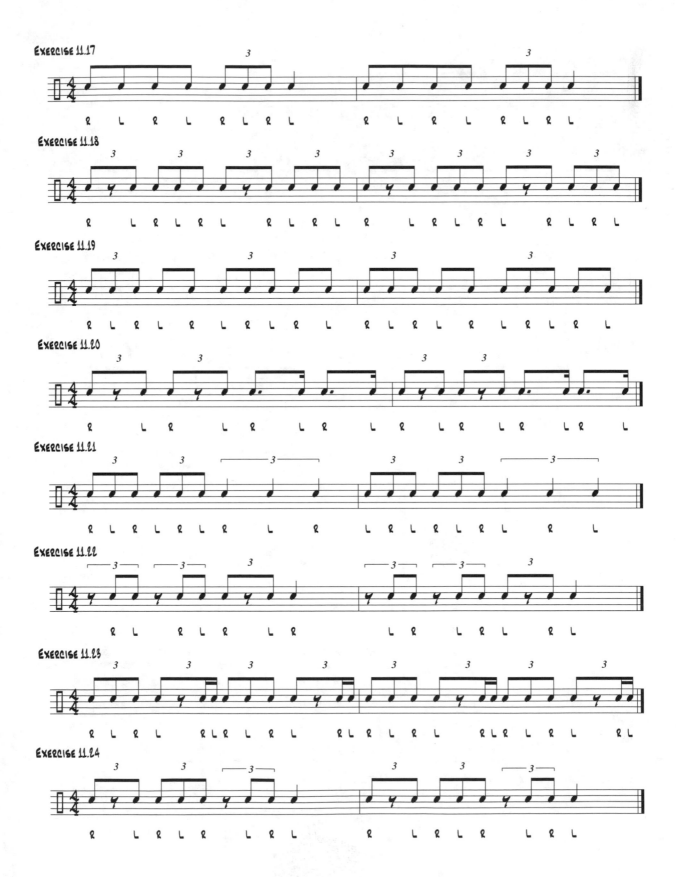

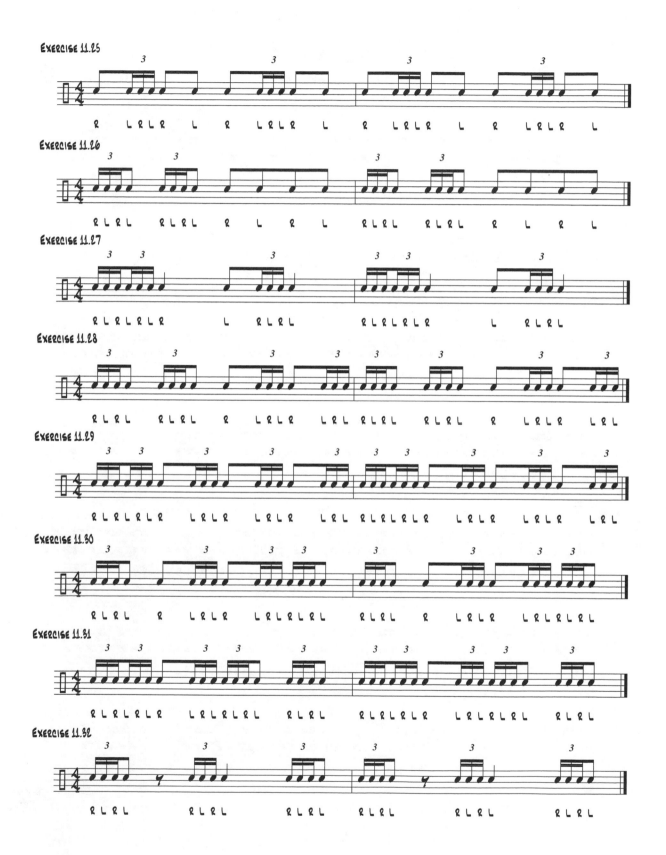

Freddie's Feet

A Study in Synopation

©Michael Miller

Chapter 12

The Big Bounce: Open and Closed Rolls

In This Chapter

➤ The playing of an open roll—without bouncing your sticks

➤ The difference between open and closed rolls

➤ A drum solo that really rolls

One of the key tools in a drummer's toolbox is the roll. A roll is the way to get a long note out of an instrument that can play only short notes, and you produce a roll by playing lots of short notes really fast, all in a row.

There are two types of rolls you can play—open rolls and closed rolls. When you play an open roll, you should be able to hear every stroke; it's essentially a series of thirty-second notes, played with double strokes. When you play a closed roll, you shouldn't be able to hear every stroke; the sound you produce should sound more like a continuous buzz. (This is why closed rolls are sometimes called "buzz rolls"; they're also called "press rolls," since you press your sticks hard into the drumhead.)

Keep It Clean: Open Rolls

Open rolls are typically used in rudimental drumming, although you'll often use variations of open rolls when you play fills around the drumset. Think of an open roll as starting with a group of sixteenth notes. When you play each hand twice in the same space (instead of RLRL, you play RRLLRRLL), you're playing double-stroke thirty-second notes—which is all an open roll really is.

One way to think of a roll is to think of the individual sixteenth notes, but play two strokes (on the same hand) for each sixteenth note. For example, where you'd play two sixteenths and an eighth (RLR), you'd double up on the sixteenths to play four thirty-seconds and an eighth (RRLLR), like this:

Turn sixteenth notes into a roll by playing each sixteenth note "two for one" with the same hand.

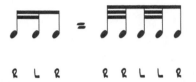

Drum Tip

It's easy—*too* easy—to bounce your strokes when practicing rolls. To make sure you're playing (not bouncing) every stroke, practice playing rolls with your sticks on a pillow. This will force you to play every stroke separately; there's no way to bounce on a pillow!

Some instructors will say you should bounce your double strokes, and they might call an open roll a "bounce roll." I disagree with this approach, particularly when you're first learning how to roll. Even though you're playing double strokes (two rights or two lefts), which would be easy to do by letting your stick bounce off the head, a true open roll is created by playing each stroke separately, in a controlled fashion. So when you play RRLL, you actually *play* two rights, followed by two lefts. This will produce a very clean, very distinct, very controlled sound.

To be fair, the faster you play an open roll, the more tempting it is to bounce your sticks to keep up. At very fast tempos, this is acceptable—and perhaps the only way to play the roll. However, you should always practice your rolls from slow to fast, and at the slower tempos, take care to play each note without bouncing.

Open rolls are designated by the number of strokes in the rolls. The name is always an odd number because the final single stroke at the end of the roll is counted as part of the roll. Thus, a roll with four thirty-second notes and a final tap is called a five-stroke roll. The figure on the next page shows the different open rolls—how they're commonly written and how they're actually played.

The Five-Stroke Roll

The five-stroke roll is one of the most common open rolls. A five-stroke roll fits in the space of a single eighth note and can start on the downbeat, on the upbeat, or (for a syncopated effect) on either the "e" or "ah" between the beat. Sticking is either RRLLR or LLRRL, and the final tap is often accented.

The Seven-Stroke Roll

The seven-stroke roll is a sixteenth note longer than the five-stroke roll. It typically starts on the "e" after the beat, although this isn't a hard-and-fast rule. More often than not, sticking is LLRRLLR, although you'll sometimes see the alternate RRLLRRL sticking.

The Nine-Stroke Roll

The nine-stroke roll takes up an entire beat. It usually starts on one beat and ends on the next, although it can also be syncopated to start on the "and" after the beat and carry through to the next "and." Either RRLLRRLLR or LLRRLLRRL is acceptable.

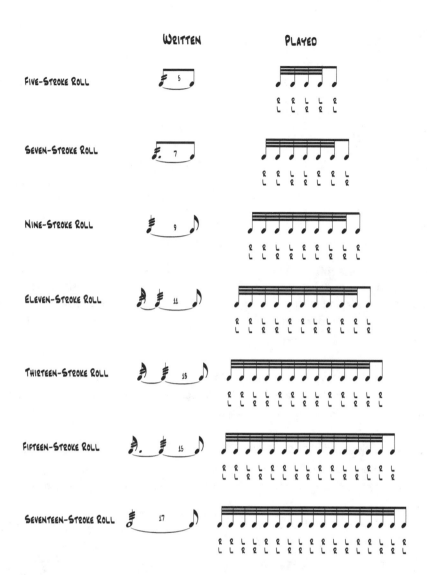

The Eleven-Stroke Roll

The 11-stroke roll is a sixteenth note longer than the nine-stroke roll and typically starts on the "ah" after the beat, carrying through to the second downbeat. Sticking is normally LLRRLLRRLLR, although the reverse sticking is also acceptable.

The Thirteen-Stroke Roll

In terms of length, you can think of a 13-stroke roll as kind of like a five-plus-nine. It almost always starts on the downbeat or the "and," carrying forward for one and a half beats. Sticking can be either RRLLRRLLRRLLR or LLRRLLRRLLRRL.

The Fifteen-Stroke Roll

If the 13-stroke roll is like a five-plus-nine, then the 15-stroke roll is like a seven-plus-nine. You'll typically start this puppy on the "e" after the beat and carry forward to the second downbeat. More often than not, sticking is LLRRLLRRLLRRLLR, although the reverse sticking is acceptable.

The Seventeen-Stroke Roll

This is a two-beat roll, notated by a half note connected to a final note. It's typically started and ended on a downbeat, with either RRLLRRLLRRLLRRLLR or LLRRLLRRLLRRLLRRL sticking.

Drum Note

To be fair, trying to play each stroke of an open roll loudly or at a fast tempo can put tremendous strain on your muscles—and can actually do serious damage over the long term. So even though I preach playing each stroke of a roll separately, without bouncing, I recognize that most drummers do, in fact, bounce their rolls. More precisely, they use what is called a *controlled bounce*.

To play a controlled bounce, you play the initial stroke as you would normally, but instead of bringing the stick off the head manually, you let it bounce off the head back to its original position. Then you tap the stick back down for the second, repeated, stroke, and let it bounce back up to position, as well. This gives you two repeated strokes (RR or LL) with less effort than actually hitting the drum twice.

While I still recommend learning to play open rolls by hitting each stroke separately, mastery of the controlled bounce enables you to play faster and reduces the strain on your arm and wrist muscles. You can also use a controlled bounce to play fast jazz and bebop patterns on your ride cymbal.

The bottom line? Bouncing isn't always bad, even though I still believe you should use the no-bounce method when learning how to roll.

Make a Buzz: Closed Rolls

When you see the following notation, you know you're into something longer than a 17-note roll:

Notation for a measure-long buzz roll.

This notation indicates that you should play a roll that lasts an entire four-beat measure. Now, this *could* be a 33-stroke roll, but there really isn't such a beast. Instead, when you see this notation, you should play a closed roll that lasts an entire measure.

A closed roll (also called a buzz or press roll) consists of strokes that are hard-pressed into the drumhead, resulting in a multiple bounce that sounds like a "buzz." When you press one hand after another fast enough, you create the continuous buzz that makes up a closed roll.

Exercising Your Rolls

Exercises 12.1 through 12.16 provide practice for open-stroke rolls. You can also ignore the open-stroke notation and practice these as closed rolls.

The first eight exercises are specific practice for the seven types of open rolls. There's nothing hard about these exercises; they simply present each roll in a typical playing scenario.

The second eight exercises mix up the rolls to some degree and apply them in more complex patterns.

As with all the exercises in this book, start slow and work your way up to a faster tempo. Remember to *play* each stroke—don't let yourself get caught rebounding!

A Rolling Solo: *Rollin' the Hay*

With apologies to Mel Brooks (watch for Teri Garr's first appearance in *Young Frankenstein* for the reference), *Rollin' the Hay* is a drum solo that applies just about every type of roll you can play.

You start the piece with a buzz roll, crescendoing from very soft to very loud over the course of a measure. The same pattern is repeated in measure 3, but this time decrescendoing from very loud to soft.

Drum Note

The pattern found in Exercise 12.14 (a five-stroke roll followed by an extra note) is sometimes called a six-stroke roll.

Similar crescendos appear in measure 7, this time over the course of two 11-stroke rolls. Play this pattern carefully; it's difficult to create a convincing crescendo with so few notes.

Measure 9 sees the first of several applications of the syncopated five-stroke roll you saw back in Exercise 12.14. You'll see this pattern repeated throughout the solo. (I told you I liked this pattern!)

The final four measures of the piece is your chance to wail. Measures 21 through 24 alternated syncopated and nonsyncopated five-stroke rolls (don't get them mixed up!), and let you drive hard to the final note. If you like, you can turn up the volume on these measures so that you really whack the last beat!

The Least You Need to Know

➤ Open rolls are strings of thirty-second notes played with double strokes (RRLL and so on).

➤ While many drummers bounce their double-stroke rolls, full control requires you to play each note separately.

➤ A buzz roll is created by pressing the stick into the drumhead for a multiple bounce.

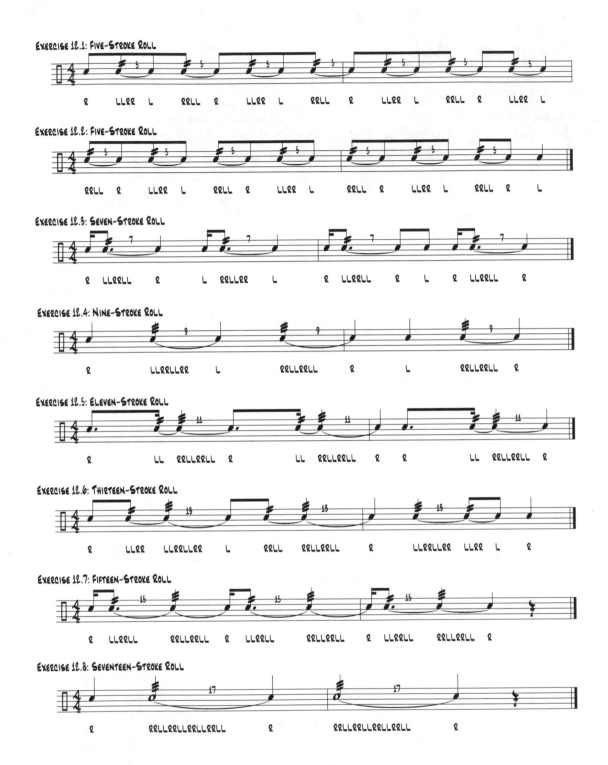

Rollin' the Hay

Snare Drum Solo

© Michael Miller

Chapter 13

Twenty-Six Things You Need to Know: The Rudiments

> ### In This Chapter
>
> ➤ Every drummer needs to learn the rudiments
>
> ➤ The use of grace notes in flams and ruffs
>
> ➤ Flamadiddles, ratamacues, and drags
>
> ➤ The mystery of Lesson 25

There are 26 fundamental patterns—combinations of single strokes, rolls, and grace notes—that every drummer needs to know. These patterns, known as rudiments, are the building blocks of your playing. In fact, as you've progressed through the previous exercises in this book, you've already been playing rudiments—it's almost impossible to play a song without playing one or more rudimental patterns.

Learning the rudiments is especially important if you'll be playing in an orchestra, concert band, marching band, or drum and bugle corps. Many of the patterns you'll play in a typical snare drum part are based on the patterns found in the 26 rudiments; when you know the rudiments, everything else is easier.

Getting Started: The First Thirteen Rudiments

The traditional 26 rudiments are arranged in no logical order, except perhaps in order of use. Interestingly, some of the first 13 rudiments are actually variations of basic patterns found in the second 13 rudiments!

The best way to practice a rudiment is to start slowly, playing the rudiment over and over until you've mastered the pattern and the sticking. Then you should gradually speed up the tempo, making sure not to progress to a new tempo until you've mastered the previous speed. Once you're up to your maximum speed, hold it for a few repetitions, and then gradually decrease the tempo until you're playing the rudiment at the original slow tempo at which you started. You should repeat this method with each of the rudiments until you've mastered all 26 of them.

Drum Note

The traditional drum rudiments date all the way back to the 1600s, from Switzerland's fife and drum corps of that day. These basic rudiments evolved over time (and through several countries) to become the current 26 rudiments endorsed by the National Association of Rudimental Drummers. Other groups and organizations have adapted these traditional 26 rudiments to their own needs, which is why you might encounter subtle variations of the basic rudiments, or even additional rudiments beyond the original 26.

1: The Long Roll

The long roll is simply a buzz roll of indeterminate length. While the notation indicates a double-right/double-left sticking, in reality you'll play this as you would any buzz roll, with a multiple-bounce press to create a smooth, clean, buzz.

No. 1: the long roll.

2: The Five-Stroke Roll

That most simple and most common of rolls is the second rudiment in the list. Either RRLLR or LLRRL sticking is acceptable.

No. 2: the five-stroke roll.

3: The Seven-Stroke Roll

The seven-stroke roll is the third rudiment. While most rudimental instructors teach this as a traditional dotted eighth-note roll, like the one you learned in the last chapter, there is a variation that puts all seven strokes into the same space as a typical five-stroke roll. This variation requires you to play a thirty-second-note triplet instead of straight thirty-second notes. Where you'd normally start a seven-stroke roll on the "e" after the beat, the triplet version would start on the "and" after the beat. When you play this variation, think "trip-e-let tap" and play two strokes for every syllable in the word "trip-e-let."

No. 3: the seven-stroke roll.

4: The Flam

The flam is a basic component of every drummer's arsenal—and it's easy to play! Basically, a flam is a *grace note* that you play just before another note. You play it lighter and tight up against the second, primary note so that you're almost playing both notes simultaneously.

L R   R L

No. 4: the flam.

Drum Word

A **grace note** is a short note that you play immediately preceding a regular note. Typically the grace note (or notes—you can play more than one) is played shorter and softer than the main note and leads you into the primary note.

The name of this rudiment comes from the sound of the pattern. When you play the two notes properly, it makes a sound like "fa-lam!" In fact, the way to practice this rudiment is with the two notes spaced wide apart ("fa——lam"), and then gradually decrease the space between the notes—until you get the "flam" sound.

While the rudiment is notated with the main note being a quarter note, the primary note of the flam can be of any duration—quarter, eighth, sixteenth—you name it.

Drum Tip

When you're playing on a drumset, try playing a flam between two different drums. For example, you might play the grace note on your small tom and the main note on your floor tom. It's a great sound!

5: The Flam Accent

The flam accent takes a flam and adds two more notes so that you're playing a pattern of three primary notes. While you typically find flam accents applied to triplets (and to patterns in 3/4 or 6/8 time—in other words, to music naturally grouped in threes), you can also apply flam accents to straight eighth notes for a syncopated effect. When you string two eighth-note flam accents together across a bar of 4/4, the second flam accent falls on the "and" after two, for an upbeat accent.

No. 5: the flam accent.

6: The Flam Paradiddle

Drum Note

The repeated sticking (RL**RR** or LR**LL**) is the "diddle" in "para-diddle."

This rudiment takes a little explaining. It's based on the twenty-first rudiment, the single paradiddle—so you might want to skip ahead and learn that rudiment *first*.

In any case, what you have with a flam paradiddle—also called a "flamadiddle" is a group of four sixteenth notes with a flam attached to the front. What makes this pattern unique is that the last two sixteenth notes are played with the same hand—so you get a sticking like RLRR or LRLL (again, with a flam in front of the first note).

No. 6: the flam paradiddle.

Flamadiddles get interesting when you group two or more of them together. This is because the grace note of the second flamadiddle is played with the same hand as the last two notes of the previous one. So, if you play a RLRR pattern, you have to play a *third* stroke with your right hand to start the flam for the LRLL flamadiddle. When you try this at even a moderate speed, you'll either work up some killer technique or see your hands freeze up in a terrifying sticking accident.

7: The Flamacue

The flamacue is very similar to a flamadiddle, with three major exceptions. First, there is no double-sticking; you play a straight RLRL or LRLR pattern. Second, you accent the second sixteenth note, for a syncopated effect. Third, there's a final flam *after* the sixteenth-note pattern, just to put a capper on things.

No. 7: the flamacue.

8: The Ruff

I don't know why this rudiment is called a ruff. It doesn't sound like "ruff," or even like a dog barking—and it's not hard or "rough" to play. In fact, a ruff is almost as easy to play as a flam.

No. 8: the ruff.

Where the flam puts one grace note in front of a primary note, the ruff uses *two* grace notes and one primary. You bounce the grace notes lightly and then accent the primary note, in either a LL-**R** or RR-**L** pattern.

9: The Single Drag

The single drag is one of several "combination" rudiments in that it combines a ruff with a second, accented note. The two primary notes can be of any equal duration, and either **LLRL LLRL** or **LLRL RRLR** sticking is acceptable.

No. 9: the single drag.

10: The Double Drag

If you can have a single drag, why not a *double* drag? When you combine two ruffs and a third primary note, you have a double drag. It's a pattern in three and is typically applied to triplets or three-based time signatures (3/4, 6/8, and so on)—although you can apply this pattern to straight-eighths for a syncopated effect.

No. 10: the double drag.

This rudiment actually has two variations. The first and simplest version of the double drag has all three primary notes of the same duration—all quarters or all eighths, for example. The second version is a little more syncopated, with the first primary note being a longer, dotted note, and the second note being correspondingly shorter. Where the first version sounds like "ruff ruff tap," the second sounds like "ruff, ruff-tap."

11: The Double Paradiddle

Even though you haven't learned the single paradiddle yet (skip ahead to the twenty-first rudiment, in case you're curious), it's time to learn the *double* paradiddle—sometimes called the paradiddle-diddle. Basically, this rudiment takes a single paradiddle (which has either a RLRR or LRLL sticking) and tacks on two more strokes at the end—double-sticking the opposite hand. So, the sticking pattern is either RLRRLL or LRLLRR, depending on which had you start with.

No. 11: the double para-
diddle.

R L R L R R L R L R L L

While you might think that the double paradiddle, being a group of six notes, is ideally suited for triplets or three-based time signatures, you're more likely to encounter this puppy in straight-four time, used as a syncopated effect. When you string a few of these in a row, every other one forces an offbeat accent.

Drum Tip

An acceptable alternate sticking for the double paradiddle uses only one pair of repeat stickings—RLRLRR or LRLRLL. Some drummers prefer the alternate sticking as a little more controllable than the double–double traditional sticking.

12: The Single Ratamacue

The twelfth rudiment is another one of those that is named after its sound. When you play a ratamacue, it sounds like "ratamacue." Basically, a single ratamacue is a triplet (with a ruff attached to the front) leading into a fourth, accented note.

No. 12: the single rata-
macue.

LLR L R L   rrL R L R

13: The Triple Ratamacue

Contrary to what you might suppose, a triple ratamacue isn't three single ratamacues. Instead, it's a single ratamacue with two ruffs tacked to the front—making a sound something like "ruff ruff ratamacue." Just as with the single ratamacue, the final note (the "cue") is accented.

No. 13: the triple rata-
macue.

LLR   LLR   LLR L R L   rrL   rrL   rrL R L R

Drum Note

Having played the *single* ratamacue and the *triple* ratamacue, you're probably wondering what happened to the *double* ratamacue. Since the double ratamacue, which is a three-based pattern, is less widely used than either the single or the triple, it slips into place as the very last rudiment, number 26.

Drum Tip

While the rudiments were created with snare drummers in mind, these patterns are so fundamental that you'll find plenty of application on a full set of drums. You can play rudimental patterns on any drum or cymbal (including your hi-hat!), or you can "break up" the rudiments and play them on multiple drums or between a drum and a cymbal.

For example, the simple five-stroke roll becomes a classic Motown fill when you play the first four notes on your snare and the last note on your small tom. The paradiddle becomes a funky beat when you play the right-hand part of the pattern on your bass drum and the left-hand part on your snare. You're limited only by your imagination—and your technique!

Finishing Up: The Second Thirteen Rudiments

There's no particular reason that the 26 rudiments are split into a first 13 and a second 13, other than that it's nice to take a break midway through. So, assuming that you've had your break, let's get back to work!

14: The Single-Stroke Roll

The first of the second 13 rudiments, the single-stroke roll, is very similar to the first of the first 13 rudiments, the long roll. The long roll is a buzz roll using double-sticking, while the single-stroke roll uses single-sticking. (Duh!) The difference is that the long roll sounds like a buzz, while the single-stroke roll sounds like a very fast machine gun.

No. 14: the single-stroke roll.

147

You practice the single-stroke roll by slowly alternating left and right strokes and then gradually increasing your speed until you're playing right-left-right-left as fast as you can. You should then hold your maximum speed for as long as you can—you're now playing a real single-stroke roll, by the way—and then gradually decrease your tempo. In the real world, you'll be expected to launch right into a single-stroke roll at full speed, with no time for "acceleration."

15: The Nine-Stroke Roll

The fifteenth rudiment, the nine-stroke roll, is identical to the one you learned back in Chapter 12, "The Big Bounce: Open and Closed Rolls." Either RRLLRRLLR or LLRRLLRRL sticking is acceptable.

No. 15: the nine-stroke roll.

16: The Ten-Stroke Roll

The 10-stroke roll is one you *didn't* learn in the last chapter because it really isn't a straight roll. Instead, it's a nine-stroke roll with an extra tap (*not* a bounce!) at the end. When you play it correctly, you get kind of a "roll-tap-tap" effect, with the final tap accented.

No. 16: the 10-stroke roll.

Drum Don't

Make sure that you play the last two notes of the 10–stroke roll as sixteenth notes (on different hands), not as thirty-second notes.

17: The Eleven-Stroke Roll

This rudiment is identical to the 11-stroke roll you learned in the last chapter. You can start with either the left or the right hand.

No. 17: the 11-stroke roll.

18: The Thirteen-Stroke Roll

This rudiment is identical to the 13-stroke roll you learned in the last chapter. You can start with either the left or the right hand.

No. 18: the 13-stroke roll.

19: The Fifteen-Stroke Roll

This is another one of those rudiments that is identical to a roll you learned back in Chapter 12. Again, you can start with either the left or the right hand.

No. 19: the 15-stroke roll.

20: The Flam Tap

The flam tap is a flam with an extra tap added to the end. The tap is played with the same hand as the primary note of the flam and is *not* accented. (The primary note of the flam is accented, not the tap.) It sounds something like "flam-tap."

No. 20: the flam tap.

This rudiment can be a real bear when you play a bunch in a row at a fast tempo; it's a similar challenge to that of playing repeating flamadiddles. This is because the grace note for the second flam tap is played with the same hand that just got done playing the two primary notes—L-**RR** R-**LL** L-**RR** R-**LL**, and so on. Once you get in a rhythm, however, this rudiment really rocks.

Drum Tip

For a cool sound, play repeating flam taps between two different tom-toms on your drumset, with your left hand on your small tom and your right hand on your large tom.

21: The Single Paradiddle

For the life of me, I don't know why the single paradiddle is rudiment number 21. I mean, you've already learned the flam paradiddle (rudiment 6) and the double paradiddle (rudiment 11)—both of which are based on the simple single paradiddle! On top of that, the paradiddle is perhaps the most commonly encountered nonroll rudiment; if it were up to me, I'd have put it in the top five.

By now, you know how this rudiment works. It's simply a group of four equal notes, with the last two notes played with the same hand—RLRR or LRLL. It's pretty simple, but it produces a much different sound than if you were simply alternating hands across the same four notes.

No. 21: the single paradiddle.

Drum Tip

For a great example of rudiments used in the real world, check out any old video of Buddy Holly and the Crickets playing "Peggy Sue." **Jerry Allison,** the Crickets' drummer, is playing alternating sixteenth-note paradiddles around his toms—and it rocks!

22: The Drag Paradiddle No. 1

This is another combination rudiment. Take a single paradiddle, add a ruff (two grace notes) in front of it, and then add another note *before* the grace notes. (It's kind of a drag attached to a paradiddle, but not exactly—despite the implication of the name.)

No. 22: the drag paradiddle No. 1.

23: The Drag Paradiddle No. 2

Even though it's labeled "no. 2," this rudiment is the more commonly encountered drag paradiddle. In this case, you put two taps in front of a single paradiddle, with ruffs attached to the second tap and the beginning of the paradiddle. It's a driving pattern when played right—one that just propels itself forward.

No. 23: the drag paradiddle No. 2.

24: The Flam Paradiddle-Diddle

This rudiment is simple. Take a double paradiddle (also called a paradiddle-diddle), and put a flam in front of it. (You can also think of this as a double flamadiddle.)

No. 24: the flam paradiddle-diddle.

25: The Lesson 25

Okay, of all the goofy names for rudiments, this one takes the prize. Instead of calling this pattern a "ratatat" or a "diddledoo," the drummers of old who devised this list came up dry. Hence, we have the only rudiment named after its number—the Lesson 25. (One can only assume that if this fell into place elsewhere in the list, it might be called the "Lesson 12" or the "Lesson 26.")

No. 25: the Lesson 25.

There's nothing particularly tricky about the Lesson 25. It's a group of three notes with a ruff in front of them and the last note accented—typically on an upbeat. (You could say that it sounds like "twen-ty-five," but that would be a real stretch.)

26: The Double Ratamacue

You learned the single and triple ratamacues, so now we have the double version. This is a three-based pattern, so you're likely to encounter this one in triplets if you're playing in 3/4, 6/8, or other three-based time signatures.

No. 26: the double ratamacue.

The Least You Need to Know

➤ Rudiments are common patterns that are the building blocks of most drum parts.

➤ You should practice each rudiment from slow to fast and then back down again.

➤ Many rudiments are actually combinations of other rudiments—such as adding a flam to a single paradiddle and calling it the flamadiddle.

➤ While you should learn the rudiments on the snare drum, you can apply rudiments around your entire drumset, by alternating hands on different drums or cymbals.

Chapter 14

Marching Along: Basic Rudimental Beats

In This Chapter

➤ Combine the rudiments in interesting patterns

➤ Apply rudimental patterns to marching band and drum corps beats

➤ Learn to play a rudimental solo

In the last chapter, you learned all 26 traditional drum rudiments. Now let's apply those rudiments with some rudimental beats!

Rudimental drumming is essential to marching band and drum and bugle corps drumming. The exercises in this chapter are typical of the types of beats you'll find in most marching bands or drum corps.

Rudimental Exercises

The 16 exercises in this chapter utilize a variety of different rudiments, in a number of variations. Here are some things to watch for as you practice:

➤ **Exercise 14.1** uses five-stroke rolls to create the typical marching beat. Bands (and armies!) often use this very simple beat, repeated over and over, when they're marching from one location to another.

➤ **Exercise 14.2**, which uses flams and a 17-stroke roll, is sometimes called a "roll-off." Bands traditionally use a roll-off to signal the start of a new piece of music.

➤ **Exercise 14.3** is another simple beat, utilizing nine-stroke rolls. When you repeat this phrase, let the last roll lead back to the first note of the first measure.

➤ **Exercise 14.4** is an exercise in five-stroke rolling. Pay close attention to the accents, which are different in each measure.

➤ **Exercise 14.5** has lots of paradiddles. Note the accents on every downbeat.

Drum Don't

A common mistake many beginning drummers make is starting at too fast a tempo and then slowing down when they reach a difficult passage. You should *never* slow down or stumble in the middle of an exercise; if you do, that means you're playing too fast! Slow down and take the entire exercise—even the easy parts—at a speed you're comfortable with.

Drum Tip

If you practice your rudiments with heavy sticks, you'll build up endurance and be able to play faster when you switch to lighter sticks later on.

➤ **Exercise 14.6** consists of two double paradiddles followed by a single paradiddle. You might also want to try this with the alternate RLRLRR/LRLRLL sticking for the double paradiddles.

➤ **Exercise 14.7.** Try playing this pattern really fast—then watch your hands freeze up! The flam taps on the third beat will slow you down, so make sure you start at a tempo you can hold throughout the entire exercise.

➤ **Exercise 14.8** is all about accents—and please note the changeup on the third beat. By sticking a flamacue after two flamadiddles, you get the syncopated accent on the "e" after three.

➤ **Exercise 14.9**, you can see the interesting patterns that emerge simply by combining two rudiments—in this case, two single ratamacues with a triple ratamacue.

➤ **Exercise 14.10** contrasts the straight sixteenth notes of Lesson 25 with the sixteenth-note triplets of a single ratamacue.

➤ **Exercise 14.11** is another interesting combination—drag paradiddle no. 2, a flamacue, a flam, and a five-stroke roll.

➤ **Exercise 14.12** applies the three-beat flam accent across straight sixteenth notes for a syncopated effect.

➤ Play **Exercise 14.13** up to speed, and you'll hear the famous "Wipe Out" beat—in single and double paradiddles! For even more fun, practice starting with the left hand.

➤ **Exercise 14.14** shows another contrast between straight sixteenths and sixteenth-note triplets.

➤ **Exercise 14.15.** It's tempting to start this exercise too fast and then get all caught up when you come to the repeating flamadiddles. Have the discipline to start the first measure slow enough to enable you to get through the second measure without stumbling.

➤ **Exercise 14.16.** This final exercise attempts to reproduce the "speed up" technique you use when accelerating a single-stroke roll. For even greater effect, tack a 17-stroke roll onto the end—and then repeat the exercise *backward* so that you're slowing down the roll!

A Rudimental Solo: *Rudimentary, My Dear Watson*

This is a fun solo, combining everything you've learned up to this point. Watch out for these sections:

➤ **Measure 4**, the syncopated flam accents

➤ **Measure 5**, the sudden decrease in volume

➤ **Measure 7**, the syncopated flam accents—at a soft volume

➤ **Measures 8 and 9,** the sudden increase in volume on the last triplet of measure 8 leading into measure 9

➤ **Measure 12,** a tricky syncopated application of a double drag

➤ **Measures 16 through 19,** unusual off-beat five-stroke rolls with accented sixteenth notes in between

➤ **Measure 18,** the "shuffled" sixteenth-note triplets with rests in the middle

➤ **Measure 20,** the quick crescendo on the nine-stroke roll

➤ **Measure 22,** the hard accent on the final flam

Drum Tip

You can create your own rudimental beats and exercises by combining two or more of the 26 rudiments. Try it!

Remember to practice at a slow tempo until you've mastered all the patterns and stickings, and then gradually move the tempo up to something more moderate.

The Least You Need to Know

➤ Combining different rudiments can create interesting patterns.

➤ Since some rudiments are easier to play than others, make sure you play the entire piece at a pace that enables you to play the hardest parts without stumbling.

➤ Most marching band and drum corps drumming is rudimental in nature.

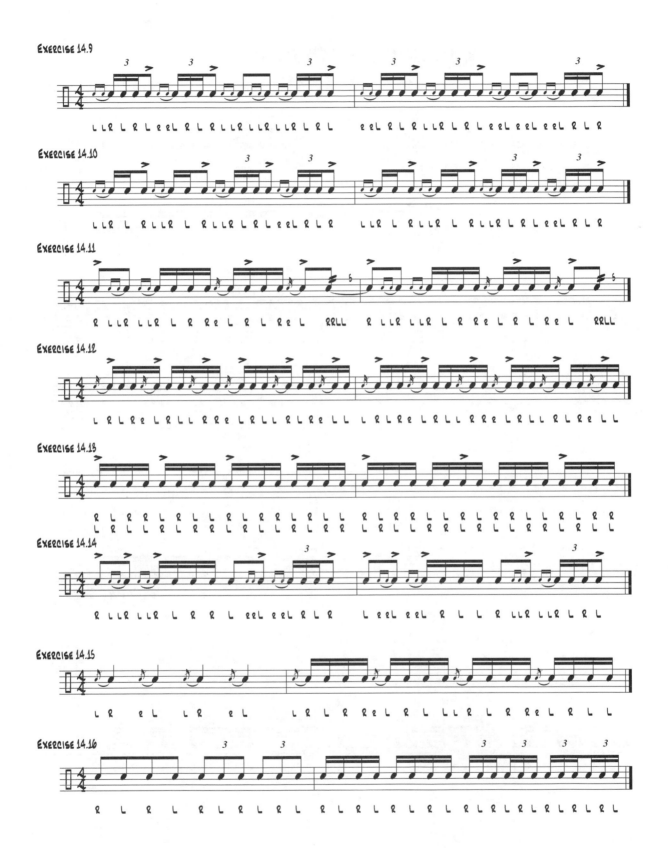

Rudimentary, My Dear Watson

A Rudimental Snare Drum Solo

© Michael Miller

You Got the Beat: Drumset Basics

Progress from basic hand-foot coordination to playing in odd time signatures. Part 3 is an essential resource for both beginning and working drummers—complete with over 100 different rock and jazz beats! You'll learn basic rock beats, dance beats, country beats, R&B beats, shuffle beats, and jazz beats—and a whole lot more!

Chapter 15

In the Driver's Seat: Moving Around the Drumset

In This Chapter

➤ The typical way to set up and position your drumset

➤ Ways to avoid physical fatigue and injury

➤ The importance of a comfortable seat

Once you've mastered a single drum (your snare), you can apply that technique across multiple drums—and cymbals. This means, *finally,* that it's time to start playing the complete drumset!

Before you can play your set, however, you first have to set it up. While most kits are set up in a similar fashion, there are no hard-and-fast rules for where to put all your drums and cymbals. Basically, personal preference rules. If you think your snare drum belongs to the far right of your large tom, then by all means put it there. Just about any type of setup is acceptable, as long as it facilitates your playing style.

Still, it's very important to make sure that your set is properly set up and adjusted so that you can easily reach all the drums and cymbals without straining or stretching. Your goal should be to position all the components of your kit so that they're easy to reach and easy to play.

Take a Seat

Let's start with where you sit—on your butt! Your rear end needs to reside on a comfortable, adjustable seat. The seat should be padded to help you make it through those long gigs, constructed of a material that both gives and breathes, and sturdy enough to withstand your bouncing around on it for long hours on end.

A drummer's chair is called a throne. Really. (If you sit on a throne, you must be the king of the band!) Drum thrones come with traditional round seats or with more form-fitting bicycle-type seats. You can also find thrones with backrests, which can increase your comfort level between songs in especially long gigs.

When in doubt, set up your drums to look like this typical right-handed five-piece kit.

How high should you position your throne? This is a personal matter (as is most drumset positioning), but you should set the height so that you can easily reach your pedals with both the heel and the ball of your feet. A good rule of thumb is that you should sit high enough so that your knees are bent no more than 90 degrees, but low enough so that the throne carries most of your weight.

When you sit on your throne, you should sit straight and tall, as far forward on the seat as is comfortable. You want to be light on your feet, pedal-wise, while maintaining good posture.

Spread Your Feet

Once you've positioned your throne, you need to spread your legs, making close to a 45-degree angle. Now, with your legs spread, position your snare drum stand directly between your legs.

With your snare drum in place, adjust the height of the stand to a comfortable level, a few inches above the top of your legs. Most drummers leave the snare drum flat, although some like to tilt it toward them (to avoid accidental *rimshots*) or away from them (to facilitate deliberate rimshots). If you play traditional grip, you may want to tilt the snare from left to right to make it easier to play rimshots with your left hand.

Now it's time to work with your pedals. Let's start with your left foot, which will be working your hi-hat. Place your hi-hat pedal directly under your left foot, and adjust the height of the hi-hat cymbals so that you can play them easily with either hand. Make sure to set them high enough so that there's adequate clearance for your left hand (on the snare drum) when you're crossing over to play the hi-hat with your right hand.

Drum Tip

Good posture is important for a drummer, as is being in good physical condition. If you sit all bent over, you'll have trouble hitting the farthest parts of your set—and you'll end up with a sore back after a long gig! Sit up straight and tall, strengthen your limbs, and make sure you've had plenty of aerobic exercise—you'll need all the endurance you can get!

Drum Note

If you're playing a double-bass kit, you'll put the left bass drum where you'd normally position your hi-hat so that you and your snare drum are centered between the two bass drums. Your hi-hat then scoots to the left a tad so that your left bass drum pedal and hi-hat pedal are side by side.

If you don't have room (or money) for a second bass drum, consider buying a double-bass pedal. These pedals, from Drum Workshop and others, use two pedals (one on either side of your snare drum) to drive two beaters into a single bass drum—and enable you to play double-bass licks with a single drum!

Next up is your right foot. This is where you position your bass drum and the bass drum pedal. Your bass drum should be close enough so you can place your right heel on the bass drum pedal, but not so close that your foot gets cramped. You may also need to move your bass drum to the left or the right a tad to avoid any uncomfortable angles with your feet.

Spread Your Toms

With your feet firmly planted in place, let's position your tom-toms. Most sets today have two small toms, either mounted directly on the bass drum or hanging off separate stands over the bass drum. The tom you'll be using the most is the one directly in front of your snare (the smallest, left-side small tom), so make sure that this drum is positioned within easy reach. One good way to do this is to close your eyes and reach out as if you were starting a fill around the toms. Where your hand naturally starts out should be where you position the center of your left-side small tom.

The right-side small tom should go next to the left-side tom, positioned so that the two drums don't quite touch. (You should also take care so that the left-side tom doesn't touch your snare drum—and that neither small tom drops down onto your bass drum.) You may need to position this tom at a slightly different height or angle than your other small tom, for best playability.

The angle that you set your small toms is, like all this setup stuff, a matter of personal preference. If your bass drum is small enough and your throne is high enough, you could set up your small toms to be perfectly flat. (This is the way **Keith Moon** used to set up

Drum Word

A **rimshot** is when you hit the head and the rim of the drum simultaneously. Learn more about rimshots in Chapter 24, "Different Strokes: Beyond Sticks."

Drum Note

These instructions apply to traditional right-handed setups. If you're left-handed, you may want to set up your kit from right to left instead.

his kit.) However, with the advent of larger bass drums and the penchant of most drummers to sit lower behind the kit, you'll probably need to tilt your toms forward to some degree. Just make sure that they're horizontal enough to allow a proper stroke off the head; if they're tilted too far forward, you'll be punching them like you would a wall!

You may also want to tilt your small toms inward (toward each other) to some degree. Your left-side tom may need to tilt slightly in from left to right, and your right-side tom may need to angle from right to left. Just take whatever time is necessary to get a smooth left-to-right flow across these toms.

Drum Note

Some drummers use two snare drums in their kit, one typically tuned low and fat, and the other tuned higher and ringier. If you use a second snare drum, position it to the left of your hi-hat, at about the same height as your main snare.

Drum Don't

If you constantly hit your left hand with your right when you're playing hi-hat, your hi-hat cymbals are set too low. A higher hi-hat will mitigate this type of accidental hit—although positioning your hi-hat *too* high will make it harder to play two-handed sixteenth-note patterns between your hi-hat and your snare.

The final drum in your kit is your large tom. This tom may have its own set of legs or may be suspended from a separate tom stand. You should be able to reach this drum comfortably with your right hand without twisting your body and with your left hand with a minimal twist and reach. In most setups, the large tom is positioned at roughly the same height as the snare drum and with minimal tilt—although, again, your personal preference may be different.

Stack Your Cymbals

You can almost think of your set as existing on different horizontal planes. Your feet are on one plane; your snare is on a second plane; your tom-toms are on a third plane; and your cymbals are up above on a fourth plane. Even though your cymbals are the highest points of your kit, they should still be within easy reach—you don't want to have to stand up to hit a crash!

In fact, it's important that your ride cymbal be *very* easy to reach with your right hand, since you'll be playing it a lot. Back in the days of four-piece kits, some drummers positioned the ride cymbal on their bass drum, where the right-hand small tom typically is today. This allowed them to play *down* on the ride cymbal and afforded maximum speed from the right hand. While you can't put your ride cymbal that low if you have a full rack of toms, you should still place it as low and as close as possible on your right side, somewhere over your right-hand small tom and large tom. It should also be angled to provide a proper strike from your sticks.

Your crash cymbals will probably be positioned slightly higher than your ride. You may or may not want to angle your crashes (again, a matter of personal preference), but you'll probably find that you get a more forceful crash if you have to reach for them a little (but just a little!). Just make sure that there is enough clearance between your cymbals and your toms (and your other cymbals) to withstand the vibrations from a hard crash.

If you have only a single crash cymbal, you'll probably put it to your left, off to the side of your left-hand small tom. If you have two crashes, one typically goes on the left of your kit and the other is placed to your right—either to the left or to the right of your ride cymbal.

Drum Note

Cymbal positioning is highly personal and varies according to how many cymbals you have. In contrast to the "accepted" left-right crash setup, I have both of my main crash cymbals set up on the right side of my set, on either side of my main ride cymbal. (I'm unabashedly right-handed!) I have a secondary ride cymbal (a really sinister-sounding Sabian Dry Ride) set up on the left side of my kit, where a crash cymbal might otherwise go, and a third crash cymbal on my far left, over my hi-hat.

My right-heavy setup isn't that strange. Some drummers will place a China cymbal on their far right, past their large tom, while others will put small splash cymbals either centered between their two small toms or to the left of their hi-hat. In addition, some drummers like using two hi-hats; the second hi-hat is operated via remote pedal (placed next to their normal hi-hat pedal), with the cymbals placed somewhere on the right side of their kit.

Get Ready to Play!

Once you have your drums and cymbals initially positioned, grab your sticks and give 'em a play. Do some round-the-set fills and crashes, and make sure that everything is in the right place. You may need to do a bit of fine-tuning of placement and angle before you get everything just right.

While it's okay to turn your body slightly as you move around the set from left to right, you don't want to have to twist so much that playing the far left or the far right of your kit is uncomfortable. Not only is this physically bad for you; it will also slow you down. Ideally, you want your movement around your set to be as economical as possible. The less you have to move, the faster you can play!

Drum Don't

Drums can be loud. Rock bands can be loud. Playing drums in a rock band can be *very* loud. When you first set up your drum kit, take the time to invest in some hearing protection—your local drum shop will have some drum-specific devices, or you can use plain old earplugs. If you don't protect your ears, you can and *will* damage your hearing eventually. (I know a lot of drummers who have hearing loss in their right ears from too many cymbal crashes ....) Protecting your hearing is every bit as important as positioning your set to avoid physical strain!

The Least You Need to Know

➤ A sturdy and comfortable drum throne—adjusted to the proper height—is an essential component of your kit.

➤ Your snare drum goes directly between your legs, at about waist level, while your tom-toms should be positioned and angled for a smooth left-to-right flow.

➤ Your hi-hat pedal is positioned under your left foot, and your bass drum pedal goes under your right foot.

➤ Your ride cymbal should be on your right side, not too high and within easy reach.

➤ If you have a single crash cymbal, you'll probably position it to your right; if you have two crashes, you'll probably put one on either side of your set.

Chapter 16

For Your Hands Only: Playing Drums and Cymbals Together

In This Chapter

➤ Play a ride pattern on a cymbal or hi-hat

➤ Play backbeats on your snare

➤ Master the coordinated independence of your two hands

Up to now, you've been playing with both your hands on a single drum. Before we jump into using all your limbs, let's stay focused on your hands—but spread them out over your drumset.

Keeping Time

A drumset drummer typically uses the right hand to keep time on either a closed hi-hat or a ride cymbal. The time you keep depends on the song but is typically straight eighth notes (eight to a bar), straight quarter notes (four to a bar), or, if you're playing jazz or a shuffle beat, a *spang spang-a-lang spang-a-lang* kind of pattern.

While your right hand is keeping time, your left hand is playing backbeats (two and four) on the snare drum. Your left hand can also play other patterns—and even move around your toms—while your right hand continues to play steady time.

Your hands continue their separate ways through the better part of most songs. They really come together only when you come to the end of a phrase and need to play a fill on your toms. Because of this need to play your hands separate yet together—some call this "coordinated independence"—this chapter focuses on separating your hands and putting them together in some basic patterns.

Drum Note

You close your hi-hat cymbals by pressing down on the hi-hat pedal with your left foot. You open your hi-hat by lifting your foot up.

Typical drumset notation.

Drum Note

In drumset notation, all cymbals (and your hi-hat) have "Xs" instead of normal note heads. Crashing a cymbal (or playing a half note or longer on a cymbal) is notated with an open diamond.

Drum Tip

The right-hand ride patterns in these exercises can also be played on your closed hi-hat. Just reach your right hand over the top of your left hand (this is called "crossing over"), and play your hi-hat with your right hand while your left hand stays on the snare.

Lines and Spaces: Reading Drumset Notation

From this chapter on, you'll need to read music that has parts for more than one drum. To do this, we'll follow standard drumset notation, which uses the lines and spaces of a staff to represent the different drums and cymbals of your kit.

Here is how you decode drumset music:

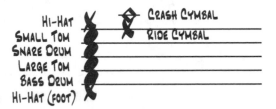

Put Your Hands Together: Practicing Independence

Exercises 16.1 through 16.16 let you practice doing different things with each of your hands. To play these exercises, use your right hand to play your ride cymbal and your left hand to play your snare drum.

The first page of exercises (16.1 through 16.8) has you playing a straight quarter-note beat with your right hand, while your left hand plays various patterns against this ride. The second page of exercises (16.9 through 16.16) shifts to a straight eighth-note pattern with your right hand, while your left continues to play contrasting patterns on the snare.

You'll find that many of these hand patterns can combine with various bass drum patterns to create full-set rock grooves. When you've mastered these hand exercises, go to Chapter 17, "Stepping Out: Adding Your Feet," to put some bottom in your grooves.

A Two-Handed Solo: Tom-Tom Time

The exercises in this chapter focus on ride cymbal and snare drum because those are the parts of your kit that you play on most songs. However, the real point of the exercises is to encourage coordinated independence between your two hands—and the exercises can actually be played on any two parts of your kit. (For example, you could play the ride pattern on your large tom and the left-hand pattern on your closed hi-hat.)

Taking that concept a tad further—and breaking up the monotony of cymbal/snare exercises—is this chapter's drum solo, *Tom-Tom Time*. In this solo, you play your large tom with your right hand and your small tom with your left hand. It's a fun little solo that demonstrates how each hand has to work separately, yet together.

When you've mastered this solo on your toms, try playing it on the bells of two different cymbals, or between your ride cymbal and your hi-hat. Once you get really good, you can try playing the right-hand part with your *foot* (on the bass drum) and the left-hand part on your snare—which is the ultimate in multilimb coordinated independence!

Drum Note

Your ride cymbal is used primarily for playing a ride pattern. Use the bead of your stick to hit the cymbal about halfway between the edge and the bell. When you play closer to the bell, you produce a more defined and "pingy" sound. (The bell itself is the ultimate in pinginess.) The closer you play to the edge, the more "wash" and ring you produce.

Your crash cymbals, on the other hand, are used to accentuate important beats, with a loud "*crash!*" You can hit a crash cymbal straight down with the bead of your stick (which tends to break sticks!), or you can give it a glancing downward hit with the shoulder of your stick. This latter method is the one I prefer because it pulls the most sound out of the cymbal. (Try to make your hit a *glancing* blow rather than a straight-down hit, or you'll risk cracking your cymbal!)

The Least You Need to Know

➤ Your right hand typically plays a steady pattern on either your ride cymbal or your closed hi-hat.

➤ Your left hand typically plays a two-and-four backbeat on your snare drum.

➤ You have to work hard to play both hands separately, yet together—a concept called coordinated independence.

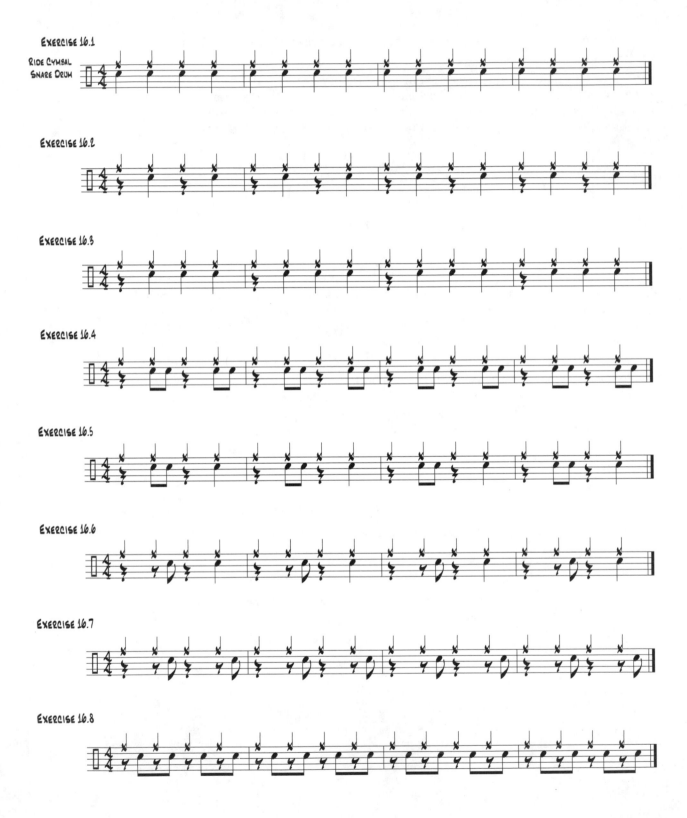

EXERCISE 16.1

RIDE CYMBAL
SNARE DRUM

EXERCISE 16.2

EXERCISE 16.3

EXERCISE 16.4

EXERCISE 16.5

EXERCISE 16.6

EXERCISE 16.7

EXERCISE 16.8

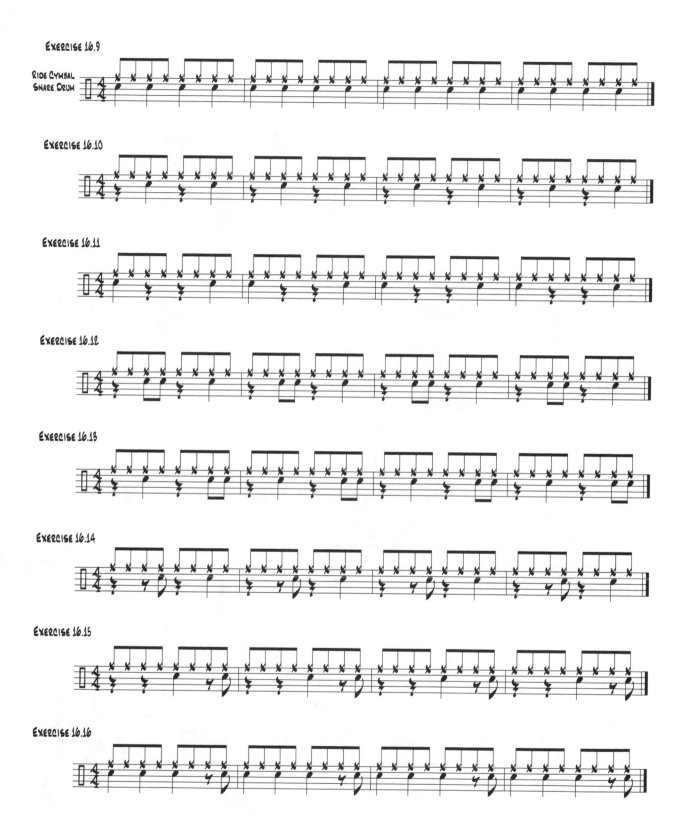

TOM-TOM TIME
A DRUMSET SOLO

© MICHAEL MILLER

Chapter 17

Stepping Out: Adding Your Feet

In This Chapter

➤ Move the groove and kick out accents with your bass drum

➤ Learn the difference between heel-up and heel-down playing

➤ Produce more than one sound from a closed hi-hat

If you're one of those folks who has trouble walking and chewing gum at the same time, you're in big trouble now. That's because it's time to add a completely new dimension to your drumming—your feet!

On a drumset, your feet are used to operate two different pedals. Your right foot operates the bass drum pedal, which uses a felt or wooden beater to strike the batter head of your bass drum. Your left foot operates the hi-hat pedal, which opens or closes your two hi-hat cymbals.

The bass drum is used to keep and accentuate the beat. It may play along with your band's bass player, or it may play a separate, steadier pattern. In certain types of jazz playing, the bass drum is used not to keep the beat, but rather to "kick" specific accents and patterns in the band. (This is why the bass drum is sometimes called the "kick drum.")

In rock music, the hi-hat is more often than not kept closed. When you do play your hi-hat with your foot, you typically use it to make a "chick" sound on two and four, in unison with your snare drum.

Pedal Pushing: How to Play Your Bass Drum and Hi-Hat Pedals

Almost all bass drum and hi-hat pedals let you adjust their springs to produce different levels of tension. A "tight" pedal is a little stiff to play but produces a pronounced rebound that some drummers feel increases their foot speed. A "loose" pedal pretty much plays what your foot plays—a more natural approach that many drummers favor.

Drum Note

To achieve the best hi-hat sound, keep your top hi-hat cymbal slightly loose and your bottom cymbal at a slight angle. Adjust the top cymbal so that, in its full-open position, there is about one to two inches of space between the two cymbals.

You should experiment with different closed hi-hat sounds. When you press the cymbals tightly together with your foot, you get a very dry "click" when you play the hi-hat with your sticks. You can also apply slightly less pressure to the closed cymbals so that they produce more of a "chunk" sound. Open the cymbals up even more and you get a very washy "sizzle," like the sound **Ringo Starr** popularized on early Beatles songs.

Some beats require you to open and close the hi-hat while you're playing it with your sticks. Hitting an open hi-hat and then quickly closing it produces a "shoop" type of sound that often fits well at the end of a phrase—or, if you're playing disco music, on every upbeat.

There are two basic approaches to bass drum or hi-hat playing:

➤ **Heel down.** With this method, you place your entire foot on the pedal and rock your foot up and down from the ankle.

➤ **Heel up.** With this method, only the ball of your foot meets the pedal; you push down with your foot to move the pedal.

Many drummers favor the heel-down method for control and speed, while other drummers prefer the heel-up method for its power. The choice is yours!

Drum Dancing: Exercising Your Feet

The first eight exercises in this chapter (17.1 through 17.8) focus solely on your feet—you don't have to worry about using your hands! Practice the coordinated independence of your two feet, focusing on keeping a steady beat with your left foot while your right foot plays different patterns. Exercises 17.1 through 17.6 have you playing two and four with your hi-hat, while Exercises 17.7 and 17.8 shake things up with your left foot playing all the upbeats.

The next exercises (17.9 through 17.16) add your hands to the mix. These are very simple patterns—nothing to tax your newfound independence; concentrate on putting everything together, with every note in its proper place and time. Go slowly at first, and make sure that all the notes are falling precisely on the beat or upbeat, as notated.

Drum Don't

When you play your bass drum, *don't* press the pedal all the way into the drum head. Strike the bass drum as you'd strike your snare drum—a very quick hit-and-release so that the pedal rebounds off the head immediately after the hit. If you allow the beater to remain against the head after striking, this will dampen the sound of your bass drum and slow down your foot.

After you've mastered these exercises, you're ready to learn some real-world rock beats—which you'll find in Chapter 18, "In the Pocket: Basic Rock, Country, and R&B Beats."

Your First Drumset Solo: *Top to Bottom*

This chapter's solo is the first to use the entire drumset. To make things easier for you, your right hand (ride cymbal) and left foot (hi-hat) remain relatively constant throughout the entire solo; the focus is on the coordinated independence between your right foot (bass drum) and left hand (snare drum).

You might find this type of "separate but together" playing difficult at first. (You may even find it hard to read all those different parts at the same time!) This is normal. You might want to try playing the snare drum and the bass drum *without* the ride cymbal or hi-hat; you can always add these back later, after you've mastered the other patterns.

Drum Tip

To develop optimal left/right independence, try setting up your drumset backward and then playing all the exercises in this chapter with the opposite hands and feet.

The Least You Need to Know

➤ You play your bass drum with your right foot and your hi-hat with your left.

➤ The bass drum is used to play patterns and accents; the hi-hat (when played with your foot) is used to reinforce two and four.

➤ The heel-down method places your entire foot on the pedal and is good for control and speed; the heel-up method uses the ball of your foot to play the pedal and is good for power.

➤ You can change the sound of a closed hi-hat by changing the pressure you apply to the hi-hat pedal.

EXERCISE 17.1

BASS DRUM
HI-HAT (FOOT)

EXERCISE 17.2

EXERCISE 17.3

EXERCISE 17.4

EXERCISE 17.5

EXERCISE 17.6

EXERCISE 17.7

EXERCISE 17.8

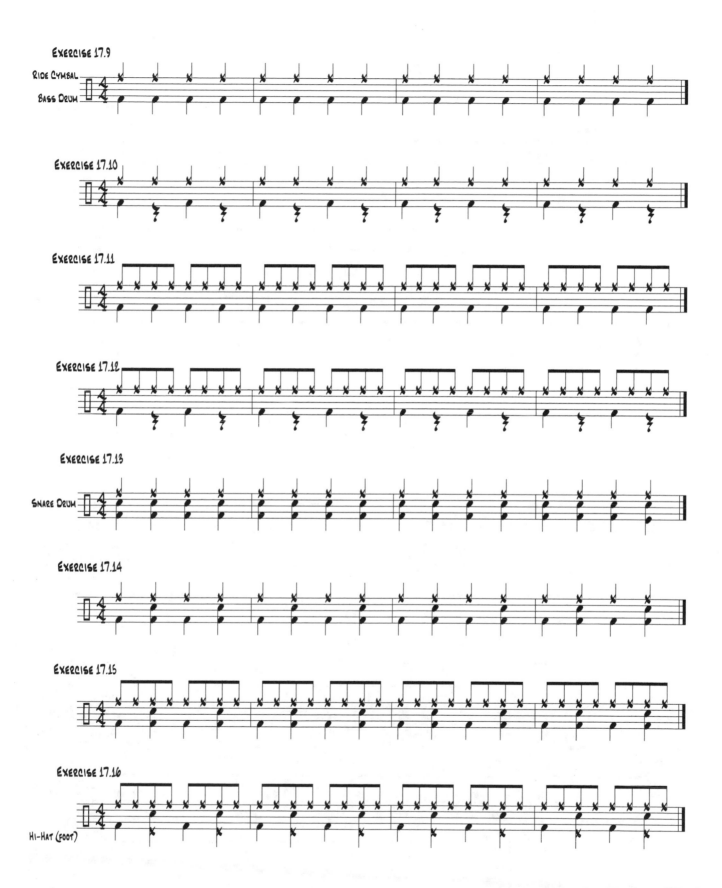

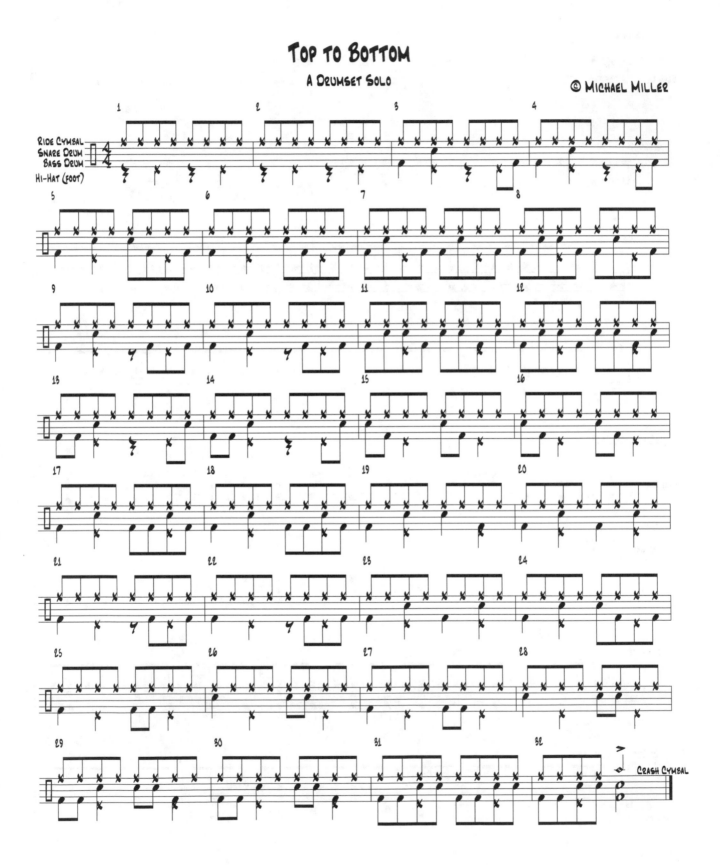

TOP TO BOTTOM
A DRUMSET SOLO

© MICHAEL MILLER

Chapter 18

In the Pocket: Basic Rock, Country, and R&B Beats

> ## In This Chapter
>
> ➤ Basic eighth-note rock beats
>
> ➤ Patterns for 1960s tunes and surf music
>
> ➤ Sizzlin' funk grooves
>
> ➤ Dance and disco patterns
>
> ➤ Shuffle beats

This is the chapter you've been waiting for—putting it all together and cranking out the grooves! Wait no more, dear drummer, because this chapter features no fewer than 64 different beats that you can use for rock, country, and rhythm and blues playing!

Groovy, Baby!

There are eight pages of exercises in this chapter—everything you need to make it through the most demanding gig, no matter what kind of group you're playing with! You should learn each of these grooves separately and then experiment by combining ride, snare, and bass parts from different exercises to create your own personal grooves.

Basic Eighth-Note Grooves

We'll start out with some basic grooves you can play on just about any rock, country, or soul tune. Exercises 18.1 through 18.13 feature straight-eighth notes on the hi-hat and a solid two and four on the snare. The big difference between grooves is where the bass drum is placed; some of these grooves drive a little more, while others have a more solid feel. Pick the groove that's right for a particular song, and then let it rip!

Four-to-the-Floor Grooves

For a more driving version of the straight-eighth groove, try playing your snare drum on all four downbeats, as in Exercises 18.15 and 18.16. Many Motown tunes (The Four Tops' "Bernadette" is a great example) use one or both of these grooves.

Drum Note

Exercise 18.14 is a special variation of a straight-eighth beat I call the Phil Spector Groove. As with many of those great old wall-of-sound records (with the legendary **Hal Blaine** on drums), there is no snare drum backbeat on two—but you wallop beat four with a vengeance!

Drum Note

What's different about Exercise 18.17? In this groove, you avoid playing your hi-hat and snare drum together. The theory is that you're making enough noise with your snare that you don't need to add to it with a relatively unheard hi-hat hit. **Charlie Watts** of The Rolling Stones popularized this approach, although other drummers—including session whiz **Kenny Aronoff**—also play this way on occasion.

Sixties Grooves

Many songs from the early 1960s—including tunes from The Beatles, The Beach Boys, and others—used a variation of the straight-eighth beat that put the snare drum on both two and the upbeat after two. Exercises 18.18 through 18.21 demonstrate some of these grooves—with 18.21 dropping the backbeat on two altogether!

Quarter-Note Grooves

Not every groove has to have a straight-eighth ride pattern. Exercises 18.22 through 18.27 feature a quarter-note ride pattern, which sounds even better when played heavy on the bell of your ride cymbal. Several of these beats further shake things up by shifting the snare from the backbeat to an unanticipated syncopation just before or after the downbeat.

Funky Grooves

Anytime you throw in a bit of syncopation, you have the foundations for a funky beat. When you're playing a soul or R&B gig, check out the grooves in Exercises 18.28 through 18.40 for some funky patterns with a lot of syncopated bass drum and snare drum work.

When you play these exercises, start slowly and count all the parts of the beat ("one-e-and-ah"). This way you can precisely fit each note into its proper place. It may help to write out four dots above each beat so that you can line up the syncopation against its place within each beat.

The Three-Legged Dog Groove

Back in 1975, Nashville session great **Larrie Londin** showed me a beat he called the Three-Legged Dog. This beat—typified in the groove heard on Jerry Reed's "Amos Moses"—has you play the hi-hat on every upbeat but rest on every downbeat. This makes for a beat that jerks along "like a three-legged dog." (It was also the precursor to the disco beat, as I found out a few years later!)

Exercises 18.41 through 18.43 present a few examples of Three-Legged Dog beats. Note the little "o" above the last hi-hat note in Exercises 18.42 and 18.43; this indicates that you should slightly open your hi-hat when you play that note. You close the hi-hat again when you see a "+" sign.

Dance Grooves

Dance music—what we called "disco" back in the 1970s—features a heavy four-on-the-floor bass drum accompanied by accented upbeats on the hi-hat. Sometimes the bass drum is slightly syncopated, but the heavy groove should continue nonetheless.

More often than not, dance music is played with sixteenth notes on the hi-hat. You should use both hands on the hi-hat and drop your right hand down to the snare to hit two and four. Exercises 18.45 and 18.46 present two popular dance grooves.

Sixteenth-Note Grooves

Lots of different types of tunes use sixteenth notes on the hi-hat to propel the beat forward. For example, "That's Just the Way It Is," by Bruce Hornsby and the Range (which certainly isn't a dance tune!), uses the beat shown in Exercise 18.48.

When you play these sixteenth-note grooves (Exercises 18.47 through 18.51), remember to play RLRL on the hi-hat while dropping your right hand down to the snare for the backbeats. These beats are deceptively difficult because you're often playing your right foot at the same time you're playing your left hand, which is something you seldom do with a straight-eighth ride.

Drum Tip

Some patterns feature "ghost notes" on your snare drum. These notes (notated by a note head surrounded by parentheses) should be played much lighter than the main backbeat, almost like a ghost of a note—something you hear but don't quite register.

Drum Note

Exercise 18.44 is a cross between a Three-Legged Dog and a disco beat. It's very similar to the drum part played by **Rick Marotta** on Steely Dan's "Peg." For best effect, open the hi-hat slightly on the last of each sixteenth-note group, and then close it slightly on the following downbeat.

Ethnic Grooves

Outside the straight rock idiom—but still applicable—here are four sophisticated grooves that you can use in specific situations:

➤ **Exercise 18.52** uses a syncopated ride on the cymbal bell for an uptempo Latin feel.

➤ **Exercise 18.53** is kind of a reggae feel, using both the snare and the bass drum for the backbeat along with an open and closed hi-hat; this particular beat is similar to the one played by **Bernard Purdie** on Steely Dan's "Haitian Divorce," from the *Royal Scam* album.

Drum Note

Exercise 18.56 *is a beat that you hear often in country music, with kind of a double-time feel. This beat is played completely on the snare drum (no hi-hat or ride cymbal), with every upbeat accented. You can use either sticks or brushes to play this beat, depending on the song.*

Drum Note

In the pocket refers to a groove that is precisely on the beat and completely steady— something that is more difficult to do than you might think!

Drum Tip

When you first start to practice these sixteenth-note grooves, take them slowly. If you try to play them at the same tempo as you did the previous exercises, you'll probably run into a spot of difficulty.

➤ **Exercise 18.54** is the traditional Latin "clave" rhythm, played with rimclicks on the snare (turn your left stick around, put the bead in the center of your snare drum, and click the butt of the stick against the rim of the drum).

➤ **Exercise 18.55** is another uptempo Latin beat, with a double-timing bass drum and upbeat snare hits.

Shuffle Grooves

We'll end this chapter with a collection of shuffle patterns in Exercises 18.57 through 18.63. Unlike the traditional straight-eighth rock beat, a shuffle beat pulses along with a triplet feel, kind of like jazz or swing music.

Some drummers have trouble playing a shuffle beat; it's difficult to get the feel just right. It's not that the shuffle beat is that difficult to play; it's the feel that's hard to get the hang of.

The simplest shuffle beat is the "four-on-the-floor" beat in Exercise 18.57. If you think this beat is dull, think again—and take a listen to the great **Al Jackson Jr.** on "Green Onions," by Booker T. and the MG's. Al never played an eighth note on this song, yet he kept the groove so *in the pocket* that it's hard to imagine any other drum part for this song.

The other shuffle beats presented here add increased degrees of complexity. Many drummers like playing the jazzlike *spang spang-a-lang spang-a-lang* pattern on the hi-hat or ride cymbal, as in Exercises 18.60 and 18.61. Other drummers like riding with all eighths, as in Exercises 18.62 and 18.63. You can actually pick and choose among the different ride, snare, and bass drum patterns here—mix and match them to create your own unique shuffle!

Drum Note

Exercise 18.64 is the type of half-time shuffle perfected by session ace Bernard Purdie. The "Purdie Shuffle" contrasts an eighth-note shuffle on the hi-hat with a heavy half-time backbeat on the snare—with some ghost notes thrown in for good measure. You can hear "Pretty" Purdie play a version of this beat on Steely Dan's "Home at Last" (from the Aja album) and "Babylon Sisters" (from Gaucho); another famous variation of this beat was played by the late, great **Jeff Porcaro** on Toto's hit single "Rosanna."

A Groovy Solo: *The Groove Machine*

If you made through all 64 exercises, reward yourself with a fun little solo I call *The Groove Machine*. This solo starts out with **Hal Blaine**'s trademarked Phil Spector beat and then works its way through several other grooves you learned in this chapter. It even turns the beat around in a few places!

To master this solo, make sure that you start at a tempo that lets you play all the grooves precisely. If you find yourself slowing down or stumbling over a particular beat, *slow it down!*

The Least You Need to Know

➤ Most rock, country, and R&B (soul) music uses a straight eighth-note ride with a two-and-four backbeat, with variations in the bass drum part.

➤ Funk grooves feature more syncopation on either the snare or the bass drum—or both.

➤ Dance music features a "four-on-the-floor" bass drum accompanied by accented upbeats on the hi-hat.

➤ Shuffles have a triplet feel, kind of like jazz or swing music.

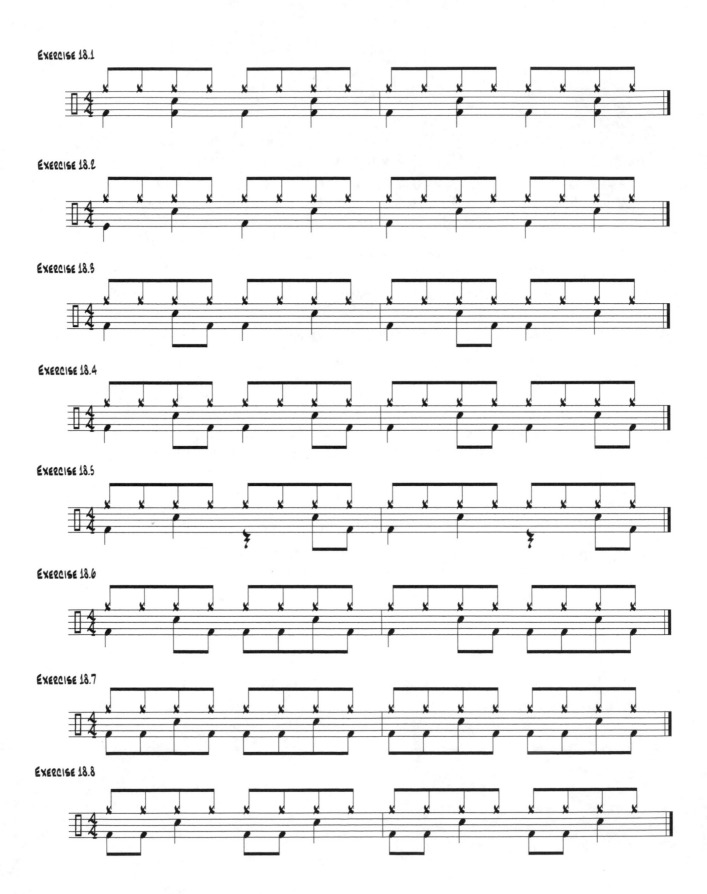

EXERCISE 18.9

EXERCISE 18.10

EXERCISE 18.11

EXERCISE 18.12

EXERCISE 18.13

EXERCISE 18.14

EXERCISE 18.15

EXERCISE 18.16

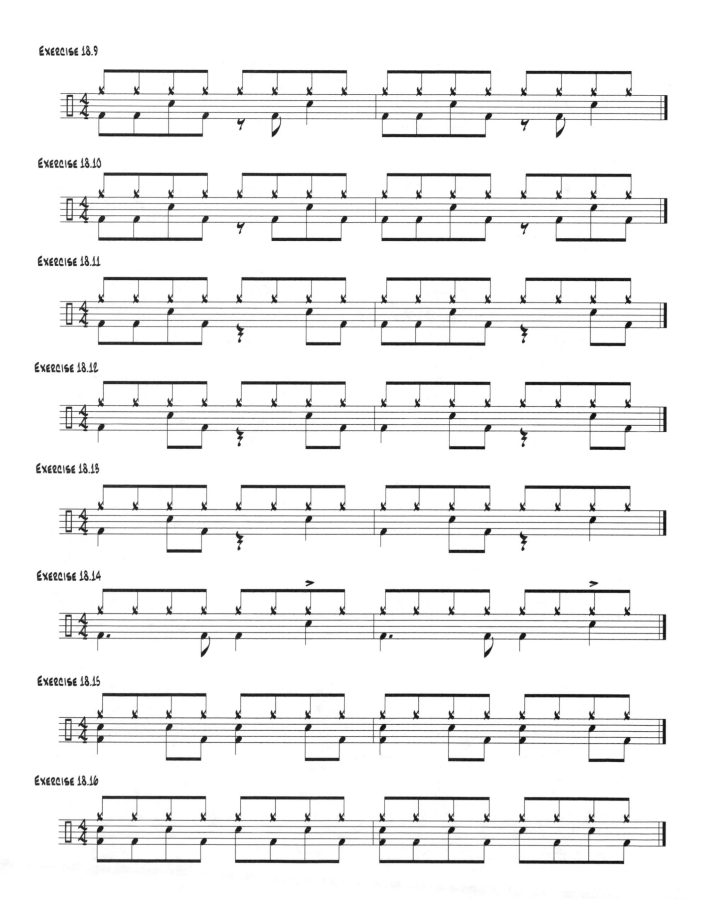

EXERCISE 18.17

EXERCISE 18.18

EXERCISE 18.19

EXERCISE 18.20

EXERCISE 18.21

EXERCISE 18.22

CYMBAL BELL

EXERCISE 18.23

EXERCISE 18.24

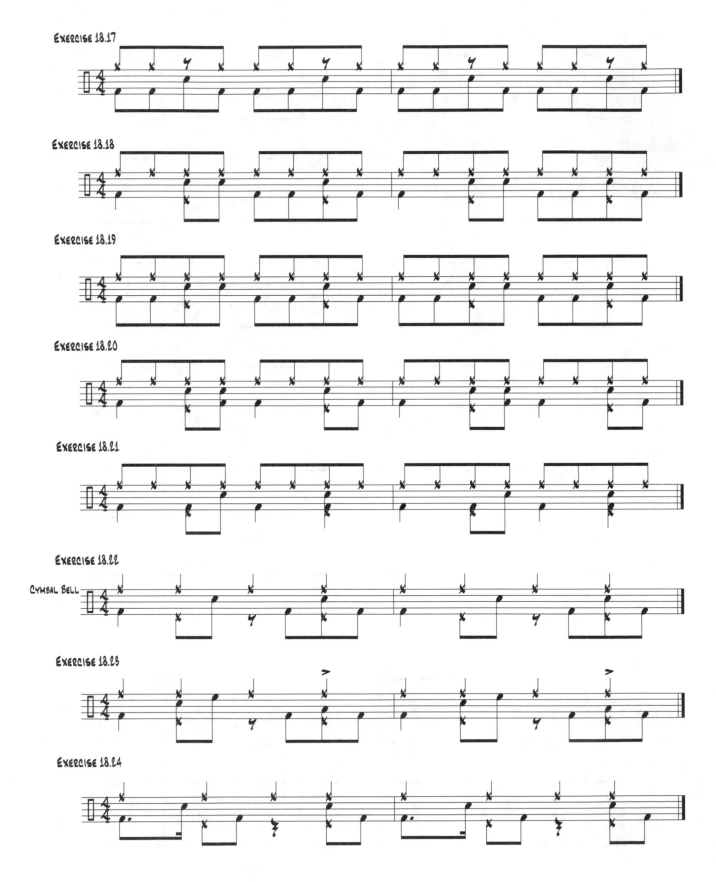

EXERCISE 18.25

EXERCISE 18.26

EXERCISE 18.27

EXERCISE 18.28

EXERCISE 18.29

EXERCISE 18.30

EXERCISE 18.31

EXERCISE 18.32

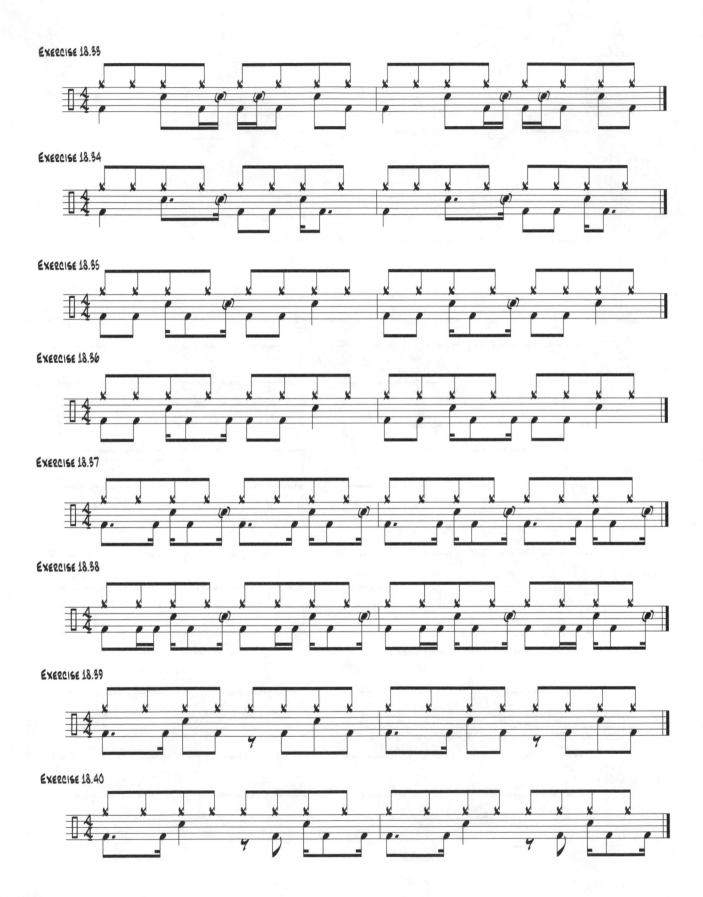

EXERCISE 18.33

EXERCISE 18.34

EXERCISE 18.35

EXERCISE 18.36

EXERCISE 18.37

EXERCISE 18.38

EXERCISE 18.39

EXERCISE 18.40

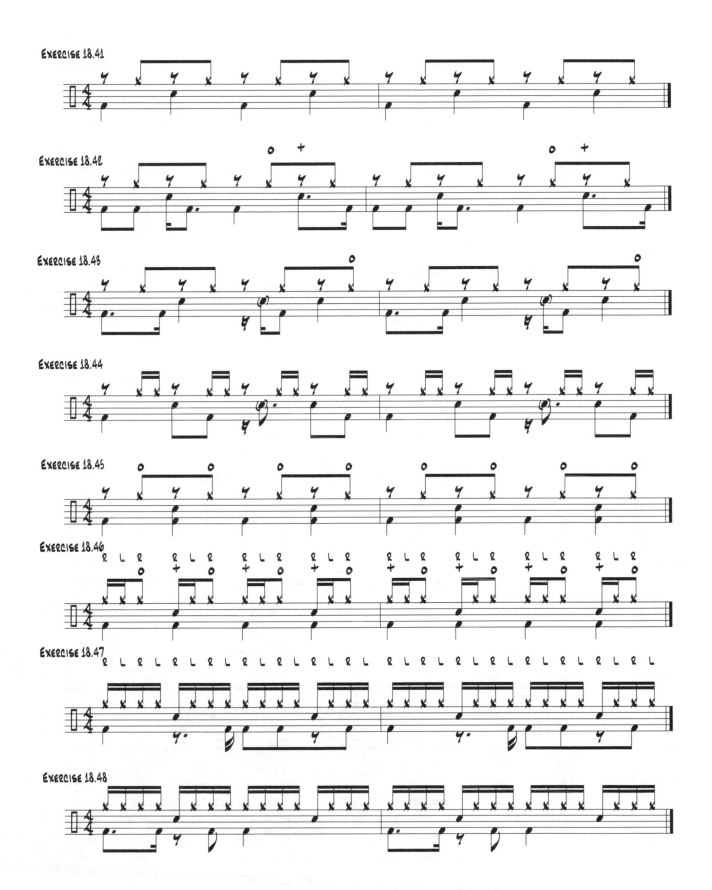

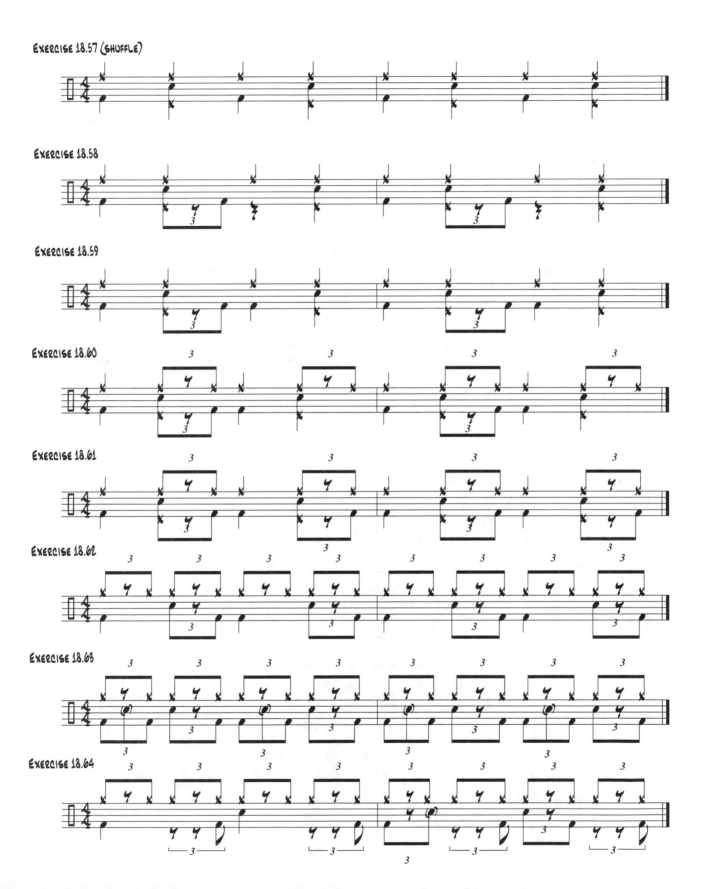

THE GROOVE MACHINE

A DRUMSET SOLO

© MICHAEL MILLER

Chapter 19

Swing Time: Basic Jazz Beats

In This Chapter

➤ The way to swing

➤ The basic jazz ride pattern—and variations

➤ Your first jazz solo

Jazz is different from rock.

Jazz is about swing. Jazz is about *spang spang-a-lang spang-a-lang* ride cymbal patterns. Jazz is about triplets instead of straight eighths. Jazz is about snare drum accents and bass drum kicks and no backbeat. Jazz is about time and feel and playing economically.

On the surface, the jazz groove is similar to a shuffle beat. It's more of a triplet feel than a straight-eighth feel—although that isn't always quite it, either. Some jazz has more of a dotted-eighth feel, while other tunes—typically uptempo bop—are played with almost straight eighths, but kind of bounced. As you can tell, it's almost impossible to notate the jazz feel, although there is a lot of jazz notation out there. Some notation uses straight eighths to represent the swing, while another notation uses dotted eighths. Throughout this book, I've opted for the triplet notation, and I'll let you determine how it's interpreted.

That said, this chapter is but a brief introduction to jazz drumming. It isn't meant to be a complete course in jazz; you can't learn jazz in just a few pages. If you're serious about playing jazz, then you'll want to supplement this book with jazz-specific method books and lots of jazz CDs. Listen to the great jazz drummers, and listen to their *feel,* their *touch.* To learn jazz drumming, you have to experience jazz—so start listening, and start playing!

Swinging the Beat: Jazz Exercises

Exercises 19.1, 19.2, and 19.3 show the basic jazz beat in its most popular variation. If you play Exercise 19.1 precisely as written, you'll have a very tight cymbal pattern that isn't quite jazz; if you see this pattern on a drum chart, you'll probably want to interpret it closer to the notation in Exercise 19.2.

Exercise 19.3 is the basic jazz groove as played on the hi-hat. Note that you slightly open the hi-hat on one and three, and then snap it closed for a firm *chick* on two and four.

Drum Note

Unlike rock drumming, jazz drumming doesn't incorporate a constant snare drum backbeat or a repeating bass drum pattern. The main groove is played with the ride cymbal, typically some variation of the *spang spang-a-lang spang-a-lang* pattern, accompanied by a two-and-four *chick* with your left foot on the hi-hat. (Sometimes the main groove is played on the hi-hat instead of the ride cymbal, with an open-and-close rhythm implying the two-and-four *chick*.)

The snare drum and bass drum, then, are used for accents. The snare might reinforce the main melody or "push" the soloist. If you're playing with a big band, the bass drum might "kick" major brass or saxophone figures. In any case, it's your right hand and left foot that get the workout; your left hand and right foot are used sparingly—and sometimes not at all!

Exercises 19.4 through 19.8 show some variations on the basic ride pattern. When you're out playing for real, you'll probably change up some combination of these basic patterns—whatever feels right for a particular playing situation.

Exercise 19.9 adds rimclicks to the basic ride pattern, played on two and four. (See Chapter 24, "Different Strokes: Beyond Sticks," for more information on rimclicks and rimshots.) For an even more driving beat, play straight snare instead of rimclicks—and reinforce the backbeat with quick hits to your crash cymbal.

Exercises 19.10 through 19.16 add some snare drum and bass drum patterns to the basic jazz groove. In the real world, you won't play these patterns per se, but they're good practice for those times where you need to add *something* with your left hand.

Drum Note

The snare drum part in Exercise 19.16 is actually playing steady quarter-note triplets—it's a nice effect against the normal jazz pattern on your ride cymbal.

A Solo in Swing Time: *Jazz Jump*

If you play a lot of jazz, you'll be playing a lot of short solos and four-bar breaks. While you can play around your entire set, it's also common to take your break with just your snare, bass, and cymbals—just as presented in this chapter's solo, *Jazz Jump*. You keep steady time throughout most of the solo with your ride cymbal and hi-hat, but work through a number of syncopated patterns between your snare and bass drum.

The key thing is to keep the steady beat going and not let yourself get thrown off when something complicated comes up with your left hand or right foot. Count through the patterns carefully—then work it up to speed and start swinging!

Drum Note

Because it's important to hear a clear and distinct ride pattern in jazz music, many jazz drummers use a dryer, darker ride cymbal (such as Zildjian's K series or Sabian's HH series) than the brighter, washier ride cymbals typical in rock music.

The Least You Need to Know

➤ Jazz has kind of a triplet feel, as opposed to rock's straight-eighth beat.

➤ Jazz drumming consists of keeping a steady *spang spang-a-lang* pattern on the ride cymbal and a two-and-four *chick* on your hi-hat; the snare drum and bass drum are used primarily for accents.

➤ Jazz patterns can be notated with triplets, straight eighths, or dotted eighths—all implying the same standard swing feel.

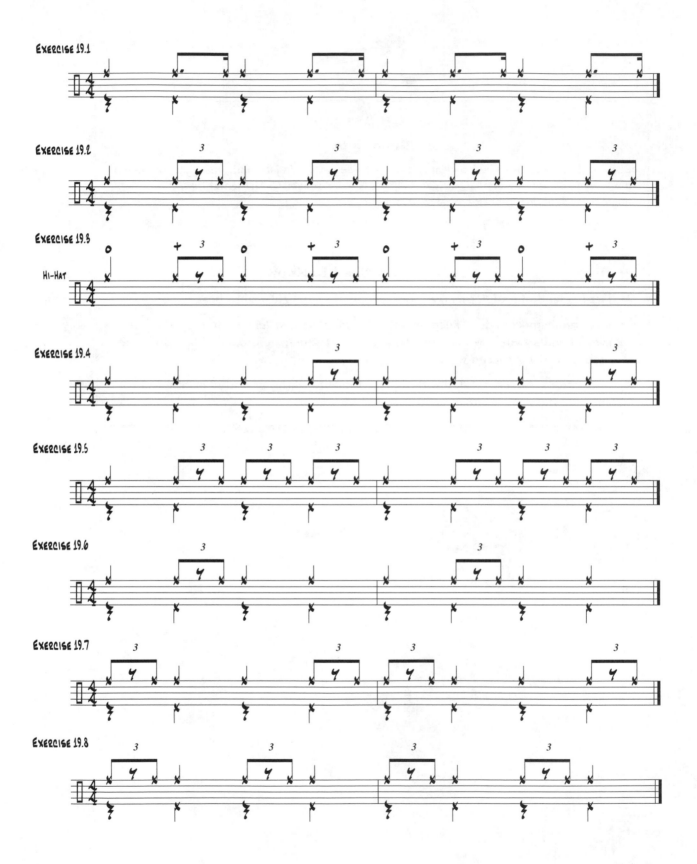

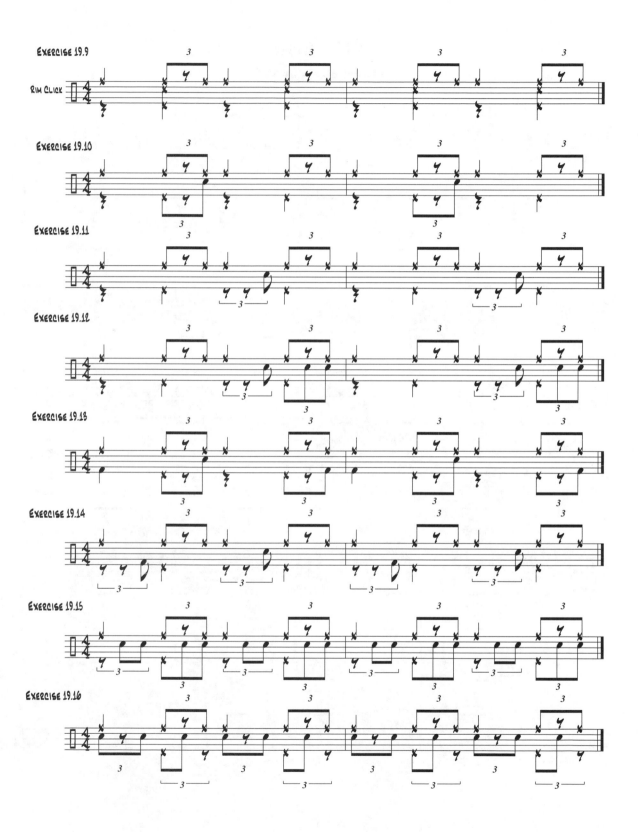

JAZZ JUMP

A DRUMSET SOLO IN SWING TIME

© MICHAEL MILLER

Chapter 20

Take Five: Playing in Odd Times

> **In This Chapter**
>
> ➤ Why odd time signatures are odd
>
> ➤ How to play a jazz waltz
>
> ➤ When to count—and when to groove—in odd times

Every bit of music you've encountered so far has been in the same, very common time signature. In 4/4 time, there are four beats in every measure, and each beat is a quarter note.

While 4/4 is the most common time signature in Western music, it's not the *only* time signature. In fact, in other cultures—Indian music, for example—time signatures other than 4/4 are the rule rather than the exception.

Even if you're playing rock or country, you're apt to encounter a least a few non-4/4 songs. This chapter, while not extensive, provides an overview of some common odd time signatures and presents some beats you can play when you run into an odd-time tune.

Counting to Something Other Than Four: Odd-Time Exercises

When you run into a song in something other than 4/4, it's time to brush up on your counting skills. You're used to *feeling* four beats in a measure; you'll have to deliberately *count* any measures with fewer or more beats—at least at the beginning. While playing a song with five beats in each measure might seem totally foreign to you now, once you start practicing and playing that 5/4 song, it will develop its own groove and feel as natural to you as a good ol' rock and roll beat.

If you remember how time signatures work (explained back in Chapter 8, "Wholes, Halves, and Quarters: Notes and Notation"), the top number indicates how many beats are in a measure, while the bottom number indicates what type of note you play on the beat. So, if you see a 5/4 time signature, that means you play five beats per measure, with a quarter note getting one beat. A 9/8 time signature indicates that you play nine beats per measure, with an eighth note getting a beat.

Since you'll probably encounter most odd time signatures in a jazz setting, most of the examples in this chapter have a jazzy flavor. However, the basic odd-time principles apply whether you're swinging or rocking—just remember to count!

Playing in 3/4

The most common odd time signature is 3/4—three quarter-note beats per measure. Songs in three are often thought of as waltzes (although the waltz is just one of many 3/4 beats). You typically play 3/4 with the "backbeat" on either two, three, or two *and* three. A good example of 3/4 in a rock tune is The Rascals' "How Can I Be Sure"; **Dino Danelli** plays a very definite jazz-waltz pattern throughout.

Exercises 20.1 through 20.8 present some basic 3/4 drum patterns. Pattern 20.8 is the type of pattern you sometimes heard **Joe Morello** playing with The Dave Brubeck Quartet; the ride cymbal actually plays a 2 + 2 + 2 pattern superimposed over two measures of three.

Drum Tip

Most odd time signatures fall into a basic pattern, or subdivision of the beat. For example, a 5/4 tune might fall into groups of 3 + 2, or a 7/4 tune might be played like 4 + 3. These subdivided patterns help you establish a groove through the song, rather than laboriously counting your way all the way through to the end.

Playing in 5/4

Five beats to a measure? How odd! If you think that's odd, consider that The Dave Brubeck Quartet's "Take Five," a 5/4 jazz tune with a drum solo in the middle, was a top 40 hit back in 1959. (If you doubt that odd time can groove, definitely listen to "Take Five"; Joe Morello deftly swings the basic pattern and then launches into one of the most tasteful drum solos you'll ever hear—all the while keeping the basic 5/4 pattern percolating with his bass drum and hi-hat.)

Exercises 20.9 through 20.12 present a number of basic 5/4 jazz patterns. As you can see, these beats invariably break down into either 3 + 2 or 2 + 3 patterns.

Playing in 7/4

Odd time isn't relegated to jazz. Sometimes you'll run into odd-time rock or fusion beats. One of the more popular odd time signatures in rock is 7/4. As you can see in Exercise 20.13, a 7/4 rock beat is typically divided into a 4 + 3 pattern—which means you can count this exercise "one-two-three-four one-two-three" instead of counting up to seven.

Playing in 9/8 and 12/8

When you move from a quarter-note beat to an eighth-note beat, you get into lots of variations. Sometimes the eighth-note really is the main beat, as in Exercise 20.14; other times, as in Exercises 20.15 and 20.16, the groove revolves around groups of three eighths, with the implied beat being a dotted quarter note.

Exercise 20.14, in 9/8, has a jazz-waltz feel, with three groups of three throughout. Exercises 20.15 and 20.16 are in 12/8, employing a pattern of four groups of three. These grooves actually have a slow feel, with a heavy "backbeat" on every second group of three notes.

To hear a great example of this "slow groove" type of 12/8, listen to The Righteous Brothers' "Unchained Melody" (with drums by the legendary **Earl Palmer**). This is a perfect beat to play for most any slow dance song.

An Odd-Time Solo: *Basic Math*

All this talk about odd-time patterns is academic—until you have to play something in five or three! This chapter's solo, *Basic Math,* is comprised of alternating measures of 5/4 and 3/4.

Now, if you do your basic math, you'd add the two together and figure out that you're actually playing eight beats of four—which, divided another way, might be two measures of 4/4. The way the patterns of this solo break down, however, you're definitely *not* playing a basic 4/4 beat! What you have instead is a 3 + 2 + 3 pattern, since each measure of 5/4 is subdivided as 3 + 2. It's a very different groove—even though you'll end up in the same place if you play a standard 4/4 rock beat along with the solo!

The Least You Need to Know

➤ An odd time signature is anything other than 4/4.

➤ When reading an odd time signature, the top number indicates how many beats are in each measure, and the bottom number indicates what type of note gets a beat.

➤ When you play an odd-time piece, start out by carefully counting your way through the song—but then find the underlying patterns and subdivisions, and use them to establish your groove.

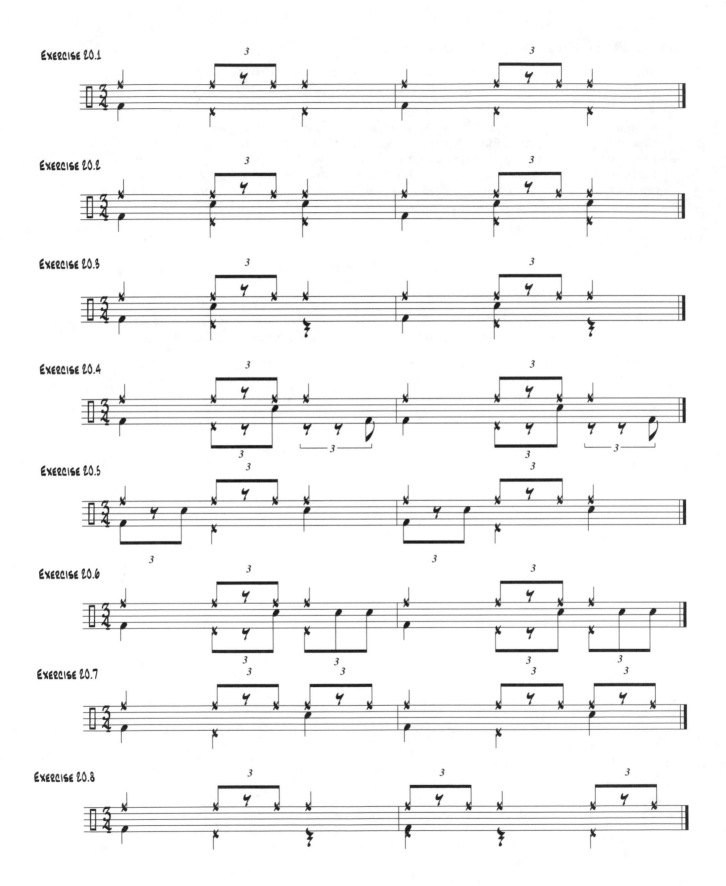

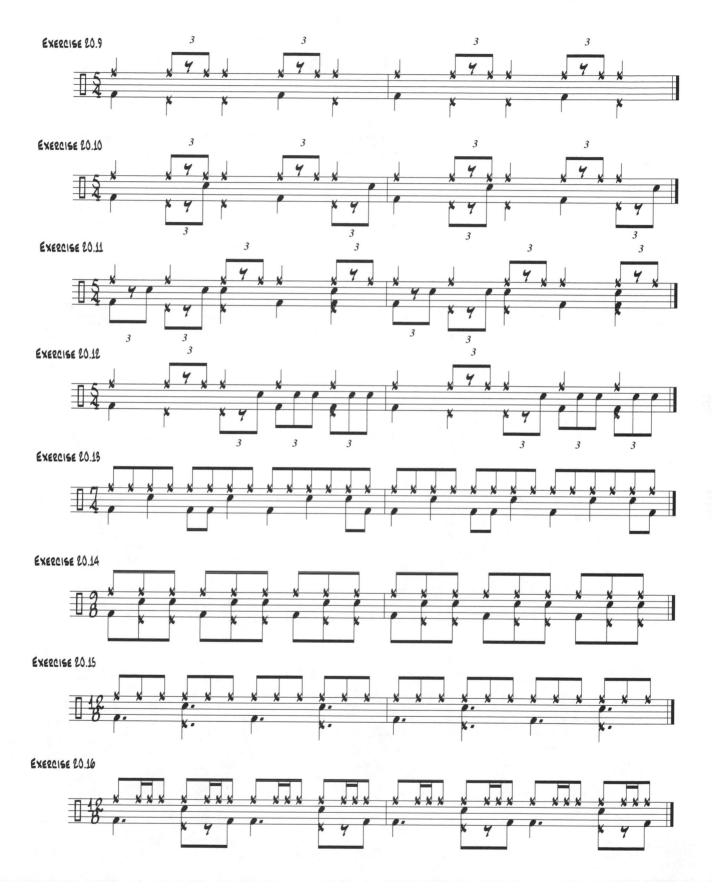

BASIC MATH

AN ODD-TIME DRUMSET SOLO

© MICHAEL MILLER

Part 4

Wipe Out: Advanced Drumset Techniques

Learn how to fill at the end of a phrase, how to construct and play a tasteful (yet impressive!) drum solo, how to play with brushes and mallets, and how to lay out when appropriate. You'll even learn some unique beats that aren't just "two and four." Special Part 4 bonus: An interview with Kenny Aronoff, one of today's most popular and in-demand drummers.

Chapter 21

Setting It Up: Fancy Fills

> **In This Chapter**
>
> ➤ Understanding phrases in music
>
> ➤ Leading into a new phrase with a fill around the drums
>
> ➤ Setting up horn accents and patterns in a big band

Most songs are made up of musical phrases. A phrase typically lasts for 4, 8, or 16 measures. Each new phrase begins a new musical idea—a new verse, sometimes, or a chorus.

To properly set up the new phrase, drummers are often called upon to play a fill to bridge the old phrase with the new. This fill is a short lead-in to the new phrase, typically using tom-toms or the snare, and generally lasting anywhere from one to four beats.

For example, if you're playing four-bar phrases, you might play a fill in the fourth measure, starting on the third or fourth beat. If you're playing longer phrases, you might start your fill on the first or second beat of the last measure of the phrase.

The goal of the fill is to drive into the next phrase. Typically, the fill carries over onto the first beat of the new phrase, often with a cymbal crash.

Sounds Great! More Filling!

Exercises 21.1 through 21.16 present some basic fills that you can use on most rock, country, or soul tunes. Some are simple, some are fancy; in a real-life playing situation, you should pick the fill that best suits the style of the song. Just remember to continue the fill to the first beat of the next (unwritten) measure, typically with a cymbal crash on one.

Exercise 21.1 shows that you can play a fill while continuing your ride pattern; just use your snare and bass drum to do something rhythmically interesting through beats three and four. Exercise 21.2 demonstrates that a fill doesn't have to include a lot of notes; a big hit on four (leading into the first beat of the following measure) might be all you need. Exercises 21.3 and 21.4 are variations on this theme.

Drum Note

The slashes (/) you see in these exercises are common notation in a lot of drum parts. The slashes indicate that you're supposed to play a standard beat—your choice—through the indicated measures or parts of measures. In the case of Exercise 21.1, you play your normal beat through all of the first measure and the first two beats of the second measure—and then play the drum part notated.

Drum Don't

It's easy to get carried away with a fill—it's the drummer's chance to shine, after all. If your fill is too flashy or not in the style of the song, it will stand out like a sore thumb. Avoid the temptation to throw all your fancy licks into a single fill; when in doubt, play something simple!

Exercises 21.5 through 21.7 introduce sixteenth-note tom patterns on a fourth-beat fill. Exercises 21.8 and 21.9 extend the tom fill across beats three and four, with sixteenth notes down your toms.

Exercises 21.10 through 21.12 present a variety of three-beat fills utilizing toms, rolls, and syncopated patterns. Exercise 21.10 utilizes two small toms and a large tom; the second group of sixteenth notes is played on your second small tom. (If you don't have two small toms, split the second group of sixteenths between your single small tom and your large tom.)

The next two exercises are famous fills from famous drummers. Exercise 21.13 is the classic **Benny Benjamin** Motown fill; you can hear this fill on dozens (if not hundreds!) of Motown tunes, including The Temptations' "Ain't Too Proud to Beg" and The Isley Brothers' "This Old Heart of Mine." (Make sure you hit beat four extra hard on your snare—use a rimshot, if you can!) Exercise 21.14 is the patented measure-long **Hal Blaine** out-chorus triplet fill—just pound your two toms together hard!

Exercise 21.15 is a funky snare-and-bass fill under a continuing ride pattern, using some heavy syncopation across an entire four-beat measure. Finally, Exercise 21.16 shows how, if you use your imagination—and a fair amount of technique!—you can create a truly inventive fill. (Just compare the fill in Exercise 21.16 with the somewhat overused fills in Exercises 21.9 and 21.10—when you start throwing in fills like this, people will sit up and take notice!) This fill uses some tom-tom deception (the triplets sound harder than they really are since you keep one hand on each tom) and some syncopated hi-hat "chirps" (fast open-and-closes as you hit the hi-hat) to both turn the beat around and drive the song right into the next phrase. Practice this one slowly and work up to speed—it's a gas when you play it fast!

Kick the Licks: Setting Up a Big Band

We'll end this chapter with something a little different. Playing in a big band requires you not only to play end-of-phrase fills but also to "set up" important brass and saxophone figures and accents. You prepare the band for the big accent by playing a short fill that leads directly to the horn figure and then "kicks" along with the horns.

How does this work? Let's say that there's a big horn accent on the "and" after two. You would set up this figure by playing a fill through beat one that ends smack on beat two—thus leading directly to the horn figure on the following upbeat. You'd then reinforce the horn accent, typically with a cymbal crash and a big kick from the bass drum.

This isn't nearly as hard as it sounds, and if you've ever listened to any big-band recordings, you know that any given tune includes dozens of these sorts of setups. To give you an idea of how this works in the real world, Exercise 21.17 presents a typical big-band chart complete with horn accent on the "and" of two in the second measure. The drum part at the bottom of the page includes full notation for a typical setup fill, but you should feel free to try your own licks here—just remember to punch that upbeat!

Drum Note

The score shown in Exercise 21.17 is typical of what you might see for a big-band arrangement. This is the music that the director or conductor reads; each instrument in the band gets its own staff.

Drum Don't

A common mistake is to rush the beat during a fill. Tape record yourself and listen carefully to your fills; if you find yourself speeding up during fills, practice with a metronome or a click track to help you keep a steady tempo.

The Least You Need to Know

➤ Drum fills are used to lead out of one phrase and into the next.

➤ Fills can last one, two, three, or four beats of the measure leading into the next phrase.

➤ Too-flashy fills draw too much attention to the drummer—and detract from the rest of the music.

➤ In a jazz group or big band, the drummer has to "set up" horn accents and patterns with minifills throughout the song.

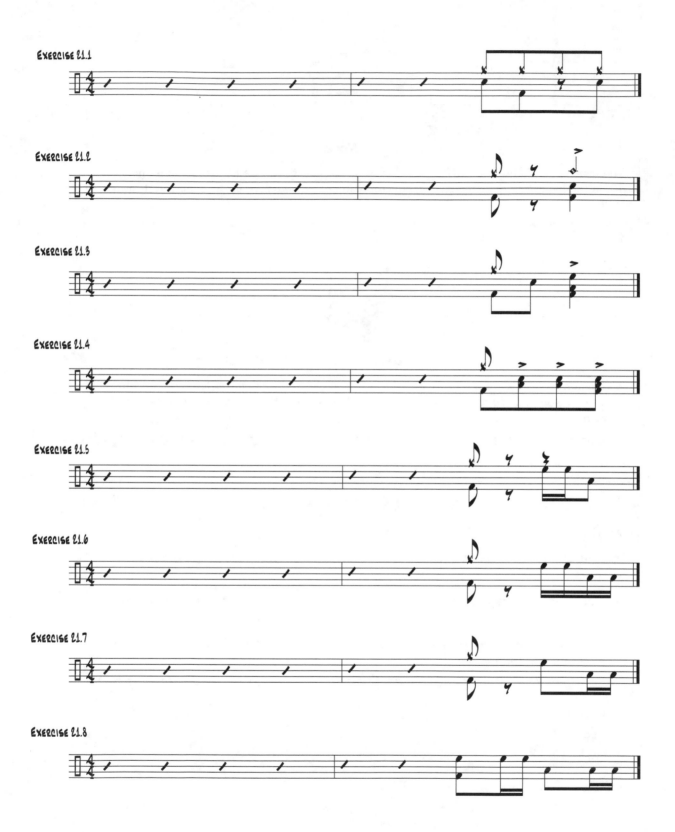

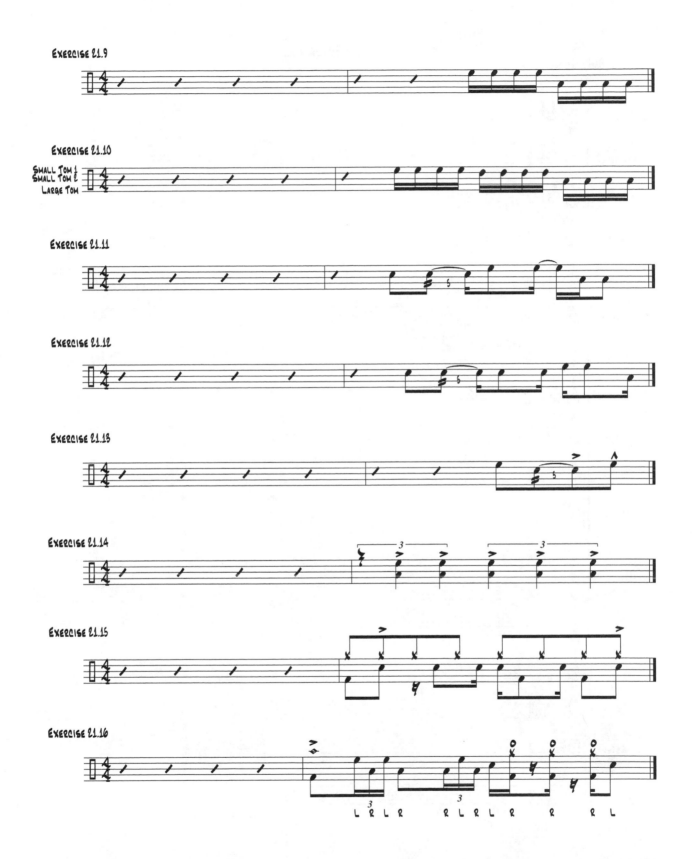

EXERCISE 21.17

Chapter 22

Take the Spotlight: Drum Solos

In This Chapter

➤ Why some solos sound great—and others suck

➤ How to structure a powerful solo

➤ What to do when you get stuck in the middle of a solo

➤ How to add flash to your solos

It's time.

You've played all night long, song after song. Finally you come to that one song that lets the entire band stretch out. You get about halfway through, past the verses and the chorus and the lead guitar solo, and then all the other instruments drop out, leaving the focus on you alone.

It's time for your drum solo.

It's Your Turn: How to Play a Drum Solo

Some drummers like playing drum solos. (Showoffs!) Others don't. (Nervous Nellies!) But whether you like it or not, the time will come when the spotlight is on you, and you're expected to demonstrate your brilliance behind the skins.

When that time comes, you'd better know how to handle it.

The Good, the Bad, and the Really Loud: Why Some Solos Are Better Than Others

I have to admit, I don't like listening to most drum solos. That's because a lot of drummers use their solo time to show off all their hot licks; they don't know how to structure a solo melodically so that it fits within the context of a song. These technique freaks play solos that are all blast and bombast but that lack musicality.

For my dollar, give me a musical solo every time.

What makes a solo musical? Here are some important factors:

➤ A musical solo often follows the structure of the song to the point that you could sing the song along with the solo and not miss a beat. A nonmusical solo puts a lot of notes in a small space, regardless of the song; you could drop one of these solos into *any* song and it wouldn't matter.

➤ A musical solo builds in intensity so that it ends on its highest point. A nonmusical solo starts high (with a lot of technical flourishes) and doesn't have anywhere to go but down.

➤ A musical solo has a form, just as a song, a novel, or a movie has a form—a beginning, a middle, and an end. A nonmusical solo rambles and meanders and eventually peters out for no specific reason.

➤ A musical solo has its own internal logic, with one part building on another in natural phrases. A nonmusical solo is just one lick after another, with no rhyme or reason.

➤ A musical solo leads naturally back into the song as part of its logical structure. A nonmusical solo just stops—and the band often has to be counted back in!

In short, the best solos are more than just pure technique. They're well-thought-out improvisations that follow a certain form and logic. Yes, they can include some flashy licks—you do want to impress the crowd, after all!—but they should be no less musical than a solo by a lead guitarist or a saxophone player.

The Best-Laid Plans of Mice and Drummers: How to Structure Your Solo

Before you start your solo, you should think about the general structure of your solo. Every solo should have three main parts—the beginning, the middle, and the end. In general, your solo should build from start to finish; you should also play something a little different in each part.

➤ **The beginning.** You should start off at about the same energy level that directly preceded your solo. In most cases, this means starting at a moderate level, in terms of both volume and complexity. In fact, some of the best solos start with the drummer still playing basic time. You should then gradually increase the volume and the complexity, working your way from "playing the song" as written to playing your own thing.

Drum Word

An **ostinato** is a rhythmic pattern that is repeated over and over.

➤ **The middle.** Here's where you really start cooking. The middle part of your solo should be where you start taking liberties with the basic song structure, by throwing in syncopated rhythms or *ostinato* patterns or rhythms that play around with the beat or that even turn the beat around. Whatever you end up playing, throughout this entire section, your solo should gradually build in intensity.

➤ **The end.** This is the climax of your solo—the point that everything builds to, the section with the highest energy level and rhythmic complexity. This is also where you toss in all your hot licks and fancy technique—within the context of the song. When you reach the climax, it's okay to play loud and fast and crash the cymbals a lot. You want to get the crowd on their feet, so a little razzle-dazzle isn't necessarily out of place.

Once your solo peaks (and the crowd gives you a standing ovation), you need to bring things back down to a more moderate level and bring the rest of the band back in to finish the song. If you've played along with the form of the song, the band will be able to easily tell when to come back in; if you left the song structure far behind, you'll have to set up their entrance in other ways—like verbally counting them in.

When in Doubt, Roll: What to Do When You Get Stuck

One of the most common questions I get from beginning drummers is this: How do you know what to play in a solo? Just where do those ideas come from?

Fellow drummers, here's a little secret that all the pro drummers know: Hot licks come from basic rudiments.

That's right, you can construct an entire drum solo from the 26 basic rudiments, applying the rudiments in constructive ways around the entire drumset.

Not sure what to play at the start of your solo? Try some paradiddles—or maybe a series of five-stroke rolls! Pick a rudiment, start with it on your snare, and then start playing on your toms and between your toms. You can then let your imagination—and long hours of rudimental practice!—take over. If you're playing paradiddles, the next thing to do is to play double paradiddles, or flamacues, both of which follow logically yet add rhythmic complexity and a degree of syncopation. You can even take a rudiment and play it on an unexpected beat—like starting a paradiddle on the upbeat rather than the downbeat.

When you find a rhythm that works, keep playing it! Create your own phrases—play one rhythm, repeat it, turn it around, alternate it with another—all the while listening to the song's melody in your mind. Fit those rudiments into the song in the most natural way possible, the way a tap dancer dances patterns around the beat.

And if you can't think of *anything* to play—if you just freeze out there, all alone—remember the old drumming adage: *When in doubt, roll!* That's right, if you can't think of anything else to play, start a buzz roll on your snare drum. Keep it going long enough to get your wits back, and then use that roll to get you back into the flow of things. Play some crescendos and decrescendos with the roll, reach out and hit a cymbal to accent a beat, maybe even throw some tom hits in as appropriate. Use that roll as a life preserver—and a little bit more!

Drum Tip

During the entire solo—beginning to end—it helps if you keep the song's melody and chord structure playing through your mind. In some instances, you may even want all or part of the band's rhythm section (or maybe just the bass player) to continue playing through your solo. By having the song structure in the front of your mind, you'll always know where you are in the solo, without having to count out measures or admit that you're playing totally free-form.

Drum Tip

While you probably shouldn't vary the song's tempo during your solo—the tempo is the tempo, after all—you *can* vary the song's dynamics. You can keep a solo interesting by playing with varying degrees of loudness and softness; repeating the same pattern at different volume levels is a great way to create your own phrasing.

Flash with the Pans: How to Add Sizzle to Your Solo

How do you get the crowd on its feet? Simple—by doing something that appears hard and looks flashy!

Note that I said playing something that *appears* hard. The end of your solo might actually be very simple to play, but it will get the crowd cheering if it looks like something difficult to play.

Here are some sure-fire crowd pleasers that won't make you work too hard:

➤ **Crash the cymbals.** A lot. If you have two crashes, hit them one after another, right-left-right-left, with your right hand, while your left hand continues playing some sort of pattern on your snare or toms.

➤ **Roll around the drums.** Repeatedly. Play fast sixteenths or an open roll around your toms, from top to bottom and back again.

➤ **Hit lots of drums really fast.** It might not be melodic, but breaking up a sixteenth-note pattern between four drums sounds impressive and looks really flashy.

➤ **Throw in some bass drum licks.** If you can, learn a few licks that use your bass drum to complete a simple pattern. (For example, play four sixteenths alternating small tom to large tom to bass drum to large tom.) This adds a lot of power to a lick and, if you do it right, sounds like your right foot is really flying. (If you're playing a double-bass setup, you can also throw in some fast double-bass licks—a definite wow for the crowd!)

➤ **Cross-stick.** This is where you alternate a pattern between two drums on opposite sides of your kit, bringing your arms up and over each other as you repeat the pattern. Again, this looks harder than it is—and appears really flashy from the audience.

Just remember—build your solo to its highest point, using whatever techniques you have at your disposal!

Solo Practice: Three Drumset Solos

To help you hone your soloing skills, this chapter includes three, count 'em, *three* drumset solos—in three totally different styles!

Ringo's Right Foot: The Beginning

This solo is in the spirit of **Ringo Starr**'s brief solo on "The End." (**Ron Bushy**'s "In-A-Gadda-Da-Vida" solo takes a similar approach.) The bass drum keeps a steady eighth-note pattern, while you play different patterns on top of it. Things wrap up with a heavy series of eighth notes stomping the band back in.

Gene's Toms: Sing³

This solo is patterned after **Gene Krupa**'s groundbreaking solo on "Sing Sing Sing." It's a solo played almost exclusively on your large tom, with a four-on-the-floor bass drum and a two-and-four hi-hat. Play the eighth notes with a swing feel, and make sure to really pound the accents and underplay the unaccented notes. The solo ends with some kicks using the snare and the crash cymbal, and then a loud series of triplets and a final *bang!*

Danny Around the Drums: **Made Ya Smile**

The final drum solo in this chapter is a take-off on **Danny Sera-phine**'s brief solo on Chicago's "Make Me Smile." The first two measures are taken directly from what Danny played on record, and the rest of the solo builds from there. The end of the solo (starting with measure 21) reprises the beginning pattern, and the last measure ends just the same as the song, with a long roll on the large tom. Play this as a single-stroke roll, and take your time to crescendo from very soft to as loud as you can play.

In between the start and the finish are some really neat patterns. This solo uses three tom-toms; if you only have two toms, combine the two small toms into a single small tom part. The key to playing this solo effectively is to watch the sticking. If you try to play this puppy with alternating rights and lefts, it won't work. You have to play a fair number of doubles to get your hands positioned properly around your kit.

Drum Tip

It's okay to use parts of your set in your solos that you don't nor-mally play when keeping a beat. If you have lots of toms, multiple crash cymbals, and an extra snare drum, use 'em!

The Least You Need to Know

➤ The best solos are musical and structured.

➤ Your solos should progress through three "movements"—the beginning, the middle, and the end.

➤ Solos should build in intensity and complexity from beginning to end.

➤ It helps to keep the song's structure or melody playing in your head as you play your solo.

➤ Save all your fancy licks for the very end—then pull out all the stops and get the crowd on its feet!

The Beginning
A Drumset Solo

© Michael Miller

SING³

A DRUMSET SOLO

© MICHAEL MILLER

MADE YA SMILE
A DRUMSET SOLO

© MICHAEL MILLER

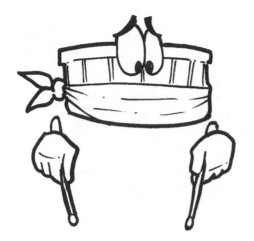

Chapter 23

Less Is More:
When *Not* to Play

> ### In This Chapter
>
> ➤ Discover some cool beats that aren't just a ride with a backbeat
>
> ➤ Learn when to lay out
>
> ➤ Find out how to keep the beat without a ride pattern—or without using your snare drum
>
> ➤ Play without using your drumset

Some of the best drum parts are where the drummer doesn't play—or at least doesn't play a traditional beat. While it's easy to fall into playing straight-eighths with a heavy backbeat, some songs require something different than just two and four. This chapter is all about knowing when to play something different—and knowing when not to play at all!

Play a Different Beat

When you want a song to sound a little different, play something a little different. Forget about playing a traditional two-and-four with accompanying ride, and think about other patterns you can play around your set.

Back when I was playing two or three wedding receptions a weekend, I didn't have the time or the inclination to really listen to some of the songs we were playing—I just muscled my way through every song with a traditional two-and-four rock beat. One of these songs was Fleetwood Mac's "Rhiannon," which I played like any other rock song in our repertoire, with a straight-eighths ride on the hi-hat and backbeats on two and four. Imagine my surprise when I actually *listened* to the beat **Mick Fleetwood** played on the record and discovered that he was playing on the *toms* throughout most of the song! I heard it as a traditional beat, when what he played was something else entirely. What he played—although it varied a little from measure to measure—went basically like this:

Mick Fleetwood's tom-tom beat on "Rhiannon."

Playing on the toms instead of the snare is a sure-fire way to create a unique beat. Just listen to the tom-tom beat (in paradiddles!) played by **Jerry Allison** on Buddy Holly's "Peggy Sue"—and copied by **Hal Blaine** on Tommy Roe's "Peggy Sue"–esque "Sheila"—for a good example of a tom-based groove. Of course, the granddaddy of all rock tom-tom beats is the one played by drummer **Frank Kirkland** on Bo Diddley's self-named tune, "Bo Diddley."

The "Bo Diddley" tom-tom beat.

This beat has been copied and copied and copied over time; you've probably heard it on Buddy Holly's "Not Fade Away" (drummer: **Jerry Allison**), Johnny Otis' "Willie and the Hand Jive" (drummer: uncredited), The Who's "Magic Bus" (drummer: **Keith Moon**), and Bruce Springsteen's "You're the One" (drummer: **Max Weinberg**).

Another good example of a really different beat is The Beatles' "Come Together." **Ringo Starr** starts off with a surprisingly intricate sixteenth-note triplet pattern between his hi-hat and tom-toms, and then switches to a simple bass drum and tom-tom beat on the verses. Only during the big instrumental break does Ringo go to the cymbals and snare to play a somewhat trashy traditional beat. In spite of this lack of a traditional two-and-four throughout, there's no doubt that this is one of the hardest-rocking songs from The Beatles catalog.

Ringo Starr's distinctive beat for "Come Together."

Ringo played a lot of nontraditional beats on Beatles songs. Take "Ticket to Ride," for example. Throughout most of the song, he plays a simple pattern with his bass drum, snare drum, and small tom—no ride cymbal or hi-hat. This is easily one of the most recognizable beats in pop music; you can play this pattern all by itself with no other instruments, and most people will be able to tell you the name of the song!

Another distinctive Beatles beat: "Ticket to Ride."

Sometimes the different beat is *really* different—and really difficult. **Steve Gadd** is known for his amazing technique and coordination, and it shows on what has become his signature drum part: Paul Simon's "50 Ways to Leave Your Lover." This part is extremely complex—until you realize that it's kind of a marching beat played between snare drum and hi-hat with the hands changed up. That is, the left hand plays the hi-hat while the right hand plays the main beats on the snare drum, which is just the opposite of how you'd normally approach things. If you want to learn this beat, start very slowly, and pay close attention to the sticking:

One of the most distinctive drum grooves of all time—Steve Gadd on "50 Ways to Leave Your Lover."

Drum Tip

The key to learning this beat is to play the entire beat on a single drum. What you then discover is that it's nothing more than a basic rudimental beat split between snare drum, hi-hat, and bass-drum. Once you feel the basic beat on a single drum, then you can adapt Steve's sticking and split your hands between snare and hi-hat (and your right foot on the bass drum).

Alternately, you can learn this beat one hand at a time. When you isolate the right-hand and left-hand parts, either one looks really simple. Master each hand separately, then—at an appropriately slow tempo—start adding them together.

Whichever approach you take, you'll discover that **Steve Gadd** pretty much keeps each hand in a specific place throughout the groove, so it's a matter of learning where each hand falls. It's only when you put both hands together that it gets tricky!

Lay Out—Until the Chorus

Lots of times a song really doesn't need a steady beat throughout the entire song. This is often the case with ballads and softer songs; the drummer lays out during the verse, coming in with some big fills just before the chorus.

A good example of this approach can be found on Carly Simon's "That's the Way I've Always Heard It Should Be." Drummer **Jimmy Johnson** rests through several long verses, making his presence known with some powerful tom fills leading into each chorus. Jimmy resists the temptation to chick his hi-hat during the verses—he lays out completely until the fills. Even during the chorus, he doesn't really play a traditional beat; it's basically a series of big tom fills, adding some emotional punch to the song.

Drum Note

You'll sometimes see the two flams in "Ticket to Ride" notated as the last two beats of a quarter-note triplet. For simplicity's sake, I notated them as straight-eighth upbeats. In reality, Ringo plays something a little in between straight eighths and triplets. Listen to it closely to try to duplicate his exact feel!

223

As noted elsewhere in this book, **Hal Blaine** was the true master of playing only when needed. Listen to Simon and Garfunkel's masterpiece, "Bridge Over Troubled Water." The song goes through several verses before Hal even makes his presence known—and when he does, it's bass drum and snare drum only, with heavy reverb. As the song builds, the backbeat keeps getting bigger, until Hal is adding tire chains (!) to the mix to get the biggest, echoiest sound imaginable. It's an awesome drum track, truly majestic and powerful—just like the song itself.

Drop the Ride

Why some drummers feel that they have to hit something on every eighth note, I'll never understand. Sometimes you don't need to keep a ride pattern going throughout the entire song—a simple backbeat will do.

There are lots of examples of nonride playing in the Phil Spector catalog—with Spector's favorite drummer, our old pal **Hal Blaine**, sitting behind the skins. One of the best examples of a "rideless" beat is The Ronettes' "Be My Baby." On this tune, the ride pattern is kept with maracas, while Hal essentially plays just "four" on his snare drum throughout the verses. On the choruses, Hal switches to two and four, played on his snare and large tom together. Never once in this song does he play a cymbal or a hi-hat. (He does play some *terrific* fills leading into each chorus, however, and in the song's out-chorus.)

Another example of not playing a traditional ride pattern is The Beach Boys' "Good Vibrations." **Hal Blaine** (yeah, he played on just about everything back then) plays a lot of tom fills and accents, and a heavy snare drum backbeat in a few places, but no ride cymbal or hi-hat. What little "ride" there is throughout the song is played on maracas, sleigh bells, or tambourine. (There are also some interesting bongos-hit-with-sticks effects throughout—there's a lot of cool stuff going on in this song!)

Ignore the Snare

Sometimes all or part of a song can be driven by a ride pattern only, without the snare beating out two and four. For a good example of this, listen to Petula Clark's "Downtown." The late New York session ace **Gary Chester** plays big chunks of this song with just his ride cymbal, leaving the heavy snare backbeat for the choruses. What's interesting about this tune is that you probably *think* you hear a snare drum—the drummer is so adept at playing just the right thing that it's only on closer listening that you hear the change-up.

Another example of a no-snare song is the Carpenters' classic "Close to You." Now, you might think of this as a dopey song by a dopey group (I did, when I was younger), but you'd be wrong. First of all, the song itself is classic Burt Bacharach–Hal David, actually written back in 1963 before they became famous. Second, the drumming is the epitome of drummer **Hal Blaine**'s "less is more" approach. (You thought Karen Carpenter played drums on her own albums? Wrong!) Hal doesn't play

Drum Note

For another great example of big-sounding tom–tom fills, listen to another famous Carly Simon song, "Anticipation." On this song, drummer **Andy Newmark** plays a drum part that is almost all fills, with lots of big sounds from a relatively small set.

Drum Tip

Another way to change things up is to put down your sticks and play with brushes. To learn more about brush technique and application, see Chapter 24, "Different Strokes: Beyond Sticks."

a single note on the snare drum throughout the entire song, not even a rimclick. (This is harder than it sounds—have *you* ever gone an entire song without hitting your snare drum?) Instead, he uses the hi-hat for both ride and backbeat—and plays some of the most tasteful tom-tom fills ever recorded, using his massive set of Octaplus concert toms. (To me, the best part of the song is the out-chorus, where Hal fills on his *hi-hat*—just a few notes, but absolutely perfect!)

Leave Your Kit at Home

If you really want to shake things up, consider not playing your set at all. Instead of snare drum, bass drum, and hi-hat, try playing congas or bongos or claves or tambourine—or something even less traditional.

There are numerous instances of hit songs without traditional drums. Take The Beatles' "And I Love Her"; on this early Beatles tune, **Ringo** leaves his kit in the corner of the Abbey Road studio, opting instead to play a quasi-Latin beat with bongos and claves. This is surprising musical sensitivity from a time when The Beatles were thought to be just a loud, beat-driven rock band—but indicative of Ringo's burgeoning rhythmic versatility.

A similar example is The Rascals' "Groovin'." Drummer **Dino Danelli** sets the perfect mood with congas and tambourine—including some shell clicks, where he hits the conga shell with a drumstick. The song really does groove, but without a single note from a snare or a cymbal.

Probably the best example of nondrumset playing comes on The Beach Boys' *Pet Sounds*, with drumming by the incredibly versatile **Hal Blaine.** Listen to the beginning of "God Only Knows," and you'll hear sleigh bells, tambourine, and something that sounds a little like woodblocks. That clack-clack-a-clack sound is actually made by orange drink bottles, emptied out, turned upside down, and played with sticks. It provides just the perfect beat and is a nice contrast for when Hal does sit down behind his set—for fills only, *not* to play the beat!

Another innovative song on *Pet Sounds* is "Caroline No." On this tune, Hal plays a kind of backward rhythm between a tambourine and an empty Coke can (with lots of reverb!). It's hard to imagine this song played with a traditional two-and-four beat; it needs this unusual treatment. (Also, as with "God Only Knows," Hal drops in a few tom-tom fills later in the song—the perfect complement at that point in time.)

The bottom line is that you shouldn't be wed to the traditional two-and-four backbeat. Listen to the song, and use all your musical skills to come up with the most perfect percussion part possible—even if it means *not* playing your drums!

The Least You Need to Know

➤ You don't need to hit two-and-four on your snare drum to drive a song.

➤ Playing different patterns around your drumset can create an effective—and unique—beat.

➤ It's possible to play a song without playing a ride pattern on your cymbal or hi-hat—especially if there are other instruments, such as tambourine or sleigh bells, playing quarters or eighths.

➤ Laying out for the early or softer parts of a song is sometimes preferable to playing a bunch of annoying rimclicks; you can always come in strong on the chorus!

Chapter 24

Different Strokes: Beyond Sticks

In This Chapter

➤ The way to make your snare drum softer or louder with rimclicks and rimshots

➤ The correct way to play brushes—and how to play "incorrectly" for special effect

➤ New alternatives to sticks and brushes

Most of the songs you play require the power and finesse that you can get only with a good pair of drumsticks. Some songs, however, require different types of sound—which can be produced by using your sticks in different ways or by using some sort of beater other than a stick.

Shots and Clicks: Using Your Sticks in Different Ways

The normal drum stroke puts the bead of your stick smack dab in the center of the drum. There are other ways to use the stick, however, to create different sounds.

A Softer Backbeat with Rimclicks

On some soft songs, a heavy backbeat on the snare drum may be overkill. For a softer sound, try playing a rimclick instead.

You play a rimclick by turning your left stick around so that you're holding on to the top end, not the butt. Now place the bead (which should be near the palm of your hand) on the head of the snare drum, slightly off-center. Raise the butt of the stick off the drum, and then bring it down on the opposite rim for a soft "click" sound.

Playing a rimclick on your snare drum.

That's a rimclick.

You can vary the tone of a rimclick by changing where you place the bead of the stick on the head—and where on the stick you click against the rim. If you choke up on the stick, your rimclick will sound dry and constrained. It's better to find a position that produces optimum ring for a very open and woody sound.

A Louder Backbeat with Rimshots

For a more pronounced backbeat or a louder snare drum accent, try playing a rimshot. You play a rimshot by hitting the head of the drum and the rim simultaneously; the sound is part normal snare and part loud, woody accent.

Play louder accents by using rimshots.

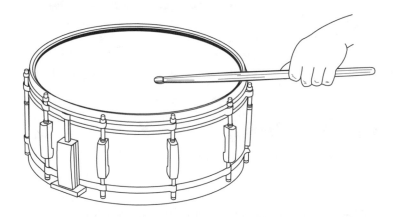

Some drummers play rimshots on every backbeat—and angle their snare drums slightly forward to make it easier to hit every rimshot.

Sweeping the Head: Playing with Brushes

If you play a lot of jazz—or a lot of soft ballads—you need to learn how to play with brushes. Brushes incorporate a "fan" of steel bristles, typically retractable, and are usually housed in a rubber-covered handle. When you hit a drum with a brush, the sound is softer and more diffused than when you hit it with a stick.

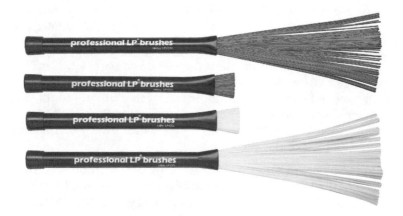

A selection of brushes from LP Music.

(Photo courtesy of LP Music Group)

Jazz brush technique incorporates a steady swishing movement with one hand while the other hand is used for backbeats and accents. The swish provides the "background noise" that would otherwise be provided by a ride cymbal or hi-hat.

Most drummers will swish with the left hand in a continuous pattern, as shown in the following figure:

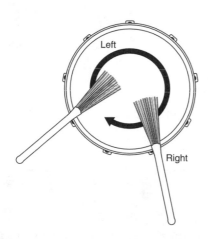

Play a circular pattern with your left hand, and hit the drum squarely with your right.

Of course, you don't have to play brushes in this traditional way. There are plenty of examples of nontraditional brushwork in pop songs—to successful effect.

Brushes are quite common in country music. Listen to Rosanne Cash's version of "Tennessee Flat Top Box," with drums by Nashville great **Eddie Bayers**, and you'll hear this popular brushes-and-bass-drum beat.

A country pattern played with brushes on the snare drum.

229

Drum Don't

You can also play a rimclick with the butt of the stick on the snare head (which, to be fair, a lot of drummers do), but you won't get the same wooden ring as you do with the bead on the head.

Eddie played this song with brushes, but on other tunes you might hear a similar beat played with sticks. The key here is that you're using brushes as you'd use a pair of sticks; you're hitting, not swishing.

Russ Kunkel played one of his most famous drum parts with brushes on James Taylor's "Fire and Rain." Legend has it that the musicians on the album were rehearsing in producer Peter Asher's living room, and several neighbors complained about the loud noise. Russ took to brushes in response, and the result is a classic drum track—with some of the tastiest fills ever put on record.

Several Burt Bacharach tunes seemed to be written with brushes in mind. One of the more interesting tracks is Dionne Warwick's "Do You Know the Way to San Jose?" with drums by **Gary Chester.** The groove is all bass drum and snare drum—with the snare played *upside down(!)* and with brushes. Listen to this one carefully; Gary really grooves with some very interesting snare-and-bass fills.

Do you know the way to San Jose? You get there with brushes!

Drummer **Liberty DeVito** is known for his hard-hitting playing—hard enough to break cymbals on a regular basis! It was surprising, then, to listen to Billy Joel's *The Stranger* album and hear Liberty playing brushes on the rocker "Only the Good Die Young." Liberty pushes the shuffle groove along with brushes, playing a ride pattern on the snare and the bass drum playing the backbeat. Knowing how hard Liberty plays, you have to wonder if he found a way to break a pair of brushes!

A shuffle pattern with brushes—and the backbeat on the bass drum!

The lesson here? Even if you're playing rock and roll, brushes should be an important part of your percussive arsenal.

Rolling Along: Playing with Mallets

Aside from sticks and brushes, you probably should have a pair of soft mallets in your stick bag. Mallets—like the kind used by timpani players in orchestras and concert bands—produce a much softer sound than drumsticks and are great for playing smooth cymbal rolls and timpani-like rolls on your large tom.

Drum Tip

If you play traditional grip, you can also play a rimshot by pressing the left stick down into the snare head and then hitting the left stick with the right stick.

Different Sounds: Other Types of Beaters

Over the past few years, several innovative new types of drum beaters have been developed. Most of these beaters were designed for use in an acoustic environment and became popular with the influence of MTV's "unplugged" concerts.

Most of these alternative beaters combine, in one way or another, the concept of sticks and brushes, putting multiple thin rods together in the way brushes use steel bristles. For example, LP's Wood Whacks are bundles of wood rods surrounded by a rubber grip. The movable sleeve midway down the bundle enables you to produce different sounds; move the sleeve toward the batter end for a tight, sticklike sound, or move the sleeve toward the handle for an open, wooden brush sound.

Drum Note

Vic Firth's version of the Wood Whack is called the Rute; Regal Tip's version, using plastic rods, is called the Blastick.

LP's Wood Whacks let you play softer—and produce an interesting multiple-hit effect on your drums.

(Photo courtesy of LP Music Group)

On your next trip to your local drum shop, check out some of these alternate beaters—you might just find a sound that you like!

Drum Note

There is no hard-and-fast rule for how to play brush patterns. You can swish with either hand, using any number of circular and noncircular patterns, as long as you produce the proper sound.

The Least You Need to Know

➤ A rimclick is played by laying the bead of the stick in the center of the snare drum and clicking the butt against the rim.

➤ A rimshot is played by striking the snare drum head and rim simultaneously—and loudly!

➤ Jazz brushes are played by swishing one brush around the snare head and using the other brush for accents and backbeats.

➤ Mallets are great for playing smooth cymbal and tom-tom rolls.

➤ Alternative beaters—such as Wood Whacks, Rutes, and Blasticks—use bundles of wooden or plastic rods to produce a sound somewhere between a brush and a stick.

Chapter 25

Parting Advice from One of Today's Hottest Drummers: An Interview with Kenny Aronoff

> **In This Chapter**
>
> ➤ Kenny Aronoff's philosophy of drumming—and how it drives the way he practices
>
> ➤ Ways to protect yourself physically when drumming
>
> ➤ Qualities you need to make it as a professional drummer

Kenny Aronoff is one of the most in-demand drummers working today. He first gained prominence in the 1980s as the hard-hitting drummer for John Mellencamp, and he has developed an impressive resumé built on both touring and recording. In addition to Mellencamp, Kenny has worked with Ricky Martin, Smashing Pumpkins, Celine Dion, Rod Stewart, Meatloaf, Elton John, Bob Dylan, Mary Chapin Carpenter, Neil Diamond, John Fogerty, Joe Cocker, the Rolling Stones, Bob Seger, Stevie Nicks, and many others.

Kenny has earned a reputation for being one of the hardest-working drummers in the business and for playing exactly the right beat for whatever song he's playing. His peers recognize his talent; the readers of *Modern Drummer* magazine named him the number-one Pop/Rock Drummer for five consecutive years and the number-one Studio Drummer for four consecutive years.

My Kenny Aronoff Story

I first heard Kenny Aronoff around 1977 in Bloomington, Indiana. I was attending the Indiana University music school at the time, and Kenny was back in town after graduating a year or so earlier. He was playing with some former band mates of mine in a jazz-fusion group called Streamwinner, and he impressed the heck out of me with his blazing fusion drumming technique. Imagine my surprise a few years later when I heard that Kenny was going to be the new drummer for the artist then known as John Cougar—after all, Cougar was a solid rock gig, and Kenny was a jazz fusion drummer!

Drum Note

You can catch up with Kenny's more recent activities at his Web site. www.kennyaronoff.com.

Well, Kenny adapted his style to such a degree that I couldn't tell that it was the same guy. His playing with Cougar/Mellencamp was powerful and deceptively simple, just what the band and the songs needed. Listening to Kenny's playing over the years reveals a drummer with incredible musical intelligence, great ears, and a total lack of ego—he plays exactly what's needed, even if he's using only a fraction of his total technique. It's no wonder that Kenny Aronoff is so in demand among today's top artists.

For a sampling of the "best of Aronoff," you can listen to Jon Bon Jovi's *Destination Anywhere*, Garth Brooks' *The Life of Chris Gaines*, Belinda Carlisle's *Heaven on Earth*, Mary Chapin Carpenter's *Stones in the Road*, Shawn Colvin's *Cover Girl*, Celine Dion's *Let's Talk About Love*, Melissa Etheridge's *Your Little Secret*, John Fogerty's *Premonition*, Ricky Martin's *Ricky Martin*, Meatloaf's *Bat Out of Hell 2/Back Into Hell*, Michael Penn's *March*, Iggy Pop's *Brick by Brick*, Bob Seger's *The Fire Inside*, Rod Stewart's *A Spanner in the Works*, or any of John Mellencamp's earlier albums, including *American Fool*, *Uh-Huh*, and *Scarecrow*. In addition, Kenny was the uncredited drummer behind "The Wonders" (or was that "The Oneders"?) in the movie *That Thing You Do!* and he played on both *Burning for Buddy* Buddy Rich tribute albums.

From the initial planning of this book, I wanted Kenny to somehow be a part of what I was writing. I liked the idea of including a fellow Hoosier drummer and IU grad, and I knew that Kenny would reinforce the main concepts I'd be writing about. (Besides that, all the drummers here in Indiana—including my publisher's husband!—know Kenny, and not including something from him might get me drummed out of the state!)

Drum Note

As befits a drummer of his stature, Kenny Aronoff is a top endorser for several different companies. He plays Tama drums and has several signature snare drums. His Trackmaster is a 5-inch × 14-inch brass-shelled drum with lots of crack and attack, similar to the old Ludwig Black Beauties. His Super Piccolo is a unique 4-inch × 15-inch brass-shelled drum with an interesting balance of openness and control. Both drums feature black nickel shells with detailed hand engraving.

Kenny endorses Vic Firth drumsticks, and he also has his own signature stick. Kenny's Power Play stick has a unique set of grooves on the butt end to provide extra grip for the last three fingers of the hand and is ideal for heavy playing.

Kenny also has several instructional books and videos available for sale, including *Laying It Down: Basics of Rock Drumming* and the *Power Workout* series. These titles can be found at most music stores or can be ordered directly from Warner Bros. Publications (www.warnerbrospub.com).

The Kenny Aronoff Interview

I was fortunate to catch Kenny Aronoff at his home in Bloomington during a short break between a Melissa Etheridge tour and an upcoming tour with John Fogerty. As is typical, Kenny was very helpful, very informative, and just about the nicest guy you could care to talk to.

Kenny Aronoff—one of today's hottest drummers.

(Photo courtesy of Kenny Aronoff)

Mike Miller (MM): How did you get started playing?

Kenny Aronoff (KA): Well, when I was a kid I used to watch the marching bands come to town, like on Memorial Day. I always got excited about the drums and the drum line. I grew up in a little town in New England, about 3,000 people, and I got so excited. Then, in fourth grade they asked me what instrument I wanted, and I said drums. I loved it, I thought that was the coolest instrument.

When I was about 11 years old, I saw *A Hard Day's Night,* and that turned my whole head around. I mean, I just had never seen anything like that in my life. That was in 1964. I was devastated—I mean, there was nothing going on. We had, like, just three black-and-white TV channels—with an antenna! There were no video games, and there wasn't a lot of stimulation in the technology. Our only source of entertainment was sports. When music came, with The Beatles, it was like the most powerful thing I'd ever experienced in my life. So I formed a band, immediately—the next week! (laughs) I wanted to be Ringo so bad, I wanted to be in the band.

So I used to play in a band; we'd play on the weekends, and it just kept expanding. Then I saw that some guy in my hometown of Stockridge, Massachusetts, was getting really good, He was getting really, really good, and I asked him, was he studying with somebody? And he said it was this guy, Arthur Press, percussionist with the Boston Symphony Orchestra. In the summertime, the Boston Symphony Orchestra would come to a place called Tanglewood—that's right where I grew up. So I studied with Press in the summers, and he sort of directed me to become a music major.

I was kind of behind in my musical background because I didn't have much to do with the high school music program. I had a rock band! Why would I want to be playing in a symphony band when I could be playing Zeppelin? (laughs) You know, I had my own band. Ironically, that's obviously where I ended up in my career, really back to where my roots were.

Drum Note

Mike Wanchic was the long-time guitarist in John Mellencamp's band. Mellencamp, like Kenny Aronoff, lives in Bloomington, Indiana—home of Indiana University.

Drum Note

Don Was has produced albums by the B-52s, Bonnie Raitt, Bob Dylan, Paula Abdul, the Rolling Stones, Bob Seger, Brian Wilson, Carly Simon, David Crosby, Iggy Pop, Neil Diamond, Ringo Starr, Jackson Browne, and many others. He has also produced a number of soundtrack albums, including the soundtracks to *Thelma & Louise, Days of Thunder, Honeymoon in Vegas, Toy Story, Hope Floats,* and *George of the Jungle.*

MM: When I first heard you, you were playing with Streamwinner, and I knew you as a fusion drummer with some hot licks, lots of tom fills, and cymbals and stuff. Then I heard you playing with Mellencamp, and I said, "This can't be the same Kenny Aronoff!" How did you get from Streamwinner to playing with Mellencamp?

KA: Well, I had been with Streamwinner for three years, and I was getting close to turning 27, and I thought, "Man, this isn't going anywhere." So I thought, "I have to move on."

I thought I was going to move to New York, *but …* I'd just gotten a call from a friend of mine to go to L.A. to audition, believe it or not, for Lou Rawls. That would've been a change! So I got that L.A. audition, but I didn't get the gig, thank God.

So, two weeks before I was going to move to New York, I ran into somebody who mentioned to me that John Mellencamp had just fired his drummer. So I went right to a phone booth and called up Mike Wanchic, you know, just looking for another audition. I came home and I started thinking, man, what am I, nuts? This Mellencamp thing is what I've always wanted! I mean, the music was simple, much simpler, but the touring, and making records, being on TV—my whole dream had always been this! I don't know why I got so sidetracked. (laughs) So, I auditioned and got the gig.

I remember thinking how simple the parts were and everything, but, man! It was really a huge adjustment. It took me two years just to get comfortable with playing simple. It was a big adjustment. But then, slowly but surely, it became what I was known for. You know, that laying it down, straight ahead.

MM: Obviously, Mellencamp was the gig that really got you noticed. How did you go from there to all of the studio work and all the other touring you've done?

KA: In 1988, John decided to quit the music business, and that's exactly when I got divorced. I was like, "How am I gonna make a living?"

I only knew so many people in L.A., but we were so hot that I could at least make phone calls and get through to some people. I happened to be in L.A. doing a Jefferson Airplane reunion album—not Starship, but the original Airplane—and there was this guy, Don Was, who was the producer and he was also the main guy with Was (Not Was). Well, he wanted to have a meeting with me. I was like, "Cool!"

So I had the meeting, and he wanted to know if I wanted to do an Iggy Pop record. I was flippin' out—you bet I do! Then we became real good friends, and he started hiring me for everything—Elton John, Bob Dylan, Bob Seger, Glenn Frey, you name it. That's how I met Bog Seger; hence, that's how I hooked up to go on tour with him. And I suddenly became "the dude."

Then, in the early 1990s, I went after Nashville a little bit. So I was working in Nashville, in L.A., in New York—everywhere. It was really cool. That's how I sort of launched that second career, and it's never stopped since.

MM: With all the playing you do, how do you keep yourself in the best physical shape for drumming?

KA: One of the main things I have going for me is just genetics. I was lucky enough to be born with a strong constitution and a lot of energy. But, beyond that, if you have a race car and you don't take care of it, it'll fall apart. So diet is a big part of it. Exercise is a big part.

I try to eat a certain kind of diet low in sugar, low in processed foods. I eat proteins, I eat carbohydrates, and I eat fats, but they're the right kinds. It's really tough on the road, but I do the best I can, and I know what's good and what's bad. Most places you can get vegetables, chicken or fish, and some form of grain. It's better to have, like, brown rice, as opposed to fried bread or something. (laughs) You can get a little bit of fruit somewhere and then drink lots of water. I take a lot of supplements to make sure that my immune system stays strong.

I try to eat six meals a day to keep the blood sugar down. There's a lot of these new diets, you know, the protein diet and all that stuff, but the main thing is to eat as much clean food as you can. If you eat good foods and you keep your motor running, and as your motor's running you're burning fuel, you're burning your food up. If you don't eat at all, your whole metabolism slows down, and you do lose some weight, but you actually start losing muscle, too. So the idea is to eat the right amount for the kind of activity and the metabolism you have—and constantly, which keeps your motor running, which will digest the food and the things you want to digest, and not start eating your own muscle.

Then there's the exercise part, cardio and muscle strengthening. Cardio I get from playing drums, or if I'm not on tour and I need more cardio, I do things like the StairMaster. Then I lift weights, for muscle strength. Plus, I stretch. I try to add yoga in there, too.

MM: Drumming, if you don't do it right, can be a physically hazardous profession—to your hearing and to your hands and arms and all that. What steps can a drummer take to protect himself or herself when they're playing?

KA: Everything I've just mentioned does protect you, does help you to not hurt yourself. Particularly stretching, as far as avoiding carpal tunnel problems and stuff like that. That can be a major problem with a lot of drummers. It's just basically if you're tight, not limbered up, you can hurt and strain the tendons and muscles in your arms.

Not only that, but you have to consider your back. Drummers, sitting all the time, pounding a bass drum, you can get sciatic problems. You can get back problems from sitting on a stool, playing like that, slumping over. You can get neck problems or anything to do with the shoulders, arms, hands, fingers.

You've got to really be aware of what's going on. If you're starting to get problems, you've got to address them pretty quickly.

MM: Have you ever had any major problems?

KA: Not major. Every so often you run into maybe a little numbness in your hand, or you tighten up, or you feel strained. Like, I'll play real hard, and my hands will puff up. My forearms and tendons get strained and swollen, you know, inflamed a little bit. I'm just pushing too much.

MM: What do you do when that happens?

KA: Well, the injuries I've had are where I've just overdone it, and my hands are puffed up or I feel that tension and tightness in my ligaments. I do self-massage on my arms, I know just where to go. If I have to, I'll take some ibuprofen for the inflammation. Icing and stretching help a lot. I do certain stretches for all those areas.

Drum Note

Hearing can be measured in terms of sensitivity at various frequencies. When Kenny says "3 to 4K" he's talking about the frequency range between 3,000 and 4,000 kilohertz—which contains the primary frequencies produced by crash and ride cymbals.

MM: What protection do you use for your hearing?

KA: When I practice, I use headphones. When I play live, I wear ear monitors. The problem with that is you can still turn the speakers up, you know.

There's no question that I've lost some hearing. Let's just put it this way—I have good ears, considering what my profession is. (laughs) But I have lost hearing in the 3 to 4K area.

MM: You certainly do a lot of traveling. Whether you're at home or on the road, what kind of practice routine do you do?

KA: I have a certain technique that I use. Now, anytime I play the drums, I usually include all four limbs. I really believe in that. Even if I'm practicing on a pad, I like to include my right foot and my left foot with something because when you play the drums, you always use all four limbs. So I try to do that, try to incorporate everything.

Then I work on my single-stroke roll. I work on some rudiments—not always, but they're there. I work on certain wrist techniques with double, triple, and quadruple speed groupings.

I don't have a lot of time, so I try to be very economical and efficient with my practicing. I try to practice the techniques that are going to be useful for what I do.

I try to do all this on the drumset, if I can. If I've gotta watch a football game or something on TV and I need to practice, I put a pad in front of me—but I use feet *and* hands. I do exactly what I would normally do on a set, but I do it on a pad.

Once I've done some of the technique stuff, I start working on my philosophy of drumming, which is beat, time, groove, and creativity. I sit down and I work on a beat that I might be working on, and work it and work it and work it. I play it over and over again, and whenever I hear anything that's not sounding right, I go back and work on it. Then I focus on just the kick drum, just the snare drum, just the hi-hat; then I mix it up. Then I start to stretch out and develop that beat.

I try to learn a beat, not just to play it; I want to try to incorporate it into my playing so I can *use* it when I do play. You know that feeling of practicing and practicing all this stuff, and you never seem to be using any of it? Well, I got sick of that. (laughs) I like to work things up so that I can use them.

MM: Practice what you use.

KA: Yeah—or use what I practice. And I try to integrate new ideas into the playing that is already familiar to me. There is so much to work on!

MM: How many hours a day do you practice, generally?

KA: There are times when I don't practice at all because I'm touring. When I'm on the road and I do a three-hour show, let's say with Melissa, I'd have like an hour sound check—with her or without her, I'd do it—then I practice maybe 15 minutes before I go on stage. That'll be about four hours a day, maybe even more, because maybe in the hotel I do something. That gets anywhere from four to four-and-a-half hours a day there.

When I'm off the road, I like to get two to three hours in, you know, and that's not enough. There's so much to learn!

MM: When you're giving a clinic and talking to drummers, what kinds of typical mistakes do you see beginners making?

KA: Well, beginners typically don't like to groove. They don't like to stay with one beat. They don't value taking a beat and keeping it steady, making it feel good, and being creative with that beat. You know, adding things to it, like decorating a cake. They tend to want to do all the flashy stuff. They don't want to build the cake and then put icing on it; they want just the icing. You can't have icing without the cake, you know what I mean? (laughs)

MM: If you could give a word or two of advice to beginning drummers, what would you say to them?

KA: You really want to have fun, but realize that it takes hard work for a long, long period of time to be great. That's the advice I'd give to any kid about anything. Have fun, have the best time in your life, but know that to really be successful where you can support yourself and make a living and do great, it's gonna take years and years and years and years of work. That's just the facts, you know? You don't have to take it on as a profession, like I did, but you do have to realize if you want to do it professionally, that it's gonna take a lot of work.

MM: That's great advice. Is there anything else you want to get across to the readers of this book?

KA: I have a philosophy of success, that the key to success, in my mind, is hard work. That's a given. It's like a vehicle, like a car that gets you somewhere, an airplane that gets you somewhere. Hard work gets you somewhere.

Then, to fuel that hard work, is passion. If you find something in life that you're passionate about, it's easier to get on board and work your a** off. That's my key advice to people. Find a passion for something, because hard work is a given, then work your a** off and constantly educate yourself. *Re*-educate yourself. Constantly keep learning and pushing it, learning and reading and watching.

Don't ever expect that once you become great at something, you're set for life. It doesn't work that way.

MM: This is great stuff, Kenny. This is exactly how I wanted to end the book.

KA: Great!

Learning from the Pros

What can we learn from pros like **Kenny Aronoff** and **Hal Blaine** (interviewed back in Chapter 7)? Here are the key points I see, especially for beginning drummers:

➤ **Hard work is important.** Kenny Aronoff may be the hardest-working drummer in the business today; he doesn't turn down any job unless he has a previous commitment. Back in his heyday, **Hal Blaine** worked at least three recording sessions a day, every day. The work ethic of these top drummers shows in their playing and in their fame. If you want to be good, and if you want to be famous, you have to work hard to get there.

➤ **Practicing is important.** Kenny says he practices several hours a day, every day. Other professional drummers will tell you the same thing. You have to practice to get good at what you do and—more important—to learn new things. As Kenny says, "There's so much to learn!"

➤ **Reading is important.** Hal's key piece of advice to beginning drummers is to learn how to read music. Yes, you can play drums without reading music (**Buddy Rich** did), but you'll be able to take advantage of so many more opportunities if you can read. When you sit down with a new band or in a recording studio, you need to read that piece of sheet music to figure out what's going on—and if you can't read it, you're out.

➤ **Having a good attitude is important.** When you talk to a Hal Blaine or a Kenny Aronoff, you hear an enthusiasm in their voice that is contagious. Drumming is hard work, yes, but it's also great fun. If you work hard, practice a lot, and have a positive attitude, other musicians will want to play with you, and you'll go far.

I'll end this book with one final word. As I was writing this book, I confirmed to myself that drummers are a unique breed. Drummers, in general, are nice folks who are extremely helpful (especially to other drummers) and give graciously of their time. If you decide to become a drummer, make sure that you're as helpful to others as other drummers will be to you. It's part of what drumming is all about.

Now pick up those sticks and start practicing!

The Least You Need to Know

➤ Kenny Aronoff's philosophy of drumming is beat, time, groove, and creativity.

➤ Proper diet and physical conditioning should be an essential part of any drummer's routine.

➤ Becoming a professional drummer takes a combination of hard work and a passion for what you do.

➤ Don't expect that once you become great at something, you're set for life—you need to constantly re-educate yourself.

Drum Words: A Drummer's Glossary

accent   A note played louder or with more emphasis than regular notes.

backbeat   In 4/4 time, beats two and four, typically played on the snare drum.

bar line   The vertical line placed on the staff between measures.

bass drum   The large drum, set up vertically and played with a pedal, that provides the lowest note in the drumset.

batter head   The head of the drum that is struck, typically the top head.

bead   The tip of the drumstick.

beat   Any pulsing unit of musical time.

bell   The round, raised center of a cymbal; playing the bell results in a pingier sound than playing closer to the edge.

bomb   When the drummer in a jazz band plays an unexpectedly loud accent with the bass drum.

brushes   Fan-shaped devices made of wire strands attached to a handle, often used in soft jazz and ballads.

butt   The end of the drumstick opposite from the bead.

clef   A symbol placed at the beginning of the staff to indicate the pitch of the notes on the staff.

closed roll   A multiple-stroke roll produced by pressing the stick into the head for multiple bounces. Also called a buzz roll or a press roll.

crash cymbal   A relatively thin cymbal that, when hit hard, produces a loud burst of sound with quick decay.

crescendo   Gradually louder.

cymbal   Circular metal percussion instruments made of a bronze alloy, used to play a ride pattern or for accent crashes.

decrescendo   Gradually softer.

double bar   Two vertical lines placed on the staff to indicate the end of a section or a composition.

downbeat   The major beats in a measure; in 4/4 time, the downbeats are 1, 2, 3, and 4.

dynamics   Varying degrees of loud and soft.

fill   A pattern played, typically on the toms, at the end of one musical phrase leading into the next phrase.

flam   A grace note played almost simultaneously with the main note, from hand to hand.

four on the floor   A 4/4 beat in which the bass drum plays straight quarter notes on every downbeat.

ghost note   A note played very lightly in comparison to others.

gig   A musician's job.

grace note   One or more notes, played lightly and quickly, that precede a main note.

groove   (1) A specific beat. (2) Indicating that a song was played at just the right tempo and feel, as in "in the groove."

hi-hat   Two smaller cymbals that are closed together via a pedal and played with both the foot and with sticks—typically to keep a ride pattern.

hoop   The wood or metal "rim" that sits on top of the edge of the drum head and attaches the head to the shell.

lug   The casing that is attached to a drum shell and accepts a tuning rod.

measure   A group of beats, indicated by the placement of bar lines on the staff.

note   A symbol used to indicate the duration and pitch of a sound, as in whole notes, half notes, and quarter notes.

odd time   Any non-4/4 time signature, such as 3/4, 5/4, or 9/8.

open roll   A series of thirty-second notes played with double strokes.

paradiddle   Four notes of equal duration played with either a RLRR or a LRLL sticking. A double paradiddle consists of six notes with either a RLRRLL, a LRLLRR, a RLRLRR, or a LRLRLL sticking.

percussion   Musical instruments that you hit, beat, crash, shake, roll, scratch, rub, twist, or rattle.

phrase   Within a piece of music, a segment that is unified by rhythms, melodies, or harmonies and that comes to some sort of closure; typically composed in groups of 2, 4, 8, 16, or 32 measures.

pitch   The highness or lowness of a tone.

polyrhythm   Two or more rhythms played simultaneously, or against each other.

resonant head   The front or bottom head of a drum that is *not* struck; so named because it resonates when the batter head is hit.

rest   A symbol used to denote silence or not playing a particular note.

rhythm   The organization of sound in time; the arrangement of beats and accents in music.

ride cymbal   A large, relatively heavy cymbal that is used to keep time via a repeating "ride" pattern.

rim   *See* hoop.

rimclick   A soft, woody "click" that results from placing the bead of the stick in the middle of the drum and then hitting the middle of the stick against the rim.

rimshot   A loud, woody sound that results from hitting the rim and the head of the drum simultaneously.

roll   Several notes played rapidly in succession, typically with double strokes on each hand; a roll can be either *open* or *closed*.

rudiment   One of 26 basic rhythmic patterns.

ruff   Two grace notes attached to a main note; the grace notes are played with a double stroke on one hand, while the main note is played with the opposite hand.

score   The written depiction of all the individual parts played of each of the instruments in an ensemble.

set   (1) A kit of drums, including a snare drum, a bass drum, tom-toms, and cymbals. (2) A group of songs, played straight through without a break.

shell   The thin, hollow cylinder that comprises the main body of a drum; shells can be made from solid wood, plies of wood, fiberglass, steel, bronze, or other materials.

shoulder   That part of a drumstick that begins to taper down to the bead.

shuffle   A rhythmic feel based on triplets or a dotted-eighth-note/sixteenth-note pattern.

snare drum   A thin wood or metal-shelled drum with metal wires running alongside the bottom head to produce a crisp sound; the snare drum is used to reinforce the backbeat in rock music.

snare head   The bottom or resonant head on a snare drum.

staff   An assemblage of horizontal lines and spaces that represent either different pitches or, in the case of percussion, different percussion instruments or parts of the drumset.

straight eighths   A ride pattern, typically played on the hi-hat or ride cymbal, consisting of eight eighth notes per measure.

suspension mount   A type of tom-tom holder that doesn't attach directly to the tom's shell; instead, a suspension mount attaches the drum's tuning rods or rim, thus enabling the shell to vibrate more freely.

syncopation   An accent on an unexpected beat—or the lack of an accent on an expected beat.

tempo   The rate of speed that beats are played in a song.

tension rods   The threaded screwlike pieces that fit through a drum's hoop and screw into the lugs; tension lugs are used to adjust the tension of a drum head.

throne   A drummer's seat.

throwoff   The assembly that moves the wire snares next to or away from the snare drum's snare head.

tie   A curved line over or under two or more notes that "ties" the two notes together into one. In percussion notation, a tie is also used to indicate adjoining notes of a roll, ruff, or flam.

time signature   The fraction-like notation that indicates the basic meter of a song. The upper number indicates how many beats are in a measure, and the bottom number indicates the type of note that receives one beat.

tom-tom   Sometimes known just as a "tom," this drum produces a low-pitched sound; smaller toms produce higher pitches.

triplet   A group of three notes performed in the space of two.

upbeat   The eighth-note "and" after the downbeat.

Drum Records: Recommended Listening

The following is a selection of CDs that feature influential drummers or prominent drum parts.

Artist	CD	Drummer(s)
Al Green	*Let's Stay Together*	Howard Grimes, Al Jackson Jr.
Aretha Franklin	*Lady Soul*	Roger Hawkins
Art Blakey & the Jazz Messengers	*Moanin'*	Art Blakey
Benny Goodman	*Carnegie Hall Jazz Concert*	Gene Krupa
Billy Cobham	*Spectrum*	Billy Cobham
Billy Joel	*The Stranger*	Liberty DeVito
Blood, Sweat & Tears	*What Goes Up* (compilation)	Bobby Colomby
Booker T. & the MG's	*Green Onions*	Al Jackson Jr.
Bruce Springsteen	*Born to Run*	Ernest Carter, Max Weinberg
Buddy Holly	*Greatest Hits*	Jerry Allison
Buddy Rich Big Band	*Mercy, Mercy*	Buddy Rich
Carly Simon	*The Best of Carly Simon*	Jim Gordon, Jimmy Johnson, Jim Keltner, Andy Newmark
Chicago	*Chicago II*	Danny Seraphine
Chick Corea	*Three Quartets*	Steve Gadd
Cream	*Total Cream*	Ginger Baker
Dave Brubeck Quartet	*Time Out*	Joe Morello
Dave Grusin	*The Gershwin Collection*	Sonny Emory, Dave Weckl
Dave Matthews Band	*Live at Red Rocks 8-15-95*	Carter Beauford
Fleetwood Mac	*Fleetwood Mac*	Mick Fleetwood
Frank Zappa	*Joe's Garage: Act 1*	Vinnie Colaiuta
Gregg Bissonette	*Submarine*	Gregg Bissonette

Artist	CD	Drummer(s)
Hall & Oates	*Abandoned Luncheonette*	Bernard Purdie
Herbie Hancock	*Maiden Voyage*	Tony Williams
Herbie Hancock	*Headhunters*	Harvey Mason
Jackson Browne	*Running on Empty*	Russ Kunkel
James Taylor	*Sweet Baby James*	Russ Kunkel
Jimi Hendrix Experience	*Are You Experienced?*	Mitch Mitchell
Joe Cocker	*Mad Dogs and Englishmen*	Jim Gordon, Jim Keltner
John Coltrane	*A Love Supreme*	Elvin Jones
John Cougar Mellencamp	*Uh-Huh*	Kenny Aronoff
King Crimson	*Discipline*	Bill Bruford
Led Zeppelin	*Houses of the Holy*	John Bonham
Little Richard	*Here's Little Richard*	Earl Palmer
Mahavishnu Orchestra	*Birds of Fire*	Billy Cobham
Max Roach	*Freedom Now Suite*	Max Roach
Michael Penn	*March*	Kenny Aronoff, Jim Keltner
Miles Davis	*Milestones*	Philly Joe Jones
Miles Davis	*Bitches Brew*	Charles Alias, Jack DeJohnette, Lenny White
Miles Davis	*Four and More*	Tony Williams
Paul Simon	*Still Crazy After All These Years*	Steve Gadd, Roger Hawkins, Grady Tate
Phil Spector & Various	*Back to Mono* (boxed set)	Hal Blaine, Earl Palmer
Rush	*Exit … Stage Left*	Neil Peart
Simon & Garfunkel	*Bridge Over Troubled Water*	Hal Blaine
Stan Kenton & His Orchestra	*Fire, Fury and Fun*	Peter Erskine
Steely Dan	*Aja*	Steve Gadd, Ed Greene, Paul Humphrey, Jim Keltner, Rick Marotta, Bernard Purdie
Steely Dan	*Katy Lied*	Hal Blaine, Jeff Porcaro
Steely Dan	*Pretzel Logic*	Jim Gordon, Jim Hodder, Jeff Porcaro
Steely Dan	*Royal Scam*	Rick Marotta, Bernard Purdie
The 5th Dimension	*Up-Up and Away: The Definitive Collection* (compilation)	Hal Blaine
The Beach Boys	*Pet Sounds*	Hal Blaine
The Beatles	*A Hard Day's Night*	Ringo Starr
The Beatles	*Abbey Road*	Ringo Starr
The Four Tops	*The Ultimate Collection*	Benny Benjamin
The Police	*Zenyatta Mondatta*	Stewart Copeland
The Rascals	*Anthology (1965–1972)*	Dino Danelli
The Rolling Stones	*Exile on Main Street*	Charlie Watts

Artist	CD	Drummer(s)
The Staple Singers	*Bealtitude: Respect Yourself*	Roger Hawkins
The Temptations	*The Ultimate Collection*	Benny Benjamin
The Who	*Tommy*	Keith Moon
Toto	*Toto IV*	Jeff Porcaro
Wilson Pickett	*In the Midnight Hour*	Al Jackson Jr.
Various	*Burning for Buddy*	Kenny Aronoff, Bill Bruford, Billy Cobham, Steve Ferrone, Steve Gadd, Omar Hakim, Joe Morello, Simon Phillips, Max Roach, Ed Shaughnessy, Marvin "Smitty" Smith, Steve Smith, Matt Sorum, Dave Weckl
Various	*Burning for Buddy Vol. 2*	Kenny Aronoff, Gregg Bissonette, Bill Bruford, Steve Gadd, Joe Morello, Neil Peart, Simon Phillips, Marvin "Smitty" Smith, Dave Weckl
Various	*Let There Be Drums! Vol. 1: The '50s*	Jerry Allison, Fred Below, Cozy Cole, Preston Epps, Panama Francis, Billy Guesack, Buddy Harman, Dickie Harrell, Frank Kirkland, Joe Marshall, Sandy Nelson, Earl Palmer, Bill Savitch, Milt Turner, James Van Eaton
Various	*Let There Be Drums! Vol. 2: The '60s*	Johnny Bee, Hal Blaine, Gary Chester, Doug Clifford, Dino Danelli, Jerry Edmonton, Bobby Elliot, Buddy Harman, Roger Hawkins, Levon Helm, Al Jackson Jr., Howie Johnson, Don Stevenson, Ron Wilson
Various	*Let There Be Drums! Vol. 3: The '70s*	Bill Bruford, Andre Fischer, Steve Gadd, Mickey Hart, Roger Hawkins, Robert Johnson, Jim Keltner, Billy Kreutzmann, Russ Kunkel, Michael McBride, Andy Newmark, Bernard Purdie, Bobby Ramirez, Charlie Watts, Max Weinberg, Earl Young

Drum Books: Supplemental Instruction Books

What follows is a list of some of the most popular drum instruction books and videos. My personal recommendations are in **boldface.**

Advanced Funk Studies (Rick Latham)

***Advanced Techniques for the Modern Drummer* (Jim Chapin)**—the essential book for coordinated independence

Alfred's Drum Method Book 1 (Sandy Feldstein and Dave Black)

Art of Bop Drumming, The (John Riley)

Basics of Rock Drumming (Kenny Aronoff—video)

Bass Drum Control (Colin Bailey)

Best of Concepts, The (Roy Burns)

Complete Modern Drum Set (Frank Briggs)

***Contemporary Studies for the Snare Drum* (Fred Albright)**—advanced-level studies to improve sight-reading skills

Cross-Sticking Studies (Ron Spagnardi)

Double-Bass Drumming (Joe Franco)

Drum Concepts and Techniques (Peter Erskine)

***Encyclopedia of Reading Rhythms* (Gary Hess)**—hundreds of drum charts, from basic rhythms to more sophisticated studies

***Haskell W. Harr Drum Method Book One* (Haskell W. Harr)**—probably the best book for learning rudimental drumming; a true classic

Intermediate Contest and Recital Solos for Drum Set (Jake Jerger)

Lessons with the Greats, Vol. 1 (John Xepoleas)

Lessons with the Greats, Vol. 2 (John Xepoleas)

Linear Time Playing (Gary Chaffee)

Master Studies **(Joe Morello)**—a terrific book for control and technique that includes studies for accents, buzz rolls, single and double-stroke combinations, sticking, flams, endurance, and velocity

Master Technique Builders for Snare Drum (Anthony J. Cirone)

Modern Rudimental Swing Solos for the Advanced Drummer **(Charlie Wilcoxin)**—advanced solos that apply all the rudiments

Modern Snare Drummer, The (Ron Spagnardi)

New Breed **(Gary Chester)**—a series of "systems" for improving your reading skills and coordination, great for both beginners and more advanced players

New Breed II (Gary Chester)

New Directions Around the Drums (Mark Harmon)

Playing, Reading and Soloing with a Band (Gregg Bissonette)

Polyrhythmic Studies for the Snare Drum (Fred Albright)

Portraits in Rhythm **(Anthony J. Cirone)**—a true classic with 50 snare drum etudes for intermediate and advanced drummers

Progressive Independence (Ron Spagnardi)

Rhythmic Patterns for the Modern Drummer (Joe Cusatis)

Drum Tip

If you have trouble finding any of these books at your local drum shop or music store, you can order most of them online at Forever Drumming (www.foreverdrumming.com) or The Drum Place (www.drumplace.com).

Rudimental Patterns for Full Drum Set Studies (Joe Cusatis)

Rudiments to Rock (Carmine Appice)

Snare Drum for Beginners (Morris Goldenberg)

Standard Snare Drum Method **(Benjamin Podemski)**—a comprehensive snare drum book containing exercises and solos emphasizing both rudimental and orchestral drumming

Stick Control **(George Lawrence Stone)**—the essential method book for improving snare drum technique; possibly the most-used drum book ever written

Twelve Progressive Solos for the Snare Drum (Morris Goldenberg)

Under the Table and Drumming (Carter Beauford—video)

In addition to these instruction books and videos, here are a handful of informative reference books about drums and drummers:

Backbeat: Earl Palmer's Story **(Tony Scherman)**—an "oral biography" of the pioneering rock and studio drummer

Best of Modern Drummer: Rock (Modern Drummer)

Drum Book, The **(Geoff Nicholls)**—photo-packed hardcover book covering the history of the drumset and trap drummers

Drum Hardware: Set-Up and Maintenance **(Andy Doerschuk)**—tips and practical advice for buying, tuning, and taking care of your drums

Drummer's Studio Survival Guide, The (Mark Huntly Parsons)

Drummer's Time: Conversations with the Great Drummers of Jazz (Modern Drummer)

Give the Drummers Some! The Great Drummers of R&B, Funk & Soul (Jim Payne)—a terrific book full of interviews and articles about great soul drummers, including Earl Palmer, Roger Hawkins, and Al Jackson Jr.

Great American Drums (And the Companies That Made Them), The (Harry Cangany)—interesting history of vintage drums and drum companies

Great Jazz Drummers, The (Ron Spagnardi)

Great Rock Drummers of the Sixties, The (Bob Ciani)

Guide to Vintage Drums (John Aldridge)

Hal Blaine and the Wrecking Crew (Hal Blaine, with David Goggin)—an anecdote-filled reminiscence from the premier studio drummer of the top 40 era

History of the Ludwig Drum Company (Paul William Schmidt)

Star Sets (Jon Cohan)

Traps, the Drum Wonder: The Life of Buddy Rich (Mel Torme)—a vivid biography of Buddy Rich, the drummer and the man, from his friend the late Mel Torme (who happened to be a pretty good drummer in his own right!)

Working Drummer, The (Rick Van Horn)

Zildjian: The History of the Legendary Cymbal Makers (Jon Cohan)

Drum Links: Other Percussion Resources

Want to learn even more about the drums? Then check out these resources. (My personal recommendations are in **boldface**.)

Magazines and Newsletters

Drum! (www.drumlink.com)

Drum Corps World (www.drumcorpsworld.com)

Latin Percussionist (www.latinpercussion.com)

Modern Drummer (**www.moderndrummer.com**)—the premier magazine for drummers of all ages and styles

Not So Modern Drummer (www.notsomoderndrummer.com)

Percussive Notes (www.pas.org/Publications/notes.html)

Stick It (www.stickitonline.com)

Web Sites for Drummers

anewdrummer (**www.anewdrummer.cjb.net**)—a site with lots of information for beginning drummers

The Complete Idiot's Guide to Playing Drums (**www.molehillgroup.com/drums.htm**)— where you'll find all the exercises and solos from this book in digital audio format

Concepts in Drumming (www.cidrumming.com)

Cyber-Drum (www.cyberdrum.com)

Drum Bum (www.drumbum.com)

Drum Center Forum (forum.drumcenter.com)

Drum Club (www.thedrumclub.com)

Drum Network (www.drumnetwork.com)

Drum Place (www.drumplace.com)

Drum Ring International (www.drumring.org)

DrummerGirl (www.drummergirl.com)

Drummers Web (www.drummersweb.com)

drummerstuff (www.drummerstuff.com)

DrummerWorld (www.drummerworld.com)

Drums Online (drumzonline.com)

Drums.com (www.drums.com)

DrumSet.com (www.drumset.com)

DrumWeb.com (www.drumweb.com)—one of the most comprehensive drum-oriented sites on the Web; includes drum charts (tabs), tips and techniques, and lots of links to famous drummers and drum manufacturers

Electronic Drum Web (www.edrumweb.com)—the Web's leading site for electronic percussion

Encyclopedia of Percussion (www.cse.ogi.edu/Drum/encyclopedia/)

Fife and Drum.com (www.fifeanddrum.com)

Forever Drumming (www.foreverdrumming.com)

Harmony Central: Drums & Percussion (www.harmony-central/Drums/)—news, reviews, FAQs, and lots of drum links

Hip Rhythm Digest (www.cactusjack.com)

International Drummer Page (www.kay.nu/drum/)

Percussion World (percussion.simplenet.com)

Professor Sound's Drum Tuning Bible (www.drumweb.com/profsound.shtml)—the single best source for instructions for and information about tuning your drums

Rec.Music.Makers.Percussion (www.rmmpfaq.club24.co.uk)

ThePercussionist (www.thepercussionist.com)—a full-service site from drummers, featuring everything from online lessons to message boards and a directory of drum teachers

Vintage and Custom Drum Page (web2.airmail.net/thompson/vdrum.htm)

Web Association of Percussionists (www.tupelonet.com/wap/home.htm)

Working Drummer (www.workingdrummer.com)

World of Drums and Drumming (www.nowopen.com/drums/)

Organizations

Drum Corps International (www.dci.org)

NAMM: International Music Products Association (www.namm.org)

Percussion Marketing Council (www.playdrums.com)—the trade organization for the drum and percussion industry, complete with links to drummers and manufacturers, as well as special programs, contests, and promotions for educators and beginning drummers

Percussive Arts Society (www.pas.org)—a not-for-profit organization formed to promote drums and percussion through a network of performers, students, educators, and the annual PASIC convention

General Music Resources

About.com Jazz (jazz.about.com)

All-Music Guide (www.allmusic.com)—a terrific database of musicians and music and the best place to find out who played with whom on what records; also includes a comprehensive music glossary

Fortissimo! A Program for Musical Development (library.thinkquest.org/2791/index.html)

Harmony Central (www.harmony-central.com)

Jazz Glossary Plus (guitarmain.com/index_gl.html)

Online Music Dictionary (www.austinsymphony.org/musicterms.html)

Drum and Cymbal Manufacturers

Ayotte (www.ayottedrums.com)

Brady (www.bradydrums.com)

ddrum (www.clavia.se/ddrum.htm)

Drum Workshop (www.dwdrums.com)

Evans Drumheads (www.evansdrumheads.com)

Fibes (www.fibes.com)

GMS (www.gmsdrums.com)

Gretsch (www.gretsch.com)

LP Music Group (www.lpmusic.com)

Ludwig (www.ludwig-drums.com)

Mapex (www.mapexdrums.com/home.html)

Noble & Cooley (www.noblecooley.com)

Pacific Drums and Percussion (www.pacificdrums.com)

Paiste Cymbals (www.paiste.com)

Pearl (www.pearldrum.com)

Peavey (www.peavey.com/mi/drums.html)

Premier (www.premier-drums.com)

Promark Drumsticks (www.promark-stix.com)

Regal Tip Drumsticks (www.regaltip.com)

Remo (www.remo.com)

Roland (www.rolandus.com)

Sabian Cymbals (www.sabian.com)

Slingerland (www.Slingerland.com)

Sonor (www.sonor.de)

Sunlite (www.sunlitedrum.com)

Tama (www.tama.com)

Vic Firth Drumsticks (www.vicfirth.com)

Yamaha (www.yamaha.com/drum.htm)

Zickos (www.zickosdrums.com)

Zildjian Cymbals and Drumsticks (www.zildjian.com)

Index

Symbols

10-lug drums, tuning, 64
12/8 time signature exercises, 200
"25 or 6 to 4" (Chicago: Seraphine, Danny), 76
26 rudiments, 141-151
    double drag (rudiment ten), 145
    double paradiddle (rudiment eleven), 145-146
    double ratamacue (rudiment twenty-six), 151
    drag paradiddle no. 1 (rudiment twenty-two), 150
    drag paradiddle no. 2 (rudiment twenty-three), 151
    eleven-stroke roll (rudiment seventeen), 148
    fifteen-stroke roll (rudiment nineteen), 149
    five-stroke roll (rudiment two), 142
    flam (rudiment four), 143
    flam accent (rudiment five), 143-144
    flam paradiddle (rudiment six), 144
    flam paradiddle-diddle (rudiment twenty-four), 151
    flam tap (rudiment twenty), 149
    flamacue (rudiment seven), 144
    history, 142
    Lesson 25 (rudiment twenty-five), 151
    long roll (rudiment one), 142
    nine-stroke roll (rudiment fifteen), 148
    ruff (rudiment eight), 145
    seven-stroke roll (rudiment three), 142
    single drag (rudiment nine), 145
    single paradiddle (rudiment twenty-one), 150
    single ratamacue (rudiment twelve), 146
    single-stroke roll (rudiment fourteen), 147-148
    ten-stroke roll (rudiment sixteen), 148
    thirteen-stroke roll (rudiment eighteen), 149
    triple ratamacue (rudiment thirteen), 146-147
3/4 time signature exercises, 200
5/4 time signature exercises, 200
"50 Ways to Leave Your Lover" (Simon, Paul: Gadd, Steve), 222-223
7/4 time signature exercises, 200
9/8 time signature exercises, 200

A

Abbey Road (The Beatles: Starr, Ringo), 65, 75
accent marks, 105, 116
acoustic jazz drumming, 7
African percussion, 53
"Ain't Too Proud to Beg" (The Temptations: Benjamin, Benny), 208
Aja (Steely Dan: Gadd, Steve), 76
All-Music Guide, 255
Allison, Jerry
    "Not Fade Away" (Holly, Buddy), 222
    "Peggy Sue" (Holly, Buddy), 150, 222
alternative playing methods, 227
    brushes, 229-230
    drum beaters
        Wood Whacks, 231
    laying out, 223-224
    mallets, 230
    no-snare playing, 224-225
    nondrumset playing, 225
    nonride playing, 224
    rimclicks, 227-230
    rimshots, 228-230
    unique patterns, 221-223
American Fool (Mellencamp, John: Aronoff, Kenny), 234
anewdrummer Web site, 253
"Anticipation" (Simon, Carly: Newmark, Andy), 76, 224
"Aquarius/Let the Sun Shine" (The Fifth Dimension: Blaine, Hal), 82
Aronoff, Kenny, 5, 91, 180, 233
    American Fool (Mellencamp, John), 234
    author's story, 233-234
    Bat Out of Hell 2/Back Into Hell (Meat Loaf), 234
    Brick by Brick (Iggy Pop), 234
    Burning for Buddy (Buddy Rich tributes), 234
    Chapin Carpenter, Mary, 233
    Cocker, Joe, 233
    Cover Girl (Colvin, Shawn), 234
    Destination Anywhere (Bon Jovi, Jon), 234
    Diamond, Neil, 233
    Dion, Celine, 233
    Dylan, Bob, 233
    endorsements, 234
    Fire Inside, The (Seger, Bob), 234
    Fogerty, John, 233
    Heaven on Earth (Carlisle, Belinda), 234
    interview, 235-239
    John, Elton, 233
    Laying It Down: Basics of Rock Drumming, 234
    Let's Talk About Love (Dion, Celine), 234
    Life of Chris Gaines, The (Brooks, Garth), 234
    March (Penn, Michael), 234
    Martin, Ricky, 233
    Meat Loaf, 233
    Mellencamp, John, 77, 233
    Nicks, Stevie, 233
    Power Workout series, 234
    Premonition (Fogerty, John), 234
    Ricky Martin (Martin, Ricky), 234
    The Rolling Stones, 233
    Scarecrow (Mellencamp, John), 234
    Seger, Bob, 233
    Smashing Pumpkins, 233
    Spanner in the Works, A (Stewart, Rod), 234
    Stewart, Rod, 233
    Stones in the Road (Chapin Carpenter, Mary), 234
    Uh-Huh (Mellencamp, John), 234
    Web site, 234
    Your Little Secret (Etheridge, Melissa), 234
The Association: Blaine, Hal, 77
attack, 33
auxiliary percussion instruments, 53-54
    African, 53
    Indian instruments
        tablas, 53-54
    Latin, 51-53
        bongos, 52
        claves, 52-53
        conga drums, 52
        LP Music Group, 52
        maracas, 53
        Santana, Carlos, 51
        shakers, 53
        shekeres, 53
        timbales, 52
    melodic, 56
        marimbas, 56
        vibraphones, 56
        xylophones, 56
    sleigh bells, 54
    symphonic, 55
        gongs, 55
        timpani, 55
        triangles, 55
    tambourines, 54-55
    woodblocks, 54

B

Back to Mono box set (Spector, Phil: Blaine, Hal), 82
The Band: Helm, Levon
  "Cripple Creek," 113
  "Weight, The," 113
basic eighth-note grooves, exercises, 179
Basic Math solo exercise, 201
bass drums
  playing
    exercises, 174-175
    pedals, 173-174
  selecting, 27-28
  setting up drumsets, 163
  tuning, 68-69
Bat Out of Hell 2/Back Into Hell (Meat Loaf: Aronoff, Kenny), 234
Bayers, Eddie, "Tennessee Flat Top Box" (Cash, Rosanne), 229
"Be My Baby" (The Ronettes: Blaine, Hal), 82, 224
The Beach Boys: Blaine, Hal, 77
  "Caroline No," 54
  "God Only Knows," 82
  "Good Vibrations," 224
  Pet Sounds, 82
beads (sticks), variations, 34-35
The Beatles: Starr, Ringo, 74-75
  Abbey Road, 65, 75
  "Come Together," 222
  "Ticket to Ride," 222-223
Beginning, The, solo exercise, 216
"Beginnings" (Chicago: Seraphine, Danny), 76
Benjamin, Benny, 9, 83, 208
  The Isley Brothers
    "This Old Heart of Mine," 208
  Motown, 78
  The Temptations
    "Ain't Too Proud to Beg," 208
Benson, George: Newmark, Andy, 76
big band drummers, 71
  Cole, Cozy, 72
  Krupa, Gene, 71
  Nelson, Sandy, 72
  Rich, Buddy, 72-73
big-band drumming, 7
  fills, 208-209
  setting up other players, 208-209
Birds of Fire (Mahavishnu Orchestra: Cobham, Billy), 74
Bissonette, Gregg, 91
Bitches Brew (Davis, Miles: Williams, Tony), 74
Blaine, Hal, 6, 9, 77, 180, 183, 208
  accomplishments, 81
  America, 77
  "Aquarius/Let the Sun Shine" (The Fifth Dimension), 82
  The Association, 77
  attributes, 81

  creativity, 82
  quantified success, 82
  signature sound, 82-83
  versatility, 82
"Be My Baby" (The Ronettes), 82, 224
The Beach Boys, 77
  "Caroline No" (Pet Sounds album), 54
"Bridge Over Troubled Water" (Simon and Garfunkel), 82, 224
Buh-Doom!, 81
The Byrds, 77
"California Dreamin'" (The Mamas and The Papas), 83
Carpenters, 77
Clark, Petula, 77
"Close to You" (Carpenters), 83
"Da Doo Ron Ron" (The Crystals), 82
Denver, John, 77
Diamond, Neil, 77
"Dizzy" (Roe, Tommy), 77, 82
The Fifth Dimension, 77
"God Only Knows" (The Beach Boys), 82
"Good Vibrations" (The Beach Boys), 224
The Grass Roots, 77
Hal Blaine and the Wrecking Crew, 78, 81
Hart, Lorin, 81
"I Got You Babe" (Sonny and Cher), 82
interview, 83-93
Jan and Dean, 77
"MacArthur Park" (Harris, Richard), 83
The Mamas and The Papas, 77
"Midnight Confessions" (Grass Roots), 82
"Monday, Monday" (The Mamas and The Papas), 83
The Monkees, 77
"My Love" (Clark, Petula), 83
Ocampo, Sam, 81
Orbison, Roy, 77
Pet Sounds (The Beach Boys), 82
Presley, Elvis, 77
Roe, Tommy, 77
"Sheila" (Roe, Tommy), 222
Simon and Garfunkel, 77
Sinatra, Frank, 77
Spector, Phil, 77, 82
  Back to Mono box set, 82
The Tijuana Brass, 77
"Up, Up, and Away" (The Fifth Dimension), 83
Web site, 93
"Wedding Bell Blues" (The Fifth Dimension), 83
Wilson, Mark, 81
Blakey, Art, 73
Blood, Sweat & Tears: Colomby, Bobby, 76
"Bo Diddley" (Diddley, Bo: Kirkland, Frank), 222

Bonham, John, 24
Bon Jovi, Jon (*Destination Anywhere*: Aronoff, Kenny), 234
bongos, 52
Bonham, John, 4
Booker T & the MG's: Jackson, Al Jr, 78
books
  Hal Blaine and the Wrecking Crew (Blaine, Hal), 78
  Laying It Down: Basics of Rock Drumming (Aronoff, Kenny), 234
  Power Workout series (Aronoff, Kenny), 234
  supplemental instruction books, 249-250
  Zildjian: The History of the Legendary Cymbal Makers (Cohan), 251
Bowie, David: Newmark, Andy, 76
brands
  Drum Workshop (DW), 18
  Fibes, 18
  GMS, 18
  Gretsch, 18
  Ludwig, 18-19
  Mapex, 19
  Pacific, 19-20
  Pearl, 20
  Premier, 20
  Sonor, 20
  Tama, 20
  Yamaha, 21
Brick by Brick (Iggy Pop: Aronoff, Kenny), 234
"Bridge Over Troubled Water" (Simon and Garfunkel: Blaine, Hal), 82, 224
Brooks, Garth (*Life of Chris Gaines, The*: Aronoff, Kenny), 234
Browne, Jackson: Kunkel, Russ, 76
brushes, 228-231
Buddy Holly and the Crickets ("Peggy Sue": Allison, Jerry), 150
Buh-Doom! (Blaine), 81
Burning for Buddy (Buddy Rich tributes), 234
Burton, Gary, 56
butts (sticks), 35
buying drums. *See* purchasing
buzz rolls. *See* closed rolls
The Byrds: Blaine, Hal, 77

C

"California Dreamin'" (The Mamas and The Papas: Blaine, Hal), 83
Cangany, Harry
  advice on purchasing drums, 37-39
  Drum Center of Indianapolis, 37
  Great American Drums, The (and the Companies That Made Them), 37

Carlisle, Belinda (*Heaven on Earth*: Aronoff, Kenny), 234
"Caroline No" (The Beach Boys: Blaine, Hal), 54
Carpenters ("Close to You": Blaine, Hal), 77
cases (drum), selecting, 30
Cash, Rosanne ("Tennessee Flat Top Box": Bayers, Eddie), 229
changing drum heads, 62-63
    instructional steps, 63
    recommended time frames, 62
Chapin Carpenter, Mary (*Stones in the Road*: Aronoff, Kenny), 233-234
Charles, Ray: Palmer, Earl, 77
Chester, Gary, "Do You Know the Way to San Jose?" (Warwick, Dionne), 230
Chicago: Seraphine, Danny
    "25 or 6 to 4," 76
    "Beginnings," 76
Clark, Petula ("My Love": Blaine, Hal), 77, 83
claves, 52-53
cleaning guidelines, 57-58
    cymbals, 58-59
    drums, 58-60
    stands and pedals, 59-60
"Close to You" (Carpenters: Blaine, Hal), 83
closed rolls, exercises, 136-137
coated drum heads, 62
Cobham, Billy
    Birds of Fire (Mahavishnu Orchestra), 74
    Spectrum, 74
Cocker, Joe: Aronoff, Kenny, 233
Coda signs, 106
Cohan, Jon, *Zildjian: The History of the Legendary Cymbal Makers*, 251
Cole, Cozy, "Topsy II," 72
Colomby, Bobby, 76
Colvin, Shawn (*Cover Girl*: Aronoff, Kenny), 234
"Come Together" (The Beatles: Starr, Ringo), 222
Complete Idiot's Guide to Playing Drums, The, Web site, 253
concert drumming, 8
conga drums, 52
Cooke, Sam: Palmer, Earl, 77
Copeland, Stewart: The Police, 76
costs, 39
    electronic drums, 48
    entry-level sets, 40-41
    high-end professional sets, 42
    purchasing your first drums
        name brand versus no name, 16-21
        new versus used, 16-17
        price ranges, 14-16
        snare drums, 27
    semi-pro kits, 41-42

counting notes, 100-101
country drumming, 6-7
Cover Girl (Colvin, Shawn: Aronoff, Kenny), 234
crash cymbals, 32
crescendos, 105
"Cripple Creek" (Band, The: Helm, Levon), 113
The Crystals ("Da Doo Ron Ron": Blaine, Hal), 82
cymbals
    cleaning guidelines, 58-59
    manufacturers, 255-256
    selecting, 32-34
    setting up drumsets, 164-165
    types
        crash, 32
        hi-hats, 32
        ride, 32

D

D.C. al Coda, 106
D.C. al Fine, 106
D.S. al Coda, 106
D.S. al Fine, 106
"Da Doo Ron Ron" (The Crystals: Blaine, Hal), 82
dance grooves, exercises, 181
Danelli, Dino, 75-76, 200, 225
Darin, Bobby: Palmer, Earl, 77
The Dave Brubeck Quartet: Morello, Joe, 73
Davis, Miles: Williams, Tony
    Bitches Brew, 74
    In a Silent Way, 74
dealers, selecting, 36
    catalogs, 36
    chain music superstores, 36
    drum-only dealers, 36
    full-service music stores, 36
    Internet-based retailers, 36
decrescendos, 105
DeJohnette, Jack, 73
Denver, John: Blaine, Hal, 77
Destination Anywhere (Bon Jovi, Jon: Aronoff, Kenny), 234
DeVito, Liberty, *The Stranger* album (Joel, Billy), 230
Diamond, Neil
    Aronoff, Kenny, 233
    Blaine, Hal, 77
Diddley, Bo ("Bo Diddley": Kirkland, Frank), 222
Dinelli, Dino, 6
Dion, Celine (*Let's Talk About Love*: Aronoff, Kenny), 233, 234
"Dizzy" (Roe, Tommy: Blaine, Hal), 77, 82
"Do You Know the Way to San Jose?" (Warwick, Dionne: Chester, Gary), 230
dotted notes, 102

double drag (rudiment ten), 145
double paradiddle (rudiment eleven), 145-146
double ratamacue (rudiment twenty-six), 151
double-ply drum heads, 62
drag paradiddle no. 1 (rudiment twenty-two), 150
drag paradiddle no. 2 (rudiment twenty-three), 151
drum beaters, Wood Whacks, 231
Drum Center of Indianapolis
    Cangany, Harry, 37
    Web site, 37
drum corps drumming
    drummer types, 8
    exercises
        rudiments, 153-155
drum keys, 63
drum techs, 60
Drum Workshop (DW) drums, 18
DrumHers! Web site, 254
drummers
    advice from the pros, 239-240
    career picture, 11
    jazz, 71
        Blakey, Art, 73
        Cobham, Billy, 74
        Cole, Cozy, 72
        DeJohnette, Jack, 73
        Jones, Elvin, 73
        Krupa, Gene, 71-72
        Morello, Joe, 73
        Nelson, Sandy, 72
        Rich, Buddy, 72-73
        Williams, Tony, 74
    reasons to become a drummer, 3-5
    rock, 74
        Aronoff, Kenny, 77
        Colomby, Bobby, 76
        Copeland, Stewart, 76
        Danelli, Dino, 75-76
        Gadd, Steve, 76
        Kunkel, Russ, 76
        Moon, Keith, 75
        Newmark, Andy, 76
        Porcaro, Jeff, 76
        Seraphine, Danny, 76
        Starr, Ringo, 74-75
        Watts, Charlie, 75
    roles and responsibilities, 5-6
    steps to becoming a drummer, 9
        finding a teacher, 9-10
        learning to read music, 11
        practicing, 10
    studio, 77
        Benjamin, Benny, 78
        Blaine, Hal, 77-78
        Hawkins, Roger, 78
        Jackson, Al Jr., 78
        Palmer, Earl, 77
    TV, 78-79
        Fig, Anton, 78

Pelton, Shawn, 78
Rosengarden, Bobby, 78
Shaughnessy, Ed, 78
Smith, Marvin "Smitty," 78
Weinberg, Max, 78
types, 6
    country, 6-7
    drum corps, 8
    jazz, 7-8
    percussion and ethnic, 8
    R&B, 6-7
    rock, 6-7
    studio and show, 9
    symphonic, 8
drumming
    big band
        fills and set-ups, 208-209
    country, 6-7
    drum corps, 8
        rudimental exercises, 153-155
    ethnic, 8
    jazz, 7-8
    percussion, 8
    R&B, 6-7
    rock, 6-7
    show, 9
    studio, 9
    symphonic, 8
        auxiliary instruments, 55
drums
    basic care, 57-58
        cleaning, 58-60
        spare parts, 60
    bass
        exercises, 174-175
        playing the pedals, 173-174
        selecting, 27-28
        setting up drumsets, 163
    congas, 52
    converting acoustic drums to
        electronic, 48-49
    drum cases, selecting, 30
    electronic drums, 45
        costs, 48
        how they work, 46
        MIDIs (musical instrument
            digital interfaces), 46
        pros and cons, 47-48
        types, 46-47
    manufacturers, 255-256
    muffling, 65-67, 69
    purchasing
        advice from a pro, 37-39
        choosing where to buy, 36
        costs, 39-42
        drumsets, 21-34
        pre-purchase considerations,
            13-19, 21
    snare
        accent exercises, 116
        closed roll exercises, 136-137
        components, 25
        eighth-note exercises, 116
        no-snare playing, 224-225

open roll exercises, 133-137
price ranges, 27
quarter-note exercises,
    115-116
selecting, 25-27
setting up drumsets, 162
shells, 26-27
sixteenth-note exercises, 116
solo: *Freddie's Feet*, 126-127
solo: *Rollin' the Hay*, 137
solo: *Rudimentary, My Dear
    Watson*, 154-155
solo: *Taking Back the Beat*, 117
syncopation exercises,
    125-126
triplet exercises, 126
stands and pedals, selecting,
    30-32
strokes
    learning techniques, 112-114
    matched-grip, 112-113
    traditional grip, 112
tom-toms, selecting, 28-30
top brands
    Drum Workshop (DW), 18
    Fibes, 18
    GMS, 18
    Gretsch, 18
    Ludwig, 18-19
    Mapex, 19
    Pacific, 19-20
    Pearl, 20
    Premier, 20
    Sonor, 20
    Tama, 20
    Yamaha, 21
tuning, 60-61, 63-69
    10-lug drums, 64
    bass drums, 68-69
    changing drum heads, 62-63
    drum keys, 63
    eight-lug drums, 64
    *Professor Sound's Drum Tuning
        Bible*, 66
    selecting appropriate heads,
        61-62
    six-lug drums, 64
    snares, 67-68
    timbre, 63
    tom-toms, 68
drumsets
    alternative playing methods,
        227-231
        brushes, 228-231
        drum beaters, 231
        laying out, 223-224
        mallets, 230
        no-snare playing, 224-225
        nondrumset playing, 225
        nonride playing, 224
        rimclicks, 227-230
        rimshots, 228-230
        unique patterns, 221-223

bass drum and hi-hat pedals,
    173-174
components, 21-23
keeping time, 167-169
playing exercises, 175, 179
    basic eighth-note grooves,
        179
    Basic Math solo exercise, 201
    Beginning, The, solo, 216
    dance grooves, 181
    ethnic grooves, 181-182
    feet only, 174
    fills, 207-209
    four-to-the-floor grooves, 180
    funky grooves, 180-181
    Groove Machine, The, solo, 183
    hands and feet, 174
    hands only, 168
    jazz beats, 193-194
    Jazz Jump solo exercise, 194
    Made Ya Smile solo, 217
    odd times, 199-200
    quarter-note grooves, 180
    shuffle grooves, 182-183
    Sing³ solo, 216
    sixteenth-note grooves,
        181-182
    sixties grooves, 180
    Three-Legged Dog grooves,
        180
    Tom-Tom Time solo, 168-169
    Top to Bottom solo, 175
reading drumset notation, 168
selecting
    bass drums, 27-28
    cymbals, 32-34
    snare drums, 25-27
    stands and pedals, 30-32
    tom-toms, 28-30
setup, 161-162
    adjusting for comfort, 165
    bass drum, 163
    cymbals, 164-165
    foot and pedal positioning,
        162-163
    hi-hat, 162
    seat, 161-162
    snare drum, 162
    tom toms, 163-164
solos, 213
    adding sizzle, 216
    attributes of a good solo,
        213-214
    formats, 214-215
    suggestions for content, 215
DrumWeb.com Web site, 254
Dylan, Bob
    Aronoff, Kenny, 233
    Kunkel, Russ, 76
dynamics, markings, 105

E

eight-lug drums, tuning, 64
eighth notes, 99-100, 116
Electronic Drum Web site, 254
electronic drums, 45
  converting acoustic drums to electric, 48-49
  costs, 48
  how they work, 46
  MIDIs (musical instrument digital interfaces), 46
  pros and cons, 47-48
  types, 46-47
eleven-stroke rolls
  open roll exercises, 135
  rudiment seventeen, 148
entry-level sets, costs, 40-41
Etheridge, Melissa (*Your Little Secret*: Aronoff, Kenny), 234
ethnic grooves, exercises, 181-182
ethnic percussion, 53
  African instruments, 53
  drummer types, 8
  Indian instruments
    tablas, 53-54
  Latin instruments, 51-53
    bongos, 52
    claves, 52-53
    conga drums, 52
    LP Music Group, 52
    maracas, 53
    Santana, Carlos, 51
    shakers, 53
    shekeres, 53
    timbales, 52
evaluating drums, 23-25
exercises
  accents, 116
  closed rolls, 136-137
  drumsets, 179
    basic eighth-note grooves, 179
    dance grooves, 181
    ethnic grooves, 181-182
    feet only, 174
    fills, 207-209
    four-to-the-floor grooves, 180
    funky grooves, 180-181
    Groove Machine, The, solo, 183
    hands and feet, 174
    hands only, 168
    jazz beats, 193-194
    odd times, 199-201
    quarter-note grooves, 180
    shuffle grooves, 182-183
    sixteenth-note grooves, 181-182
    sixties grooves, 180
    Three-Legged Dog grooves, 180
    Tom-Tom Time solo, 168-169
    Top to Bottom solo, 175

eighth notes, 116
open rolls, 133-134, 136-137
  eleven-stroke rolls, 135
  fifteen-stroke rolls, 135
  five-stroke rolls, 134
  nine-stroke rolls, 134
  seven-stroke rolls, 134
  seventeen-stroke rolls, 136
  thirteen-stroke rolls, 135
quarter notes, 115-116
rudiments, 153-154
  Rudimentary, My Dear Watson solo, 154-155
sixteenth notes, 116
solos
  Basic Math, 201
  Beginning, The, 216
  Freddie's Feet, 126-127
  Groove Machine, The, 183
  Jazz Jump, 194
  Made Ya Smile, 217
  Rollin' the Hay, 137
  Rudimentary, My Dear Watson, 154-155
  Sing³, 216
  Taking Back the Beat, 117
  Tom-Tom Time, 168-169
  Top to Bottom, 175
syncopation, 125-126
triplets, 126

F

feet, positioning, 162-163
Fibes drums, 18
fifteen-stroke rolls
  open roll exercises, 135
  rudiment nineteen, 149
The Fifth Dimension: Blaine, Hal, 77
  "Aquarius/Let the Sun Shine," 82
  "Up, Up, and Away," 83
  "Wedding Bell Blues," 83
Fifty Ways to Leave Your Lover (Simon, Paul: Gadd, Steve), 76
fills, 207-209
  exercises, 207-208
  setting up a big band, 208-209
"Fire and Rain" (Taylor, James: Kunkel, Russ), 230
Fire Inside, The (Seger, Bob: Aronoff, Kenny), 234
five-stroke rolls
  open roll exercises, 134
  rudiment two, 142
flags (notes), 100
flam (rudiment four), 143
flam accent (rudiment five), 143-144
flam paradiddle (rudiment six), 144
flam paradiddle-diddle (rudiment twenty-four), 151
flam tap (rudiment twenty), 149
flamacue (rudiment seven), 144

Fleetwood Mac (*Rhiannon*: Fleetwood, Mick), 221-222
Fogelberg, Dan: Kunkel, Russ, 76
Fogerty, John (*Premonition*: Aronoff, Kenny), 233-234
four-to-the-floor grooves, exercises, 180
Franklin, Aretha: Hawkins, Roger, 78
Freddie's Feet solo exercise, 126-127
French grip variation (matched grip), 110
funky grooves, exercises, 180-181
fusion drummers, 74
fusion group drumming, 7

G

Gadd, Steve, 126
  "50 Ways to Leave Your Lover" (Simon, Paul), 76, 222-223
  Aja (Steely Dan), 76
gigs, 6
GMS drums, 18
"God Only Knows" (The Beach Boys: Blaine, Hal), 82
gongs, 55
"Good Vibrations" (The Beach Boys: Blaine, Hal), 224
grace notes, 143
The Grass Roots ("Midnight Confessions": Blaine, Hal), 77, 82
Great American Drums, The (and the Companies That Made Them) (Cangany), 37
Green, Al: Jackson, Al Jr, 78
Gretsch drums, 18
grips, 109
  matched, 7, 109-110
    drum strokes, 112-113
    French grip variation, 110
  traditional, 7, 110-112
    drum strokes, 112
Groove Machine, The, solo exercise, 183

H

Hal Blaine and the Wrecking Crew (Blaine), 78, 81
half notes, 98-99
Harmony Central: Drums & Percussion Web site, 254
Harris, Richard ("MacArthur Park": Blaine, Hal), 83
Harrison, George: Newmark, Andy, 76
Hart, Lorin: Blaine, Hal, 81
Hawkins, Richard, 83
Hawkins, Roger, 78

Franklin, Aretha, 78
Oak Ridge Boys, 78
Simon, Paul, 78
Skaggs, Boz, 78
Sledge, Percy, 78
Womack, Bobby, 78
heads (drum)
changing, 62-63
instructional steps, 63
recommended time frames, 62
selecting, 61-62
types
coated, 62
double-ply, 62
hydraulic, 62
single-ply muffled, 62
single-ply thin, 61
single-ply unmuffled, 61
uncoated, 62
heads (notes), 100
Heaven on Earth (Carlisle, Belinda: Aronoff, Kenny), 234
Hefti, Neal: Palmer, Earl, 77
Helm, Levon: Band, The
"Cripple Creek," 113
"Weight, The," 113
hi-hat cymbals, 32
exercises, 174-175
pedals, 173-174
setting up drumsets, 162
high-end professional sets, costs, 42
history
jazz drummers, 71
Blakey, Art, 73
Cobham, Billy, 74
Cole, Cozy, 72
DeJohnette, Jack, 73
Jones, Elvin, 73
Krupa, Gene, 71-72
Morello, Joe, 73
Nelson, Sandy, 72
Rich, Buddy, 72-73
Williams, Tony, 74
rock drummers, 74
Aronoff, Kenny, 77
Colomby, Bobby, 76
Copeland, Stewart, 76
Danelli, Dino, 75-76
Gadd, Steve, 76
Kunkel, Russ, 76
Moon, Keith, 75
Newmark, Andy, 76
Porcaro, Jeff, 76
Seraphine, Danny, 76
Starr, Ringo, 74-75
Watts, Charlie, 75
rudiments, 142
studio drummers, 77
Benjamin, Benny, 78
Blaine, Hal, 77-78
Hawkins, Roger, 78
Jackson, Al Jr., 78
Palmer, Earl, 77

TV drummers, 78-79
Fig, Anton, 78
Pelton, Shawn, 78
Rosengarden, Bobby, 78
Shaughnessy, Ed, 78
Smith, Marvin "Smitty," 78
Weinberg, Max, 78
Holly, Buddy: Allison, Jerry
"Not Fade Away," 222
"Peggy Sue," 222
hydraulic drum heads, 62

I

"I Got You Babe" (Sonny and Cher: Blaine, Hal), 82
Iggy Pop (*Brick by Brick*: Aronoff, Kenny), 234
In a Silent Way (Davis, Miles: Williams, Tony), 74
in the pocket grooves, 182
Indian instruments, 53-54
instruction books, 249-251
instructors. *See* teachers
The Isley Brothers ("This Old Heart of Mine": Benjamin, Benny), 208
Italian musical terms
dynamics, 105
tempo, 104-105

J

Jackson, Al Jr., 83, 182
Booker T. & the MG's, 78
Green, Al, 78
Pickett, Wilson, 78
Redding, Otis, 78
Sam and Dave, 78
Jackson, Milt, 56
Jan and Dean
Blaine, Hal, 77
Palmer, Earl, 77
jazz drummers, 71
Blakey, Art, 73
Cobham, Billy, 74
Cole, Cozy, 72
DeJohnette, Jack, 73
Jones, Elvin, 73
Krupa, Gene, 71-72
Morello, Joe, 73
Nelson, Sandy, 72
Rich, Buddy, 72-73
Williams, Tony, 74
jazz drumming
drummer types, 7-8
acoustic small-groups, 7
fusion groups, 7
exercises, 193-194
Jazz Jump solo exercise, 194
Joel, Billy (*The Stranger* album: DeVito, Liberty), 230

John, Elton, Aronoff, Kenny, 233
Johnson, Jimmy ("That's the Way I've Always Heard It Should Be": Simon, Carly), 223
Jones, Elvin, 73

K

keeping time (drumsets), 167, 169
Keltner, Jim, 90
kettledrums. *See* tympani
King, Carole: Kunkel, Russ, 76
Kirkland, Frank ("Bo Diddley": Diddley, Bo), 222
Krupa, Gene, 6, 71-72
Kunkel, Russ
Browne, Jackson, 76
Dylan, Bob, 76
"Fire and Rain" (Taylor, James), 230
Fogelberg, Dan, 76
King, Carole, 76
Ronstadt, Linda, 76

L

Late Night with Conan O'Brien (Weinberg, Max), 78
Late Show with David Letterman (Fig, Anton), 78
Latin percussion, 51-53
bongos, 52
claves, 52-53
conga drums, 52
LP Music Group, 52
maracas, 53
Santana, Carlos, 51
shakers, 53
shekeres, 53
timbales, 52
laying out, 223-224
Leim, Paul, 91
Lennon, John: Newmark, Andy, 76
Lesson 25 (rudiment twenty-five), 151
lessons, 9-10
Let There Be Drums (Nelson, Sandy), 72
Let There Be Drums! (Weinberg, Max), 74
Let's Talk About Love (Dion, Celine: Aronoff, Kenny), 234
Life of Chris Gaines, The (Brooks, Garth: Aronoff, Kenny), 234
Londin, Larry, 180
long roll (rudiment one), 142
Lowdown (Skaggs, Boz: Porcaro, Jeff), 76
LP Music Group, 52
Ludwig drums, 18-19

M

"MacArthur Park" (Harris, Richard: Blaine, Hal), 83
Made Ya Smile solo exercise, 217
magazines, 253
"Magic Bus" (The Who: Moon, Keith), 222
Mahavishnu Orchestra (*Birds of Fire*: Cobham, Billy), 74
mallets, 230
The Mamas and The Papas: Blaine, Hal, 77
    "California Dreamin'," 83
    "Monday, Monday," 83
manufacturers
    cymbals, 255-256
    Drum Workshop (DW), 18
    drums, 255-256
    Fibes, 18
    GMS, 18
    Gretsch, 18
    Ludwig, 18-19
    Mapex, 19
    Pacific, 19-20
    Pearl, 20
    Premier, 20
    Sonor, 20
    Tama, 20
    Yamaha, 21
Mapex drums, 19
maracas, 53
marcatos, 105
March (Penn, Michael: Aronoff, Kenny), 234
marching band drumming.
    See drum corps drumming
marimbas, 56
markings
    dynamics, 105
    repeats, 106
Marotta, Rick, 181
Martin, Ricky (*Ricky Martin*: Aronoff, Kenny), 233-234
Master Studies method book (Morello, Joe), 74
matched grip, 7, 109-110
    drum strokes, 112-113
    French grip variation, 110
measures, 97-98
Meat Loaf (*Bat Out of Hell 2/Back Into Hell*: Aronoff, Kenny), 233-234
Mellencamp, John, Aronoff, Kenny, 77, 233
    American Fool, 234
    Scarecrow, 234
    Uh-Huh, 234
melodic percussion instruments, 56
    marimbas, 56
    vibraphones, 56
    xylophones, 56
metronomes, 103-104
MG's, The: Jackson, Al Jr, 78
MIDIs (musical instrument digital interfaces), 46

Midnight Confessions (The Grass Roots: Blaine, Hal), 82
Monday, Monday (The Mamas and The Papas: Blaine, Hal), 83
The Monkees
    Blaine, Hal, 77
    Palmer, Earl, 77
Moon, Keith, 75, 163, 222
Morello, Joe, 73, 200
    Master Studies method book, 74
    New Directions in Rhythm method book, 73
Motown, Benjamin, Benny, 78
muffling drums, 65-67, 69
music, reading, 11
    drumset notation, 168
    dynamics, 105
    measures, 97-98
    notes, 98-103
    repeats, 106
    rests, 101-102
    staffs, 97-99
    tempo, 103-105
    time signatures, 103
musical instrument digital interfaces (MIDIs), 46
"My Love" (Clark, Petula: Blaine, Hal), 83

N

Nelson, Sandy, *Let There Be Drums*, 72
New Directions in Rhythm method book (Morello, Joe), 73
Newmark, Andy
    "Anticipation" (Simon, Carly), 76, 224
    Benson, George, 76
    Bowie, David, 76
    Harrison, George, 76
    Lennon, John, 76
    Stewart, Rod, 76
newsletters, 253
Nicks, Stevie: Aronoff, Kenny, 233
nine-stroke rolls
    open roll exercises, 134
    rudiment fifteen, 148
no-snare playing, 224-225
nondrumset playing, 225
nonride playing, 224
"Not Fade Away" (Holly, Buddy: Allison, Jerry), 222
notation reading (drumsets), 168
notes, 98
    counting, 100-101
    dotted notes, 102
    eighth notes, 99-100
    flags, 100
    grace, 143
    half notes, 98-99
    heads, 100
    pick-up, 117

    quarter notes, 99
    sixteenth notes, 100-101
    tied notes, 102
    triplets, 102-103
    whole notes, 98
numbering system (drumsticks), 35

O

Oak Ridge Boys: Hawkins, Roger, 78
Ocampo, Sam: Blaine, Hal, 81
odd-time exercises, 199-201
open roll exercises, 133-137
    eleven-stroke rolls, 135
    fifteen-stroke rolls, 135
    five-stroke rolls, 134
    nine-stroke rolls, 134
    seven-stroke rolls, 134
    seventeen-stroke rolls, 136
    thirteen-stroke rolls, 135
Orbison, Roy: Blaine, Hal, 77
organizations, 254-255
    All-Music Guide, 255
    Percussion Marketing Council, 255
    Percussive Arts Society, 255
ostinato, 214
Otis, Johnny, "Willie and the Hand Jive," 222

P

Pacific drums, 19-20
Palmer, Earl, 9, 77, 83-84, 91, 126
    Charles, Ray, 77
    Cooke, Sam, 77
    Darin, Bobby, 77
    Hefti, Neal, 77
    Jan and Dean, 77
    The Monkees, 77
    The Righteous Brothers, 77
    The Ronettes, 77
    Sinatra, Frank, 77
    Sonny and Cher, 77
    Spector, Phil, 77
    Turner, Ike and Tina, 77
    Vee, Bobby, 77
    Williams, Andy, 77
Pearl drums, 20
Peart, Neil, 5
pedals
    cleaning guidelines, 59-60
    playing
        bass drum, 173-174
        exercises, 174-175
        hi-hat, 173-174
    selecting, 30-32
    setting up drumsets, 162-163
"Peggy Sue" (Holly, Buddy: Allison, Jerry), 150, 222

Penn, Michael (*March*: Aronoff, Kenny), 234
percussion, 53-54
 African instruments, 53
 drummer types, 8
 Indian instruments
  tablas, 53-54
 Latin instruments, 51-53
  bongos, 52
  claves, 52-53
  conga drums, 52
  LP Music Group, 52
  maracas, 53
  Santana, Carlos, 51
  shakers, 53
  shekeres, 53
  timbales, 52
 melodic, 56
  marimbas, 56
  vibraphones, 56
  xylophones, 56
 sleigh bells, 54
 symphonic, 55
  gongs, 55
  timpani, 55
  triangles, 55
 tambourines, 54-55
 woodblocks, 54
Percussion Marketing Council, 255
Percussive Arts Society, 255
Pet Sounds (The Beach Boys: Blaine, Hal), 54, 82
phrases, fills, 207-209
pick-up notes, 117
Pickett, Wilson: Jackson, Al Jr, 78
playing drumsets, 227
 bass drum and hi-hat pedals, 173-174
 brushes, 228-231
 drum beaters, 231
 exercises, 168-169, 174-175, 179-183, 193-194, 199-201, 207-209, 216-217
 keeping time, 167, 169
 laying out, 223-224
 mallets, 230
 no-snare playing, 224-225
 nondrumset playing, 225
 nonride playing, 224
 rimclicks, 227-228, 230
 rimshots, 228, 230
 solos, 213-216
 unique patterns, 221-223
The Police: Copeland, Stewart, 76
Porcaro, Jeff, 183
 "Lowdown" (Skaggs, Boz), 76
 "Rosanna" (Toto), 76
practicing, 10
Premier drums, 20
Premonition (Fogerty, John: Aronoff, Kenny), 234
Presley, Elvis: Blaine, Hal, 77
press rolls. *See* closed rolls
Professor Sound's Drum Tuning Bible Web site, 66, 254

purchasing drums
 advice from a pro, 37-39
 choosing where to buy, 36
  catalogs, 36
  chain music superstores, 36
  drum-only dealers, 36
  full-service music stores, 36
  Internet-based retailers, 36
 costs, 39
  entry-level sets, 40-41
  high-end professional sets, 42
  semi-pro kits, 41-42
 drumsets, 21-23
  bass drums, 27-28
  cymbals, 32-34
  drum cases, 30
  evaluating drums, 23-25
  snare drums, 25-27
  stands and pedals, 30-32
  tom-toms, 28-30
 pre-purchase considerations, 13
  name brand versus no name, 16-19, 21
  new versus used, 16-17
  price ranges, 14-16
  snare drum versus drumset, 13-14
Purdie, Bernard, 181-183

Q-R

quarter notes, 99, 115-116, 180

R&B drumming, 6-7
The Rascals: Danelli, Dino, 75-76
reading music, 11
 drumset notation, 168
 dynamics, 105
 measures, 97-98
 notes, 98
  counting, 100-101
  dotted notes, 102
  eighth notes, 99-100
  flags, 100
  half notes, 98-99
  heads, 100
  quarter notes, 99
  sixteenth notes, 100-101
  tied notes, 102
  triplets, 102-103
  whole notes, 98
 repeats, 106
 rests, 101-102
 staffs, 97-99
 tempo, 103
  metronomes, 103-104
  terms, 104-105
 time signatures, 103
Redding, Otis: Jackson, Al Jr, 78
repeats, 106
 Coda signs, 106
 D.C. al Coda, 106
 D.C. al Fine, 106
 D.S. al Coda, 106

D.S. al Fine, 106
 Segno signs, 106
resources
 books
  Hal Blaine and the Wrecking Crew (Blaine, Hal), 78
  Laying It Down: Basics of Rock Drumming (Aronoff, Kenny), 234
  Power Workout series (Aronoff, Kenny), 234
 drum and cymbal manufacturers, 255-256
 instruction books, 249-250
  Zildjian: The History of the Legendary Cymbal Makers (Cohan), 251
 magazines and newsletters, 253
 organizations, 254-255
  All-Music Guide, 255
  Percussion Marketing Council, 255
  Percussive Arts Society, 255
 Web sites, 253-254
  All-Music Guide, 255
  anewdrummer, 253
  Aronoff, Kenny, 234
  Blaine, Hal, 93
  Complete Idiot's Guide to Playing Drums, The, 253
  Drum Center of Indianapolis, 37
  DrumHers!, 254
  DrumWeb.com, 254
  Electronic Drum Web, 254
  Harmony Central: Drums & Percussion, 254
  Percussion Marketing Council, 255
  Percussive Arts Society, 255
  Professor Sound's Drum Tuning Bible, 66, 254
  ThePercussionist, 254
responsibilities, 5-6
rests, 101-102
Rhiannon (Fleetwood Mac: Fleetwood, Mick), 221-222
rhythm and blues. *See* R&B
Rich, Buddy, 4, 6, 29, 72-73, 126
Ricky Martin (Martin, Ricky: Aronoff, Kenny), 234
ride cymbals, 32
The Righteous Brothers: Palmer, Earl, 77
rimclicks, 227-230
rimshots, 163, 228-230
rock drummers, 74
 Aronoff, Kenny, 77
 Colomby, Bobby, 76
 Copeland, Stewart, 76
 Danelli, Dino, 75-76
 Gadd, Steve, 76
 Kunkel, Russ, 76
 Moon, Keith, 75

Newmark, Andy, 76
Porcaro, Jeff, 76
Seraphine, Danny, 76
Starr, Ringo, 74-75
Watts, Charlie, 75
rock drumming, 6-7
Roe, Tommy: Blaine, Hal, 77
"Dizzy," 77, 82
"Sheila," 222
roles, 5-6
Rollin' the Hay solo exercise, 137
The Rolling Stones
Aronoff, Kenny, 233
Watts, Charlie, 75
rolls
closed, 136-137
open, 133-137
The Ronettes
Blaine, Hal, "Be My Baby," 82,
224
Palmer, Earl, 77
Ronstadt, Linda: Kunkel, Russ, 76
"Rosanna" (Toto: Porcaro, Jeff), 76
Rudimentary, My Dear Watson solo
exercise, 154-155
rudiments, 141-151, 154-155
exercises, 153-154
Rudimentary, My Dear Watson
solo, 154-155
traditional 26, 141-151
double drag (rudiment ten),
145
double paradiddle (rudiment
eleven), 145-146
double ratamacue (rudiment
twenty-six), 151
drag paradiddle no. 1 (rudiment twenty-two), 150
drag paradiddle no. 2 (rudiment twenty-three), 151
eleven-stroke roll (rudiment
seventeen), 148
fifteen-stroke roll (rudiment
nineteen), 149
five-stroke roll (rudiment
two), 142
flam (rudiment four), 143
flam accent (rudiment five),
143-144
flam paradiddle (rudiment
six), 144
flam paradiddle-diddle (rudiment twenty-four), 151
flam tap (rudiment twenty),
149
flamacue (rudiment seven),
144
history, 142
Lesson 25 (rudiment twenty-
five), 151
long roll (rudiment one), 142
nine-stroke roll (rudiment fifteen), 148
ruff (rudiment eight), 145

seven-stroke roll (rudiment
three), 142
single drag (rudiment nine),
145
single paradiddle (rudiment
twenty-one), 150
single ratamacue (rudiment
twelve), 146
single-stroke roll (rudiment
fourteen), 147-148
ten-stroke roll (rudiment sixteen), 148
thirteen-stroke roll (rudiment
eighteen), 149
triple ratamacue (rudiment
thirteen), 146-147

S

Sam and Dave: Jackson, Al Jr, 78
Santana, Carlos, 51
Saturday Night Live (Pelton, Shawn),
78
Scarecrow (Mellencamp, John:
Aronoff, Kenny), 234
seats, setting up drumsets, 161-162
Seger, Bob (*Fire Inside, The*: Aronoff,
Kenny), 233-234
semi-pro kits, costs, 41-42
Segno signs, 106
Seraphine, Danny
"25 or 6 to 4," 76
"Beginnings," 76
setting up drumsets, 161-162
adjusting for comfort, 165
bass drum, 163
cymbals, 164-165
foot and pedal positioning,
162-163
hi-hat, 162
seat, 161-162
snare drum, 162
tom-toms, 163-164
seven-stroke rolls
open roll exercises, 134-136
rudiment three, 142
shakers, 53
"Sheila" (Roe, Tommy: Blaine, Hal),
222
shekeres, 53
shells (snare drums), 26-27
show drumming, 9
shuffle grooves, exercises, 182-183
sight reading, 9
signatures (time), 103
Simon and Garfunkel ("Bridge Over
Troubled Water": Blaine, Hal), 77
Simon, Carly
Johnson, Jimmy
"That's the Way I've Always
Heard It Should Be," 223
Newmark, Andy
"Anticipation," 76, 224

Simon, Paul
Gadd, Steve
"50 Ways to Leave Your
Lover," 76, 222-223
Hawkins, Roger, 78
Sinatra, Frank
Blaine, Hal, 77
Palmer, Earl, 77
Sing[3] solo exercise, 216
single drag (rudiment nine), 145
single paradiddle (rudiment twenty-
one), 150
single ratamacue (rudiment twelve),
146
single-ply muffled drum heads, 62
single-ply thin drum heads, 61
single-ply unmuffled drum heads,
61
single-stroke roll (rudiment fourteen), 147-148
six-lug drums, tuning, 64
sixteenth-note grooves, exercises,
181-182
sixteenth notes, 100-101, 116
sixties grooves, exercises, 180
Skaggs, Boz
Hawkins, Roger, 78
Porcaro, Jeff
"Lowdown," 76
Sledge, Percy: Hawkins, Roger, 78
sleigh bells, 54
small-group drummers
Blakey, Art, 73
DeJohnette, Jack, 73
Jones, Elvin, 73
Morello, Joe, 73-74
small-group drumming, 7
Smashing Pumpkins, Aronoff,
Kenny, 233
snare drums
accent exercises, 116
closed roll exercises, 136-137
components, 25
eighth note exercises, 116
no-snare playing, 224-225
open roll exercises, 133-137
eleven-stroke rolls, 135
fifteen-stroke rolls, 135
five-stroke rolls, 134
nine-stroke rolls, 134
seven-stroke rolls, 134
seventeen-stroke rolls, 136
thirteen-stroke rolls, 135
price ranges, 27
quarter note exercises, 115-116
selecting, 25-27
setting up drumsets, 162
shells, 26-27
sixteenth-note exercises, 116
solos
Freddie's Feet, 126-127
Rollin' the Hay, 137

Rudimentary, My Dear Watson, 154-155
Taking Back the Beat, 117
syncopation exercises, 125-126
triplet exercises, 126
tuning, 67-68
solos, 213, 217
adding sizzle, 216
attributes of a good solo, 213-214
Basic Math exercise, 201
Beginning, The, exercise, 216
Cobham, Billy
Mahavishnu Orchestra's *Birds of Fire,* 74
Spectrum, 74
Cole, Cozy
"Topsy II," 72
formats, 214-215
Freddie's Feet exercise, 126-127
Gadd, Steve
Aja (Steely Dan), 76
Groove Machine, The, exercise, 183
Jazz Jump exercise, 194
Made Ya Smile exercise, 217
Nelson, Sandy
Let There Be Drums, 72
Rollin' the Hay exercise, 137
Rudimentary, My Dear Watson exercise, 154-155
Sing³ exercise, 216
suggestions for content, 215
Taking Back the Beat exercise, 117
Tom-Tom Time exercise, 168-169
Top to Bottom exercise, 175
Sonny and Cher
Blaine, Hal
"I Got You Babe," 82
Palmer, Earl, 77
Sonor drums, 20
soul music. *See* R&B
sound characteristics (snare drum shells), 26
Spanner in the Works, A (Stewart, Rod: Aronoff, Kenny), 234
spare parts, 60
Spector, Phil
Blaine, Hal, 77, 82
Back to Mono box set, 82
Palmer, Earl, 77
Spectrum (Cobham, Billy), 74
Springsteen, Bruce (*You're the One*: Weinberg, Max), 222
staffs, 97-99
stands
cleaning guidelines, 59-60
selecting, 30-32
Starr, Ringo, 4, 74-75, 174
Abbey Road album (The Beatles), 65
"Come Together" (The Beatles), 222
"Ticket to Ride" (The Beatles), 222-223

Steely Dan (*Aja*: Gadd, Steve), 76
Stewart, Rod
Aronoff, Kenny, 233
A Spanner in the Works, 234
Newmark, Andy, 76
sticks
creative uses, 227
rimclicks, 227-230
rimshots, 228-230
grip types, 109
matched grip, 109-110
traditional grip, 110-112
selecting, 34-36
bead variations, 34-35
butts, 35
manufacturer variations, 35
numbering system, 35
Stones in the Road (Chapin Carpenter, Mary: Aronoff, Kenny), 234
Stranger, The album (Joel, Billy: DeVito, Liberty), 230
strokes
learning techniques, 112-114
matched-grip, 112-113
traditional grip, 112
studio drummers, 77
Benjamin, Benny, 78
Blaine, Hal, 77-78
Hawkins, Roger, 78
Jackson, Al Jr., 78
Palmer, Earl, 77
studio drumming, 9
symphonic drumming
auxiliary instruments, 55
gongs, 55
timpani, 55
triangles, 55
drummer types, 8
syncopation, 125-127

T

tablas, 53-54
Taking Back the Beat solo exercise, 117
Tama drums, 20
tambourines, 54-55
Taylor, James ("Fire and Rain": Kunkel, Russ), 230
teachers, locating, 9-10
techs (drum), 60
tempo, 103
metronomes, 103-104
terms, 104-105
The Temptations ("Ain't Too Proud to Beg": Benjamin, Benny), 208
ten-stroke roll (rudiment sixteen), 148
"Tennessee Flat Top Box" (Cash, Rosanne: Bayers, Eddie), 229
"That's the Way I've Always Heard It Should Be" (Simon, Carly: Johnson, Jimmy), 223

ThePercussionist Web site, 254
thirteen-stroke rolls
open roll exercises, 135
rudiment eighteen, 149
"This Old Heart of Mine" (The Isley Brothers: Benjamin, Benny), 208
Three-Legged Dog grooves, exercises, 180
"Ticket to Ride" (The Beatles: Starr, Ringo), 222-223
tied notes, 102
The Tijuana Brass: Blaine, Hal, 77
timbales, 52
timbre, 63
time, keeping (drumsets), 167-169
time signatures, 103
timpani, 55
Tom-Tom Time solo exercise, 168-169
tom-toms
selecting, 28-30
setting up drumsets, 163-164
tuning, 68
Tonight Show
Rosengarden, Bobby, 78
Shaughnessy, Ed, 78
Smith, Marvin "Smitty," 78
Top to Bottom solo exercise, 175
"Topsy II" (Cole, Cozy), 72
Toto ("Rosanna": Porcaro, Jeff), 76
traditional 26 rudiments, 141-151
double drag (rudiment ten), 145
double paradiddle (rudiment eleven), 145-146
double ratamacue (rudiment twenty-six), 151
drag paradiddle no. 1 (rudiment twenty-two), 150
drag paradiddle no. 2 (rudiment twenty-three), 151
eleven-stroke roll (rudiment seventeen), 148
fifteen-stroke roll (rudiment nineteen), 149
five-stroke roll (rudiment two), 142
flam (rudiment four), 143
flam accent (rudiment five), 143-144
flam paradiddle (rudiment six), 144
flam paradiddle-diddle (rudiment twenty-four), 151
flam tap (rudiment twenty), 149
flamacue (rudiment seven), 144
history, 142
Lesson 25 (rudiment twenty-five), 151
long roll (rudiment one), 142
nine-stroke roll (rudiment fifteen), 148
ruff (rudiment eight), 145
seven-stroke roll (rudiment three), 142
single drag (rudiment nine), 145

single paradiddle (rudiment twenty-one), 150
single ratamacue (rudiment twelve), 146
single-stroke roll (rudiment fourteen), 147-148
ten-stroke roll (rudiment sixteen), 148
thirteen-stroke roll (rudiment eighteen), 149
triple ratamacue (rudiment thirteen), 146-147
traditional grip, 7, 110-112
triangles, 55
triggers, 46-49
triple ratamacue (rudiment thirteen), 146-147
triplets, 102-103, 126-127
tuning drums, 60-69
    10-lug drums, 64
    bass drums, 68-69
    changing drum heads, 62-63
    drum keys, 63
    eight-lug drums, 64
    Professor Sound's Drum Tuning Bible, 66
    selecting appropriate heads, 61-62
    six-lug drums, 64
    snares, 67-68
    timbre, 63
    tom-toms, 68
Turner, Ike and Tina: Palmer, Earl, 77
TV drummers, 78-79
    Late Night with Conan O'Brien Weinberg, Max, 78
    Late Show with David Letterman Fig, Anton, 78
    Saturday Night Live Pelton, Shawn, 78

Tonight Show
    Rosengarden, Bobby, 78
    Shaughnessy, Ed, 78
    Smith, Marvin "Smitty," 78
types (drummers), 6
    country, 6-7
    drum corps, 8
    jazz, 7-8
        acoustic small-groups, 7
        fusion groups, 7
    percussion and ethnic, 8
    R&B, 6-7
    rock, 6-7
    studio and show, 9
    symphonic, 8

U-V

Uh-Huh (Mellencamp, John: Aronoff, Kenny), 234
uncoated drum heads, 62
"Up, Up, and Away" (The Fifth Dimension: Blaine, Hal), 83
urban music. *See* R&B

Vee, Bobby: Palmer, Earl, 77
vibraphones, 56

W

Warwick, Dionne ("Do You Know the Way to San Jose?": Chester, Gary), 230
Watts, Charlie, 5, 75, 180
Web sites, 253-254
    All-Music Guide, 255
    anewdrummer, 253
    Aronoff, Kenny, 234
    Blaine, Hal, 93
    Complete Idiot's Guide to Playing Drums, The, 253
    Drum Center of Indianapolis, 37

DrumHers!, 254
DrumWeb.com, 254
Electronic Drum Web, 254
Harmony Central: Drums & Percussion, 254
Percussion Marketing Council, 255
Percussive Arts Society, 255
Professor Sound's Drum Tuning Bible, 66, 254
ThePercussionist, 254
"Wedding Bell Blues" (The Fifth Dimension: Blaine, Hal), 83
"Weight, The" (The Band: Helm, Levon), 113
Weinberg, Max
    Let There Be Drums!, 74
    You're the One (Springsteen, Bruce), 222
The Who ("Magic Bus": Moon, Keith), 75
whole notes, 98
Williams, Andy: Palmer, Earl, 77
Williams, Tony, 74
"Willie and the Hand Jive" (Otis, Johnny), 222
Wilson, Mark: Blaine, Hal, 81
Womack, Bobby: Hawkins, Roger, 78
Wood Whacks, 231
woodblocks, 54

X-Y-Z

xylophones, 56

Yamaha drums, 21
You're the One (Springsteen, Bruce: Weinberg, Max), 222
Your Little Secret (Etheridge, Melissa: Aronoff, Kenny), 234

Zildjian: The History of the Legendary Cymbal Makers (Cohan), 251

 Arts & Sciences

 Business & Personal Finance

 Computers & the Internet

 Family & Home

 Hobbies & Crafts

 Language Reference

 Health & Fitness

 Personal Enrichment

 Sports & Recreation

 Teens

IDIOTSGUIDES.COM

Introducing a new and different Web site

Millions of people love to learn through *The Complete Idiot's Guide*® books. Discover the same pleasure online in **idiotsguides.com**–part of The Learning Network.

Idiotsguides.com is a new and different Web site, where you can:

- Explore and download more than 150 fascinating and useful mini-guides—FREE! Print out or send to a friend.

- Share your own knowledge and experience as a mini-guide contributor.

- Join discussions with authors and exchange ideas with other lifelong learners.

- Read sample chapters from a vast library of *Complete Idiot's Guide*® books.

- Find out how to become an author.

- Check out upcoming book promotions and author signings.

- Purchase books through your favorite online retailer.

Learning for Fun. Learning for Life.

IDIOTSGUIDES.COM • LEARNINGNETWORK.COM

Copyright © 2000 Pearson Education